COMMUNES
AND THE
GREEN VISION

David Pepper is principal lecturer in geography at Oxford Polytechnic. Details of his other books appear on the back cover.

Nickie Hallam is part-time lecturer in geography at Oxford Polytechnic, a post-graduate student at the School of Peace Studies, Bradford University, and a former member of the New University Project.

COMMUNES AND THE GREEN VISION

Counterculture, Lifestyle and the New Age

David Pepper

Based on research by the author
and Nickie Hallam

GREEN PRINT

First published in 1991 by
Green Print
an imprint of The Merlin Press
10 Malden Road, London NW5 3HR

© David Pepper

The right of David Pepper to be identified as author of this work has been asserted in accordance with the Copyright, Design and Patents Act 1988.

All rights reserved. No part of this publication may be reproduced, stored in a retrieval system, or transmitted, in any form or by any means electronic, mechanical, photocopying, recording or otherwise, without the prior permission in writing of the publisher.

ISBN 1 85425 051 5

1 2 3 4 5 6 7 8 9 10 :: 99 98 97 96 95 94 93 92 91

Phototypeset by Computerset, Harmondsworth, Middlesex

Printed in England by Biddles Ltd., Guildford, Surrey on recycled paper

ACKNOWLEDGEMENTS

I am indebted to Peter de la Cour, lecturer and former communard who has now gone on to found the Green College, for spending many hours in conversation about this project and helping me to get it into shape. The research was made possible by a grant from Oxford Polytechnic. I would also like to acknowledge with gratitude the help and advice of Dennis Hardy, Frank Webster, John Gold, Jon Carpenter, Penny Bardsley, Andrew Rigby, Peter Harper and Fiona Hay, and of course the communards themselves. They constantly received both Nickie Hallam and myself into their homes with kindness, hospitality and humour, sparing us the worst excesses of that well-known communes phenomenon of 'visitor alienation'. Their friendliness constituted a danger to academic disinterestedness, which I hope I have guarded sufficiently against in the writing and analysis of the interviews. Conversely, I hope I have not gone too far the other way in overscepticism, and that the need to be critical has not obliterated my underlying admiration and support for this way of living. As this book was written, so many Western political commentators and journalists were telling us that 'communism is dead'. This book shows that, even in this country, *true* commune-ism is alive and – occasionally at least – kicking.

Any utopia should have to allow for the closest possible contact between people and the living earth. The second element would be harking back to a popular theme in many socialist utopias. That is the notion of decentralisation towards some kind of communitarian society in which people genuinely do have the responsibility as well as the right to put into practice their own views in their own community as to how they can best effect . . . the goals we [greens] have. I don't think you can envisage a green world which isn't decentralised at one level and internationalised at the other level.

Jonathon Porritt, on 'Visions of Utopia' (BBC2, 'The Late Show', 30 January 1990).

It's nice to talk about ecology, but to go out and do it is difficult. Not until lots of people do it will it be fun.

A communard from Monkton Wyld.

I'm calling on people to be exceptional; to step out of their constraints and set an example by living in communes. They are a leading edge of the green movement.

A communard from Redfield.

Contents

List of tables and abbreviations used viii

Introduction 1

CHAPTER 1
The Environmentally Sound Society 7

CHAPTER 2
Communes, Utopias and Green Principles 25

CHAPTER 3
Social Change and the Politics of Community and Communes 47

CHAPTER 4
Decline of Green Evangelism 69

CHAPTER 5
How Green are the Communes? Ecological Values and Practices 119

CHAPTER 6
Changing Society: or Being Changed? 157

CHAPTER 7
A Vanguard for Ecotopia? 199

Appendix 1 221

Appendix 2 227

References 231

Index 237

LIST OF TABLES

Table 1: Political philosophies of environmentalists
Table 2: 1960s communes compared with the 1980s
Table 3: Society and community
Table 4: The communes examined in this work
Table 5: Main tenets of the Findhorn consensus
Table 6: Approximate ages of the interviewees
Table 7: Length of time in communes
Table 8: An elite?
Table 9: Major training, jobs and skills before joining
Table 10: Dissatisfaction as a motive for joining
Table 11: Major reasons for joining
Table 12: Ideological beliefs
Table 13: What 'the environment' means
Table 14: Major influences
Table 15: Beliefs about nature
Table 16: Ecologically sound practices
Table 17: Summary of views on social change
Table 18: Attitudes to conventional politics

Abbreviations used

CAT Centre for Alternative Technology (The Quarry), Powys, Wales
CF Canon Frome, Herefordshire
RF Redfield, Buckinghamshire
MW Monkton Wyld, Dorset
LSF Lower Shaw Farm, Swindon, Wilts
PIC People in Common, Burnley, Lancs
CRAB Crabapple, Shropshire
LAUR Laurieston Hall, Galloway, Scotland
LSP Lifespan, Sheffield, Yorkshire
GLAN Glaneirw, Wales
ZAP Z to A Project (formerly New University Project), Handsworth, Birmingham
FIND Findhorn, Forres, Scotland

Introduction

> The rudiments of an ecological society will probably be structured around the commune – freely created, human in scale, and intimate in its consciously cultivated relationships . . .

This is what the green anarchist Murray Bookchin (1982) thinks. This book aims to see if he is correct. It reports on research done in a dozen communes in England, Scotland and Wales, which, with two exceptions, were founded in the 1970s – in the wake of the first wave of mass publicity and concern about human impact on the environment. Extended interviews (each up to two-and-a-half hours long) with over eighty communards probed their belief systems, ideologies and practices. Each conversation led up to the central concern of the work, the question: *How important are communes in leading the way to a socially more just and ecologically more harmonious society?*

Why ask it? Because a vast literature has appeared since Rachel Carson's *Silent Spring* sparked off, in 1962, the present wave of environmental concern; but much of it has been about the technicalities and causes of the problems – whether they exist and how bad they are. Relatively little has appeared on what to do, but this is undoubtedly now the most pressing topic. This book's contribution is to examine just one option, suggested by some of the more radical environmentalists, whom I call 'greens' throughout the book. They still form a minority among people who are concerned about the environment – no more than sixteen per cent of the Americans surveyed in 1980, for example, thought that 'a completely new [social-economic] system is needed' to solve our environmental problems (Milbrath 1984, p82). But I think it increasingly probable that they are right, and that the reformists – the 'technocentrics', 'cornucopians' and 'environmental managers' who believe that it is largely a matter of technological and managerial adjustments to the present system (O'Riordan 1989) – are wrong. The views of the communards reported here will amply suggest why this should be so.

When I wrote about the issue of the environment, and what different groups of people said about it, I concluded that one way towards an environmentally sound and socially just society might lie in a 'network of alternative small communities where people try consciously to live along *Blueprint [for Survival]*-style principles' (Pepper 1984, p224). I echoed many others (see Chapter 2), some of whom might go as far as Erich Fromm (1956, p361), who thought that 'our only alternative to the dangers of robotism [modern industrial society] is humanistic communitarianism'. It is, however, easy for theorists like me to say such things. This book gives the somewhat different views of those who are actually trying to *do it*. They may be more realistic about communes as green utopias and panaceas. The book does not ask *how* green are all the communes in the UK, or elsewhere; it is not a statistical survey. Rather, it enquires whether people in communes do or do not show, through their attitudes, values and deeds, sufficient evidence for us to conclude that communes could be a significant, even major, part of a green society – an *Ecotopia* (Callenbach 1978, 1981). From it one can also decide whether or not the 'green movement' (Green Party, pressure groups and so forth) should or should not put much more time and effort into publicising, assisting and establishing communes; something it has neglected to do hitherto.

Of course, much has been written already about communes, and their ideology, sociology and practical organisation. It is clear from this literature that communes have, throughout their history, embodied some green principles and practices. Nowhere, however, does there seem to be a book which examines these forms of social organisation specifically from a green perspective. That is what is done here. What is *not* attempted is another sociological study, or a history. And one set of communes which undoubtedly does embody many 'green' attitudes and practices is omitted; this constitutes the monasteries and other religious communities. This omission is because I am interested in the notion of communes as a possible way forward for the majority of ordinary people in the radical green movement, and I do not think that a life of total devotion and commitment to a religious cause is a remotely realistic option for most of us, green as it might incidentally be. Life in a spiritually-oriented commune *might* be an option, however, hence those at Monkton Wyld and Findhorn were included in the list. It also

INTRODUCTION

featured the rural communes of Redfield, Crabapple, Canon Frome, Glaneirw and Laurieston that farm and garden organically, the last being also an education centre; the communes of the Z to A Project (formerly the New University Project, now part of Radical Routes network) and People in Common, the urban-based though rurally located printing cooperative of Lifespan; the now suburban organic farm and education centre of Lower Shaw Farm; and the Centre for Alternative Technology ('The Quarry'), an education and demonstration centre in rural Wales.

These communes were picked because they were founded within the last twenty years of high general environmental awareness, and were therefore likely, among all communes, to show the effects of this consciousness. The exception is Findhorn. Founded in the 1960s, it might be said to belong particularly to that group reviewed at the end of that decade in the excellent studies by Abrams and McCulloch (1976) and Rigby (1974 a and b). They show that the sixties communes reflected many concerns – anti-materialism, pacifism, feminism, for instance (see also MacLaughlin and Davidson (1985)) – that are relevant to today's greens. But, interestingly, there are very few references to what are now the central and defining green concerns (although Rigby's model of the world view of the communitarians does include the notion of ecological catastrophe as the main threat to future society among a dozen other components of their belief system). Findhorn is different. It has persisted and grown, and its original *raison d'être* has become a major facet of green ideology in the 1980s. It cannot be omitted from any study like this one, since it is the self-proclaimed 'centre of light' for the New (ecological) Age.

Chapters 1 to 3 of this book provide a brief context and overview for the research. The first describes the beliefs, attitudes, values and practices which might characterise an ideal environmentally sound society as defined by contemporary radical green writers. Evidence of the presence or absence of these in communes was noted in the conversations with the communards (see Appendix 1 for the interview structure used to shape these conversations). Chapter 2 surveys literature on past communes and community-based movements, to note how implicitly or explicitly green their lifestyle may have been. It then demonstrates the importance that many radical green writers now attach to communes and small communities for the future. Chapter 3 examines the theory behind the key idea of communes as a major force for social change. It demonstrates, too, that future green communal society could vary considerably in its political orientation. Chapters 4 to 6 cover the communes researched here. Chapter 4 describes the original and present intentions of their members – how green they were and are. It also examines their criticisms of conventional society. In Chapter 5 their beliefs, values and practices are assessed alongside the theoretical yardstick of Chapter 1, and then Chapter 6 examines their views on social change, and what they may be doing to influence the wider society. The concluding chapter outlines what message this study has for the green movement at large.

The cental part of the research method consisted of extended 'interviews' with commune members. Mostly, these were long (but not rambling) conversations about the interviewee's beliefs concerning what the world is and should be like, how to change it, and the role of communes in the process. They covered some deep and abstract issues, as well as the practicalities of communal living and the communal enterprises. Appendix 1 lays out the schedule of questions and issues which the conversations covered. Many of them were not put directly, in order to minimise leading interviewees into discussing things that they would not otherwise have considered significant, but the interviewers had a clear idea of which questions and answers were of major relevance to the overall aim. In particular, if the communards voiced concern about environmental matters and the attitudes and actions of wider society, then this was the signal for the interviewers to press for greater detail.

Clearly this research method is not principally a quantitative one, and it does not lend itself totally to very refined quantitative statements, such as 'fifteen per cent of communards think such and such'. However, broad statements like this are sometimes made, and there are tables with 'quantitative' data. These should obviously be treated as indicative, but not without validity.

Before going any further, the minimal defining features of a commune adopted here should be given. These are contentious, but this definition is based on conversations with communards and on definitions in Rigby, Abrams and McCulloch, Shenker (1986) and Kanter (1973).

1. Membership is voluntary.
2. It is small – commonly in Britain five to twenty-five adults.
3. They are committed to living together, and their home incorporates features designed for this purpose.

4. They will share at least some of the following: housework, eating and cooking, resources, childcare, leisure pursuits and, in some way, income (for some this makes a crucial difference between a 'commune' – total income pooling – and a 'community').
5. They are relatively withdrawn from the wider society; a discrete unit.
6. The group has priority over other relations, except perhaps couple relationships.
7. There is an understood purpose: living together and sharing both for itself, and for wider social, political or spiritual purposes. This transcends the time span of individual members.
8. Values and moral concerns (which are frequently 'alternative' to those of the wider society) are, with group solidarity and relations, placed above instrumental and economic concerns.
9. Members attempt to establish an alternative social pattern, at least for themselves and perhaps with a view to setting an example for the wider society.
10. How they do things – process – is usually as important as what they do.

Some of the communities discussed here do not fall into this definition of communes (e.g. they do not income share) and some do. For convenience and shorthand, and to avoid making sometimes arbitrary judgements about which place is a commune and which a community, the terms 'commune' and 'communard' are used throughout. Hopefully this lack of precision will be forgiven by those who live in these communes (or communities): apart from Findhorn, they all figure in *Diggers and Dreamers,* the 1990-91 *Communes* Directory.

CHAPTER 1
The environmentally sound society

One aim of the work described in this book was to discover whether, and in what particular ways, the communards we interviewed were green, and to build a profile of their world views and lifestyles which could be compared with the idealised green world view and lifestyle that we had in mind.

The components of that ideal green world view and of sound green practices may be known to readers, since they have been so much publicised, discussed and developed in the literature and the media over the past quarter of a century. But they are so important to the assessment which this research makes that they are briefly recapitulated below. A fuller description may be got from the standard works on which this summary is based (e.g. Schumacher 1973, 1980, O'Riordan 1981, Capra 1982, Merchant 1982, Cotgrove 1982, Porritt 1984, Ekins 1986). The summary emphasises attitudes and values, because many greens echo Lyn White's (1967) influential 'idealistic' assessment of the problem, that it is our attitudes and values towards nature which determine what we do to it and how we treat it. Hence, if we get our ideas sorted out so as to be 'environmentally sound', the practices appropriate to averting an ecological crisis are likely to follow. This may be contrasted with a more 'materialist' approach, which emphasises how what we *do* influences what we *think*; our attitudes and values being conditioned by actions. This issue is explored in Chapter 3, and Pepper 1985.

The summary also illustrates that much of the green world view is about society rather than focusing exclusively on nature and environment. This is consistent with the greens' radical approach; at root, unsound values and actions concerning nature link with the unsound way that we in the West, as individuals and in groups, value and behave towards each other. Hence, we can conceive of a specifically green critique of conventional Western society that may have much in common with the critiques by other political ideologies, such as socialism, anarchism, or true conservatism. Then there are fundamental 'alternative' green values about nature, with corresponding broad alternative social and political principles. These, in turn, would sustain, and be sustained by, the detailed specific practices of a green lifestyle. All of these things – a changed world view, a radically different socio-political-economic system and, especially, ecologically sound personal lifestyles and practices – are the components of an ideal green society, the seeds of which may or may not be found in the communes of the 1970s and eighties.

WHAT GREENS ARE AGAINST

Greens consider that at the heart of the world's problems of pollution, resource depletion and environmental deterioration are domineering and exploitative attitudes to nature. They are thought to be particularly Western attitudes, and Western culture is seen to have a pernicious global influence. We see nature as an instrument to be used for endless material gain. We see it this way because we think we are separate from it; a view inherent in science and technology inherited from the seventeenth century, which followed Bacon's creed that by observing nature analytically (splitting it into parts), and reducing everything to its basic components (e.g. biology is a matter of chemistry, which is a matter of physics which is a matter of mathematics), we can know and manipulate natural laws for our own ends. This approach gives tremendous technological power, which is used for ends that are ignoble. It is based on an ignoble view of human nature – that it is aggressive, selfish, competitive – and a society which is seen as naturally hierarchical and unequal. Wasteful consumerism is now the false god by which both individual and social progress are measured. The spiritual, emotional, artistic, loving and cooperative sides of our nature (the 'feminine' values) are neglected for this cold materialism, which overplays the role of rationality, 'hard facts' and calculating economic utilitarianism in deciding what is good or bad. We lack any deeper moral standards.

Over-linear thinking leads to the false conclusion that if something is good, more of it is necessarily better. Hence more technology and economic growth are, unwisely, advocated as the way to cure the social and environmental ills which have been side-effects of technological and economic advancement. Indeed the very idea of progress is now equated with this, rather than moral or spiritual advancement. By extension, what is technically most complex, like nuclear power or weapons, is regarded as most progressive, regardless of how much it destroys or pollutes. So there is a widespread misapprehension that high technology cannot and should not be rejected; yet such technology often destroys the environment and is not controllable by ordinary people, so that it can be abused and used to abuse others. Greens think that such beliefs, allied to human greed, underlie industrial society, which impoverishes both nature and social morality. Industrialism is founded on the too narrow objective of profit maximisation, encouraging overconsumption. In blind pursuit of this, industries export their pollution to society at large. Given today's large-scale industrialisation, pollution and toxicity become unacceptably high. At the same time, materials recycling and pollution control are limited in the interests of cost cutting and competition. Yet resources are used as if they were limitless, though clearly they are finite. The short-sightedness of this is never fully appreciated in a system whose time perspective for planning is short — decades rather than centuries. Giantism, profit-maximisation, division of labour, the production line, mechanisation and de-skilling; all these basic features of industrial society combine to produce uncreative, unfulfilling and alienating work and drab, uniform environments in which to live. Cities and suburbs are huge and impersonal, and the countryside is dominated by monotonous agribusiness-produced landscapes that give us poisoned and low-value food and water.

The search for expanding markets, resources and cheap labour has extended the industrial-consumer society across the globe, destroying rainforest and changing climate. The Third World is polluted and materially and culturally impoverished by the international trade system, which many still see as progressive or inevitable, and essential to 'development'. It produces a political system dominated by both narrow nationalism and by uncontrollable multinational companies; a strong centralised state is also needed by every country to make the national and international economic and political systems work. But the state interferes with the rights of individuals, inhibiting our freedom, self-determination and responsibility, producing an increasingly undemocratic politics where the wishes, needs and characteristics of regions, local communities and individuals are overridden and denied. Scientific experts often play a part in the undemocratic processes, acting in defence of corporate interests against the mass of people, a role they can occupy by virtue of their special knowledge. So, ultimately, the freedom, wellbeing, health and quality of life of the majority is impaired. Frequently the nuclear family reinforces such alienation: it is unnaturally exclusive and cannot relieve or be immune from the pressures of wider society. It often becomes a structure in which people dominate and exploit each other, replicating wider society. Greens might describe that society as fragmented and self-seeking, lacking a genuine sense of community.

Thus are greens estranged from society's fundamental values, and the more radically green they are, the more estranged they are. Theirs is a protest against more than just the immediate effects of a polluted, 'overpopulated' world where natural resources are thought to be running out. It is a revolt against the alienation of urban-industrial capitalism: its materialism, competitive individualism, lack of sufficient concern for social justice and lack of real democracy; its routine and mechanical daily life; its lack of opportunities to create things and use talents; its conditioning of people to accept authority and the status quo, with all the entrapments of middle-class existence – marriage, house purchase and the social and career ladders.

Clearly the green critique is nothing new. It has affinities with all the dissenting voices that accompanied the rise of modern capitalism over the past three hundred years, ranging from traditional romantic conservatism to romantic socialism, from the rationality of Marxist critique to the views of anarchist-communists. But greens do claim a newness for their dissenting politics, based on two starting points. The first is that the natural environment is threatened, as never before (they claim), with near-total ruin and desolation, and therefore human society, being intimately part of the global ecosystem, must crash down with it. That is the pragmatic argument for building a green society. The second one is not pragmatic, but is based on the *bioethic* – a key aspect of the 'ecologism' (Dobson 1990) which greens believe in.

WHAT GREENS STAND FOR

Core values about nature

The bioethic is the most fundamental of these. It is the belief that nature has worth *in its own right*, regardless of its use value to humans.

Hence plants and animals are respected of and for themselves. We have a moral obligation to respect, even revere, nature – perhaps as a manifestation of 'God', whoever your god is. The right to existence of all species should be maintained wherever practicable, and that existence should be as 'natural' as possible. This has substantial implications: while it is not practicable for us to respect the 'rights' of the AIDS virus, for example, it is feasible to protect animals through veganism, vegetarianism, or at least non-intensive 'humane' livestock husbandry.

This ethic may be linked to the notion of Gaia – the whole earth as a living, self-regulating organism. Although humans depend on the rest of nature, are an intimate part of it, and not separate from or above it, it follows from both the bioethic and Gaia that if humans were removed from the earth, the rest of nature could continue and there would be every point in this continuation. However the reverse does not apply. But this does not mean that nature is immune from human influence. Far from it. There *is* an environmental crisis (of pollution, overpopulation and resource depletion) which threatens the global ecosystem, and society as part of that system. It calls for us to adopt an appropriate humility; seeing nature as equally important as ourselves and acting as its protector and steward. We need to recognise and abide by the pervasive laws of nature that govern all nature, including ourselves. Such laws as carrying capacity lay down limits to growth; economic, population and technological. And they tell us that both human and non-human systems derive strength from diversity: sameness (whether in agricultural monocultures or in the spread of uniform Western industrialism to the detriment of local cultures) leads to a lack of robustness, and a destructive instability.

We need to think holistically, rather than in an over-analytical and reductionist way, in order to recognise the full implication of our place in the global ecosystem, which is that whatever we do to one part of that system will affect all other parts, eventually reverberating on ourselves: the greenhouse and ozone layer effects are prime examples of this.

A strong anti-urban bias may follow from all this (since cities often contravene ecological laws), and from the critique of conventional society outlined above. This bias may come out as love, respect and even reverence for countryside and wilderness as the repository of a simple innocent life – expressed through art, emotion and mysticism – and the reverse feelings toward urban, suburban and industrial-commercial societies and environments. Some leading greens, such as Jonathon Porritt (in his 1990 BBC TV series), are currently trying to eradicate this aspect of the green image, but it remains a persistent theme in the statements of many 'rank and file' greens.

And there may be support for feminism, stemming from the ideas of nature as female (Gaia is the Earth goddess) and/or from a belief that an imbalance between 'masculine' and 'feminine' values is ultimately responsible for the environmental crisis. However, there are many other views about this ultimate responsibility, or the ultimate 'scapegoat' as Bramwell (1989) puts it. Perceptively, she suggests that the common link between them is the feeling in ecologism of humanity's 'fall from grace', as in Protestant tradition. Indeed, one frequently hears greens talk of 'our' greed, 'our' selfishness etc. as if we were sinful. They often prefer to do this rather than exploring how the economic system draws out such characteristics from people and suppresses other, better, and equally innate ones.

The social implications

Several stages of argument follow from these green concerns about what Western society does to natural and social environments, and the green view of what our values concerning nature ought to be. The first is that we must henceforth live in harmony with nature, which means that social behaviour and personal morality should observe ecological laws. The way that the rest of nature is organised should serve as a model for human society. Secondly, the broad philosophy of an environmentally sound society should de-emphasise materialism and consumerism in order to make fewer demands on the planet's resources. This should be coupled with the practical features of population control and the development of low-impact non-polluting technology (featuring biodegradability and recycling), together with the use of 'soft', renewable energy sources and conservation techniques. Economic concepts must henceforth favour these features – so that they are incorporated in criteria for economic efficiency. Geographical reorganisation is desired, into small economic, political and social structures: particularly self-reliant regions and local communities (perhaps commune-based), for these have minimal ecological impact, are socially stable and make for cultural variety.

Third, since the sum total of material wealth based on making earth's resources into goods and consuming them will not grow, such wealth must be redistributed for, at least, the sake of peace. This involves social justice and getting rid of the economic dependency of the South on the North: substituting the present trade, 'aid' and debt relationships by independent development. Fourth, none of this is achievable without deep-rooted changes in Western values, social organisation and relationships. Living in harmony and non-violently with nature demands that we do the same with each other. The feminine (yin) values – contractive, responsive, cooperative, intuitive, synthesising – should be emphasised more, while the dominant masculine (yang) values – demanding, aggressive, competitive, rational, analytic – should be de-emphasised. Just as much feminism rejects hierarchy, so a green society may be less hierarchical than the present one, and more participative for all. Holistic thought must be emphasised, so that economic accounting naturally takes in the environmental impact of human activity. And, as the ecology of our surroundings must be valued, so should our inner ecology be respected: a premium is to be put on personal health and wellbeing.

Fifth, as part compensation for lower material standards for the rich, and following these major value changes, the concept of *quality of life* becomes all-important. Again, economics must be revised to account for this, so that wellbeing and personal fulfilment should be part measures of the worth of economic activity, governing what we produce. And only socially useful activity should be recognised in concepts like gross national product. A social wage, paid to everyone, would mean that housework, caring for the sick and needy, and tending the allotment or garden would not be economically second class activities. Manufacturing – taking nature's products and changing their form – and services should be geared to social needs, rather than wants expressed solely through the market economy. Many wants are anyway artificial and inessential: deliberately inculcated through such things as advertising. Since meaningful work is a basic human need, work should be designed not to be degrading, boring or alienating where at all possible. It should emphasise craft and creativity.

Sixth, quality of life can be enhanced through giving people control over their own lives. Society should be a genuine participatory democracy. The local community should own local resources, not the state or large private corporations who will centralise wealth and power – both of these are enemies. Individuals must feel that their views are heard and respected, whether they are 'experts' or not, and that they can tangibly influence decisions about their community and local environment. Appropriate political structures and mechanisms must be evolved to enable this. There is also a need for collectivism centred round the small community and extended family, so that people can share resources, work, caring for each other and the young or old, and have a greater sense of belonging. More fulfilling personal, including sexual, relationships should be possible in the extended 'family', which may not be a blood-related family.

But, seventh, quality of life must come from self fulfilment and 'actualisation' for the individual. Respect and love for other people, the foundation for such attitudes to nature, must itself be founded in self respect and love. This requires all possible means of self discovery and development. Inner-directed philosophies and practices should be embraced, especially holistic ones which link the individual to nature. For the eighth, last, stage in the reasoning behind the features of a green society concerns the importance of the individual in social change. Personal lifestyles are important political statements. The feminist slogan 'the personal is political' obtains. Through changing lifestyle, it is held, we can contribute directly to social change. There is faith in this mechanism for change rather than in mass collective political movements, which are seen as having failed us in the past. Coupled with this is the important role given to education of the 'right' sort, for example, along holistic, Steiner principles. For, it is reasoned, the more that people know about how their own actions affect their environment, the more they are likely to change them. The more they know of how nature works, the more they will respect and value it.

Deep ecology

Radical greens at their most radical might overtly graft a political ideology such as socialism or anarchism onto their beliefs (see below). Alternatively they may emphasise the spiritual more than the material, in which case they will often describe themselves as 'deep' ecologists. The adjective 'deep' is self-assigned, to signify that they ask what they regard as 'deep' questions about what lies at the roots of our environmental predicament, whereas 'shallow' ecologists (technocentrics or materialists) do not. Of course, whether their answers really are deep is a matter of opinion: Marxists, for instance, might think them superficial because they do not seek to understand how the economic base of society conditions actions and perceptions concerning nature (see Johnston 1989).

Devall and Sessions (1985) sum up deep ecology in eight basic principles. They are:

1. The well-being and flourishing of human and nonhuman life on earth have value in themselves (synonyms: intrinsic value, inherent value). These values are independent of the usefulness of the nonhuman world for human purposes.

2. Richness and diversity of life forms contribute to the realisation of these values and are also values in themselves.

3. Humans have no right to reduce this richness and diversity except to satisfy *vital* needs.

4. The flourishing of human life and cultures is compatible with a substantial decrease of the human population. The flourishing of nonhuman life requires such a decrease.

5. Present human interference with the nonhuman world is excessive and the situation is rapidly worsening.

6. Policies must therefore be changed. These policies affect basic economic, technological, and ideological structures. The resulting state of affairs will be deeply different from the present.

7. The ideological change is mainly that of appreciating life *quality* (dwelling in situations of inherent value) rather than adhering to an increasingly higher standard of living. There will be a profound awareness of the difference between big and great.

8. Those who subscribe to the foregoing points have an obligation directly or indirectly to try to implement the necessary changes.

As such, these principles do not signify a particularly deeply spiritual approach. However, one further and vital element does, and it means that deep ecology leads into New Ageism (the elements of which are described later in connection with Findhorn). Whereas shallow ecologists believe that humans and nature are separate and that humans are the more important, deep ecologists believe that there is no separation. They have a holistic 'total-field' view. Naess (1988) declares that all organisms are 'knots in the biospherical net or field of intrinsic relations', and the very notion of a world composed of discrete separate things is denied. As Fox (1984) puts it: 'The central intuition of deep ecology is that there is no firm ontological divide in the field of existence'. 'Ontological' means concerned with the nature of being, so Fox is saying that there is no *fundamental* difference between what humans are and what the rest of nature is. So there is no division into independent 'subjects' and 'objects'; no division between human and non-human realities.

Devall says that 'deep ecology begins with the unity rather than the dualism which has been the dominant theme of Western philosophy'. Hence there is a fundamental identity of self with the cosmos. This is atheistic spirituality, for it does not mean identity with 'God'. New Ageism does make this connection, though the identity is with any and all gods. It is true to say that the epistemological divide between 'scientific objective' knowledge and intuitive knowledge is not valid either in deep ecology. Intuitive knowledge is highly valued, as are emotions, feelings and spiritual insights.

Deep ecology is compatible with the Gaia hypothesis of the Earth as a living, self-regulating system which, unusually among the known planets, adjusts itself in the face of variations in the external environment (e.g. long term increases in solar radiation) to maintain stable and optimum conditions for life. O'Riordan (1989 p85) distinguishes radical environmentalists (ecocentrics) from reformists (technocentrics), but he also subdivides the first category into 'Gaianism' and 'communalism'. The Gaian perspective is that of deep ecology, with its 'faith in the rights of nature and of the essential need for co-evolution of human and natural ethics'. The primary emphasis of 'communalism' is more on society and 'faith in the cooperative capabilities of societies to establish self-reliant communities based on renewable resource use and appropriate technologies'.

This division is reflected in the dispute between deep and 'social' ecologists. The social ecology position refutes deep ecology's relative emphases on the need for moral and spiritual changes ahead of social policy changes. Social ecology would reverse these priorities. The anarchist version of it perceives hierarchy and relationships of domination and subordination between people as the essential root of human domination of nature. It is most forcibly expressed by Bookchin, who says that spiritual and lifestyle changes by individuals and groups will do little to alter 'our grotesque imbalance with nature if they leave the patriarchal family, the multinational corporation, the bureaucratic and centralised political structure and the prevailing technocratic rationality untouched' (1980 p78).

Bookchin and others, including socialist greens, also attack deep ecology for its calls for human population decrease; a potentially reactionary and dangerous position (see Pepper 1984 pp208-211). And Bookchin (1987) also points out the potential dangers of the bioethic in elevating animal above human interests. He goes on to attack deep ecology for its intellectual flabbiness, incoherence and tendency to talk in vague, mystifying and meaningless language. The thrust of its mysticism, when applied for instance to the Gaia thesis, is to revive notions of supreme beings, gods and goddesses, or a 'Self who absorbs all real existential selves', which are founded on hierarchical concepts. They very much hark back to the Renaissance view of the human-nature relationship: monistic but at the same time founded on a hierarchical chain of being (see Cosgrove 1990).

One might add that they also, despite their shibboleths of 'oneness with nature', imply a *separateness* between humans and nature. This is apparent when one compares deep ecology with a Marxist view of the society/nature relationship. For in the latter nature is *socially* produced, everything that is 'natural' is, in fact, produced by and through social systems; but by the same token nothing that humans do to nature is 'un-natural' (Vogel 1988). The relationship of unity is metabolic – if nature is socially produced and what humans do is natural, then humans are not excluded from nature. Deep ecology's unity, by contrast, implies a nature to be revered by sinful humans who have violated 'her', so effectively nature is elevated to a separate and divine being.

Mainstream greens like Porritt, Capra and Henderson would like to embrace many elements of deep ecology as well as social ecology. This seems to make sense because superficially there is not a huge difference between the two, as Young (1990 p132) suggests. But in fact Bookchin and social ecologists are on to what amounts to a profound *political* difference between the two. For when the position of many radical greens is closely scrutinised, serious political contradictions can arise through their tendency effectively to subordinate the social to the 'natural' (again, a false separation) and to abandon the rational for the mystical. As we discuss later, a 'Findhorn tendency' permeates the whole movement.

Political variations

Not all greens think all of the things in this model of green values and ideas. What they would emphasise as important, and how they would act to change things, amounts to, and partly depends on, their political philosophy in the traditional sense of left and right, or socialism, conservatism and liberalism (with small letters; not in the sense of party political labels which may be inaccurate as measures of

Table 1: Political philosophies of environmentalists

Traditional Conservatives (*Radical*)†	Market Liberals (*Reformist*)‡	Welfare Liberals (*Reformist*)‡	Democratic Socialist (*Reformist*)‡	Revolutionary Socialist (*Radical*)†
Are Limits to growth, and enlightened private ownership is the best way to protect nature and environment from over-exploitation. Protect traditional landscapes, buildings, as part of our heritage.	The free market, plus science and technology, will solve resource shortages and pollution problems. If resources get scarce people will supply substitutes – if there's a market for them.	Market economy, with private ownership, but managed. Reform laws, planning and taxation for environmental protection.	Decentralised socialism; local democracy; town hall socialism.	Environmental ills are specific to capitalism, so capitalism must be abolished: requiring some revolutionary change, perhaps brought on by environmental crises.
Anti-industrialism: human societies should model themselves on natural ecosystems: e.g. should be stable, and change slowly and organically. Need for diversity, but hierarchical structure: bound together by commonly held beliefs. Everyone to be content with their position (niche) in society. The family (perhaps extended) is the most important social unit. Admire tribal societies. Very romantic: yearn for the past.	Don't believe in 'overpopulation' – people are a resource.

Capitalism can accommodate and thrive on protecting the environment.

Consumer pressure for environment-friendly products will play a big part. Capital will respond to this market. | Enlightened self-interest, tailored to the communal good, will solve the problems.

Consumer pressure for environment-friendly products will play a large part. Pressure group campaigns, in a pluralist, parliamentary democracy will lead to appropriate legislation. | Mixed economy and parliamentary democracy – with strict controls on capitalism. Emphasises the role of labour and trade unions. A big role for the state (especially locally). Mixture of private and common ownership of resources. Emphasis on improving the urban environment. Production for social need. Big coops sector. State subsidises environmental protection (e.g. public transport). | Rejects the state ultimately, but needed in the transition to a communal (commune-ist) society. Class conflict vital in social change to a green and socially just world – reject the parliamentary approach.

Poverty, social injustice, squalid urban environments, all seen as part of the environmental crises.

Similar visions of future to anarchists, but emphasise collective political action, and the state initially. |

*Mainstream Greens
(Radical aims, but reformist methods: including British Green Party, Friends of the Earth and other pressure groups)

A mix of welfare liberals and democratic socialists, but say they reject politics of left and right. Emphasise the importance of the <u>individual</u>, and his/her need to revise values, lifestyles and consumer habits.

Advocate a lifestyle of voluntary simplicity. Also, need to change social-economic structures, inc. putting an end to the 'industrial society'. Favour small-scale capitalism, but with profit motive secondary to production for social and environmental need. Also coops and communes. State has a role – especially locally. Romantic view of nature – spirituality important, especially in deep ecology and New Ageism, which all mainstream greens have tendencies towards. New Age irrationalism, mysticism, rejection of 'politics' and industrialism gives it a reactionary, conservative element.

*Green Anarchists and Eco-feminists
(Radical aims and methods)

Reject the state, class politics, Parliamentary democracy and capitalism. People to organise themselves: have responsibility and power over their own lives. The individual very important, but the individual gets fulfilment in relation to the community. Decentralised economy and politics: common ownership of means of production, and distribution according to needs (income sharing communes). Spontaneous and organically evolving society. Non-hierarchical direct democracy. Rural and urban communes and cooperatives. Bioregionalism.

---

*These two, together represent "ecologism" (ecocentrism), which starts, unlike others, from the *ecological*/imperative and the bioethic (nature as important as human society). But in their social prescriptions they mainly straddle liberalism and socialism (with one or two elements of conservatism).

---

† "Radical" = wanting to go back to the roots of society and change it fundamentally in some ways, and quite rapidly.

‡ "Reformist" = the present economic system is accepted: but it must be revised – in the direction of either less or more interference in and management of the economy – gradually and through parliamentary democracy.

the real political philosophy of parties – for example, the Conservatives today are mainly 'market liberals').

Greens often argue that their values amount to a distinctive green political philosophy in its own right, 'above' traditional right-left divisions. This is not quite accurate, for while nature and environment loom large in green politics, there are still some very traditional political questions to be answered, like who is to own natural resources, what is the relative role of individuals and the collective in a green society, is there a role for the state? – as Ryle (1988) points out. Furthermore greens come from conventional society from which they will have acquired prior political positions on many issues, whether they recognise this or not. There is not space here to review all the fundamental political issues, although some of them will be discussed in Chapters 3 and 6, on social change.

Table 1, however, briefly summarises some political dimensions of environmentalism. It shows that concern for the environment and views on how to solve the problems occur right across the political spectrum. It divides the concerned into those advocating radical change from our current mixed, but free-market-oriented, economy and those who would merely revise the system, in the directions of more or less intervention, to provide a better environmental future.

In terms of traditional political philosophies, the mainstream greens seem mainly to straddle the welfare liberal and democratic socialist traditions. However, the more anarchistic of them can be distinguished by their clear position on common ownership of resources and on their unequivocal rejection of the state in all forms and of traditional politics.

Lifestyle implications

Notwithstanding differences in political emphasis, most greens would probably agree on a desirable set of ecologically sound ways of daily living. These can be seen as 'first order' – directly trying to behave with, rather than against, nature, and minimising human ecological impact – and 'second order' – organising and behaving socially in a way compatible with the values of a green society. The terms first and second order, used in this way, apply only to obvious interconnectedness with environmental matters – they are not intended to imply that first order practices are more important than second order ones. Indeed, the reverse is probably the case. The first would obviously include such things as sharing resources (washing machines, TVs etc) and recycling wastes (paper, excrement, manufactured goods components) to lessen demand on raw materials. And one would de-emphasise consumption generally, living on as little money as feasible. Wholefoods can be bought collectively and cheaply through food coops, for instance, but then growing and home-producing foods may be even more preferable and would help in the ceaseless quest to avoid artificial additives, toxins and contaminants. Obvious pollutants, like CFCs in aerosols, non-biodegradable cleaners, lead in paint or fuel, or pesticides, would be inadmissible. The cruelty-free principle might be thought to require veganism, which however could be carried to almost unimaginable extremes like not using or watching films or not using or listening to instruments like drums or violins, which use animal products. Concern about North-South trade relationships could rule out all cash crops, or products with tropical hardwoods, though some environmentalists will argue that to rob the latter of a market value will be the quickest way to ensure their total destruction. Energy conservation measures range from not buying or using most electrical goods (though while most people would probably see an electric nose-hair trimmer as the ultimate in needlessness, there is a good argument that radio and TV are necessities), to cutting down on consumption generally, for example by using less light and heat through frugality and insulation. A similar approach is appropriate to transport, making fewer journeys, walking or cycling where feasible, preferring public transport to private, motor cycles to cars, small cars to larger, and so on. Alternative technology and medicine would be favoured.

Social and work practices ('second order') might include less division of labour, more work sharing, individuals combining hand and brainwork and sharing skills and expertise, while possession of the latter would not confer power over people through status or disproportionately high income or undue influence over decision making. This last is a crucial issue in the ideal green society, which wants to re-empower individuals in directly democratic ways. Democratic participative political structures may involve non-hierarchy, consensus decision making rather than majority voting, and using delegates rather than representatives in political assemblies. Mechanisms may be sought to avoid and resolve conflict, hence a consciousness of group dynamics, co-counselling, group therapy and so on may be encouraged. Attention will almost certainly be paid to the quality of relationships, with time taken specifically to preserve and enhance them. Gentle, loving and non-aggressive behaviour will be the ideal, but cultivating openness about feelings and emotions may involve putting up with aggression and bad temper in others, and feeling uninhibited about showing these in oneself from time to time. Facilitating self-assertion and helping others to assert themselves are important in creating a better quality of life. In this connection, too, creative activity, active rather than passive leisure, group recreation, and spiritual pursuits, from collective ritual to individual meditation and prayer, could be important. So may be open and uninhibited sexuality and artistic expression. A studious mix of private and public activity, and a tolerance of different viewpoints, sexual proclivities and religious convictions, would be major features of the green lifestyle, though racism and sexism would not be tolerated.

The matter of uninhibited sexuality is contentious. Some greens see an instrumental link between this, the liberation of women from gender role stereotyping and therefore a reduction in birth rates. They argue that a less inhibited approach to sexuality removes repressions and would therefore improve quality of life. But Young (1990 p36), citing studies of existing pre-industrial societies in Oceania, argues for sexual expression to be limited to the family. A powerful ingredient of success in those societies which have established the most successful relationships with the environment, he says, is *kinship*, involving bonds of obligation to a large network of relatives both living and dead: 'kinship defines social function and ensures intergenerational and communal cooperation'. Young invites those who seek a consistent environmental philosophy to re-evaluate the importance of the family (preferably extended, but also nuclear). Environmental responsibility in tribal society is not usually an abstract idea but a function of extended family responsibility, in which blood ties are reinforced by rituals and ceremonies. Duty to the next generation is a key element here: but in conventional Western society utilitarian economic thinking militates against such a perspective (see Pearce *et al* 1989, on discounting the future, i.e. how it makes economic 'sense' to shift the burden of costs to future generations).

All these things, and many more, are hallmarks of a green lifestyle. In the contemporary environment of individualistic, self-seeking materialism most of them are difficult to do and sustain. Hence it is necessary to guard against a potential feeling of constant guilt about not doing as much, as well, as one 'should' do – for guilt is ultimately disempowering and therefore politically counter-revolutionary.

Nonetheless it is becoming quite fashionable in comfortable middle class circles to adopt many 'first order' practices in a rather minimal and even ostentatious way. 'Green consumerism' has always been a waiting trap by which ecological consciousness can become de-radicalised, from the early seventies *Whole Earth Catalog* to the present *Green Consumer/Supermarket Guides* (Elkington and Hailes 1988). But the idea that through consuming we can retrieve ourselves from the mess caused by a consumer society is fatuous. While literature like *Home Ecology* (Christensen 1989) can suggest that a green lifestyle is cosy and not too difficult to attain, the reality is quite different. Truly to live out green principles may involve an asceticism more usually associated with strictest monasticism. An account by two remarkable people who get very close to it (Murtagh and Robinson 1984) amply demonstrates this. The 'living simply' lifestyle they choose to follow on account of their environmental awareness and concern to redistribute wealth to poor people worldwide involves all of the following and more:

> [Rent, second-hand clothes, cheap basic foods and basic heating/cooking costs are necessities but] . . . We cannot justify spending money on records, record-players, books, TV, radio, newspapers, laundrettes, jewellery, haircuts, drinking, restaurants, discos, theatre, cinema, concerts, art exhibitions, places of interest, holidays, hobbies, sports, Christmas/birthday presents . . . We make as few phone calls as possible [saving energy], using public phone boxes.

They try to be vegan and get fruit and vegetables from the boxes thrown away by market traders and greengrocers. They boycott produce from the South, including tea, coffee, cocoa, sugar, bananas, many sorts of rice, lentils and beans, because of the current unjust trading practices between North and South. By extension, they boycott the products of multinational corporations (including most processed and packaged foods). They would not buy from the Eastern bloc (until recently) because of human rights denials, or from the US because of its imperialism and role in the arms race. Sanitary towels and toilet paper are reluctantly used – 'though I should experiment with a sponge which would be much cheaper' in the first instance, and although in the second instance scrap paper should be used ('or better still soap and water as we did in India'). Transport is normally by walking or bike (even from the south to the north of England), though sometimes lifts are hitched (admittedly benefitting from other people's expenditure on a car) or coach transport is purchased. They boycott the big four banks, using the Co-op as a compromise, despite its literature advocating materialist buying on credit, for the 'Whose World' project which they run in Manchester. Other activities can cause much agonising:

> I went to a cheap benefit woman's disco and went to great lengths to justify the expenditure; I love dancing and I enjoyed the opportunity of being with my women friends. But deep down I knew I could not justify it and that if a woman had been outside begging for herself and her child hopefully I would not have been able to convince myself that it was alright to go in . . . I badly wanted to learn some modern history and economics to be able to understand current conflicts and injustices better, and toyed with the idea of starting an Open University course . . . I agonised over this £10 [fee] for months. I wanted to justify spending it but couldn't . . .

There are other difficulties, like going in cafes and pubs to share the company of friends – who want to drink and eat out – when they do not think it right to spend more than they need on food and will never buy or accept drinks – they 'drink water or nothing'.

All of this is done without a hint of holier-than-thou feeling, and on an extremely low income – no state benefits are acceptable or accepted. While most greens will admire the internal consistency and coherence of such a lifestyle, few will be able to achieve it for themselves, especially as members of conventional society. Whether one can come closer to it in a commune will be discussed in Chapter 5.

CHAPTER 2

Communes, utopias and green principles

THE PAST

Rudolf Bahro thinks that communes will be an integral part of a future green society. It does not matter to him that many past attempts to form and sustain communes failed. These attempts, he says, were premature, whereas the time is now ripe for communes, with the breakdown of the expansionist capitalist culture (Bahro 1986, pp92-3). In a way this argues that history is irrelevant; whatever may have happened in the past, things are different now. While there may be some truth in this, it is still instructive to consider the past, for if communes by their nature are conducive to a green utopia then we would expect to see elements of green practices and principles in past communes and the movements they were parts of: even though these were not specifically a response to a widely-perceived environmental crisis, as is the present green movement.

Before 1800

Kanter's (1973) review of communes history emphasised how the tradition of utopia in Plato's *Republic* has been passed down through the centuries to the contemporary counterculture, so that there are striking resemblances between Plato's vision and today's commune movement. Of particular interest to us is the theme of coming close to the land, which is 'to come close to all that is natural'. This anti-urban back-to-nature idea holds that utopia is found in an agrarian and simple life which emphasises voluntary poverty or asceticism to avoid competition and conflict. Plato's ideal community must also be small (maximum around 5,000 members) so as to preserve unity. Kanter says that today's communal villages often number 150 to 200 members, rural communes range between twelve and forty, and urban groups are half this size. Shared values, self-awareness and self-knowledge are other common themes linking Plato, the sixties communes described in Kanter's book and today's green movement, as is the overarching theme of wholeness and integration in a cooperative mutualistic extended family of work and living together.

These ideas all resonate with the monastic tradition which, says Mercer (1984), began with the Essenes two thousand years ago. He describes monasticism as a withdrawal from society in search of an idea, attainable by self-abnegation. Roszak (1979, pp288-292) advocates 'monasticism', meaning 'civilised, durable communities where a vital, new sense of human destiny could take root' to carry us through coming social uncertainty and economic dislocation. It involves a simple but ingenious economy, which balances 'technical innovation and ecological intelligence', a communitarian culture of nonviolence and spiritual growth, and the capacity to synthesise qualities that have become polarised in today's world (personal and 'convivial', practical and spiritual). The technology it invents has minimal ecological impact, productivity is not idolised, success does not equate with profit, while manual labour is regarded as a spiritual discipline. Though nature worship is forbidden, a commitment to the sanctity of the person leads to a respect for the rights of nature and a 'comradely relationship' with it. There is less production and consumption, and life is slower and more meditative. The green perspective does indeed incorporate such values and approaches, though it may reject the hierarchical nature of monastic society and non-nature-centred spiritualism.

Mercer also describes 'early migrating sects', from Taborites to Anabaptists to Huterites, Menonites and Amish, who set up communes and communities in Europe and North America in the seventeenth and eighteenth centuries. While not recognisably 'green', they were often ascetic, craft-based, close to the land and pacifist. They might also share work, eating, property and wealth – but they were also often hierarchical, patriarchal and prey to charismatic leaders. Then there were the Diggers, communists of the 1650s, who are often praised in green literature today for their beliefs and actions supporting land ownership as everyone's fundamental right, and the idea that the land's fertility will be improved by working it with love and a communal spirit. And Mercer's description of the Shakers and Dokhubers (founded around 1750) also evokes some green ideas, particularly in their love for all creatures and the tenderness with which they cared for plants and trees.

Nineteenth and early twentieth centuries

Many of the communes and community experiments in this period were associated with socialism, anarchism and the political left. But this does not apply to all of them; communes and the community idea are also relevant to the thinking of the right and centre. Neither do socialism or anarchism equate exclusively with 'green'. However, it does seem that when you combine socialist and anarchist ideas with the commune/community concept, you produce many principles and practices relevant to modern green perspectives.

We find socialist communes emerging strongly in the early nineteenth century. The 1830 Paris Commune, founded by Bazard and Enfantin, does not seem a good green prototype since, according to Mercer, they followed Saint-Simon (1760-1825), the founder of French socialism, who wanted communal *exploitation* of the earth. But the division between Bazard, who advocated a political road to reform, and Enfantin, who sought prior social and moral change, does seem to pre-echo the important contemporary debate between 'red-greens' and 'green-greens'.

Robert Owen's (1771-1858) utopian socialist ideas are perhaps more relevant. He wanted society re-organised into communes ranging from 500 to 3,000 (ideally 800-1,200) people, embodying such 'green' principles as self-sufficiency, an agricultural base with small industry mixed in, public kitchens and communal eating and child-care (in New Lanark community), mixing town and country, and production and distribution according to social need. Hardy's (1979) description of the Owenite commune at Harmony Hill (1839-45) refers to careful and systematic organic farming, while Concordium in Surrey (1838-48) is described as a centre for health reform that prohibited salt, sugar and tea. The latter was also mystical, believing in the power of the 'love spirit' to change society and publishing in 1843-4 a journal called *New Age*, with articles on mysticism and vegetarianism. George Ripley, who founded the non-religious Owenite Brook Farm commune near Boston in 1841, is described by Mercer as a leader of the transcendentalists, the romantic followers of nature mysticism. Rigby reminds us that mysticism infused many secular as well as religious communities early on. The Diggers and early Quakers, for instance, were influenced by mystics like Boehme and Swedenborg, while Gurdjieff, Ouspensky, Blavatsky and Steiner were other contributors to this perspective in community ventures.

Hardy goes on to describe agrarian socialism, which in some superficial ways, though not because of a root concern for nature, was ecologically sound. Communal working and control of the land was seen as the source of all economic power and therefore the key to establishing socialism. Its idyll of peasant fulfilment and village cooperation contrasted with the general reality of long-established rural enclosures and alienation of common people from the land, against which the Diggers had fought. Its first strand, of Chartism, involved Feargus O'Connor's attempt to establish many families in self-sufficiency on two- to three-acre plots practising intensive organic husbandry, with potatoes, pigs and sheep the staples of each colony. New colonists at Charterville were promised 40 tons of dung each.

The second strand was founded on John Ruskin's romantic socialism, which often resembled traditional conservatism's yearning for feudal, hierarchical communities. Lost values were to be restored through craft production; the land was to be labour-intensively farmed to restore its full potential, to save people from the alienation of industrialism and to narrow the distance between humans and nature. Ruskin's medieval-sounding Guild of St George had several community experiments, e.g. at Totley, Sheffield. But the ecological principles on which it was founded foundered on the rock of some very un-ecological disagreements among colonists and trustees. The third strand of agrarian socialism was in the home colonies/back-to-the-land movement of the 1880s and 1890s, which Gould (1988) calls

> the most fecund and important period of green politics before 1980 . . . During that period the philosophy of industrialism, the relationship between the individual and the social and physical environment, and the degree of functions and successes of the city received an extraordinary degree of critical examination.

Faced with rising unemployment, the decline of rural society and concern for Britain's political and economic world role (a context broadly paralleling that of the 1970s and eighties rise of green concerns), people turned to the natural world and the countryside to solve individual and social problems.

The back-to-nature and back-to-the-land themes were adopted by socialists as part of a recipe for radical social change. They involved the simple life, an alternative to urbanism, harmony with nature, liberal sexual and social relations, a sensitive approach to animals, and hankering for a past golden age of freedom to work on the land of one's own choice and enjoy its produce. William Morris was the most important socialist social critic affected by love of nature and romantic anti-urbanism. He wrote of London as a 'sordid loathsome place' and wanted a Britain of 'little communities among gardens and green fields'. His *News from Nowhere* utopian vision closely parallels *Ecotopia* in many geographical and social-economic features (Pepper 1988). The socialist Edward Carpenter advocated 'small communities of limited wants and needs' to cover the whole nation, while industry, too, should be run on communal or cooperative lines (Gould p24). Carpenter's concerns for inner and world consciousness, and organic unity between humans, animals, mountains, the earth and constellations, paralleled the present concerns of 'deep ecology'.

Robert Blatchford, editor of the socialist newspaper *The Clarion*, wanted, says Gould (p39), to see 'socialism and nature as established institutions'. Like today's greens, he revolted against the environmental consequences of liberal laissez-faire economics, and thought that material betterment for the working classes should be subordinate to their quality of life, including imagination, simple pleasures and nature enjoyment. Blatchford supported and visited Starnthwaite Home Colony (1892-1901) in Westmorland, one of many set up to accommodate the urban poor and unemployed. He described it as a 'small utopia of green beauty'. Hardy says it practised real communal living and eating, and carried out fruit and mixed farming in the beauty of nature.

Gould points out that creating new low-population settlements in the country to replace cities was the ultimate aim of the back-to-the-land socialists, and was entirely compatible with Marx's call in the *Communist Manifesto* to abolish town-country antagonism as one of the first conditions of communal life (modern green critics often overlook this aspect of Marxist analysis – e.g. Fry 1975). However, it also had counter-revolutionary and ameliorative implications, being a way to cope with unemployment and defuse the discontent it spawned. This movement was also compatible with Kropotkin's (1899) anarchist vision of a Britain based on self-sufficient communities – of 200 families of five people each – intensively farming, market gardening and producing craft manufactures from workshops.

One of the largest colonies of the period was at Purleigh in Essex. Tolstoy was its dominant inspiration, and its 75 members (in 1898) aimed to by-pass socialism and organise a million people into a voluntary cooperative commonwealth. A breakaway group was set up at Whiteway (Gloucestershire) in 1898, and it lasted into the 1920s, steadily forsaking collectivism and adopting private ownership. But at the beginning its members embraced feminism, vegetarianism, non-aggression, worked communally and shared all possessions. This very green pedigree seems to be shared by other 1890s anarchist communes which Hardy describes. Norton Colony in Sheffield, for example, was based on a 'return to nature', practical horticulture and crafts (sandal making). It was vegetarian, teetotal, no-smoking, and against salt, chemicals, drugs, minerals and fermenting and decomposing foods. Unlike some of the socialist communes, these had no leaders, were non-hierarchical, without majority voting, and favoured small group cooperative relationships. Perhaps more than any other communes of the period, these anarchists most closely approximated in their social, economic and political relationships to the green lifestyle, and followed 'second order' practices.

The back-to-the-land theme was continued into the twentieth century, especially in Germany. The youth movement of the 1920s

> stressed themes similar to that of today's American communal 'counterculture': the regeneration of the individual and the society; the need to leave the city and return to nature; an asceticism connected with self-purification; and the collective joy of being together in an immediate emotional way and building a new life. (Kanter 1973, p17).

Bramwell (1989) describes this movement's calls for ecological awareness and the organic farming and vegetarian communes it started. A 'bio-dynamic' commune set up near Hamburg in 1930, for example, still exists today. The message of living according to ecological ideas and maintaining ecological balance became widespread among a group of high Tories, or 'Tory anarchists', in Britain and Germany, who were anti-capitalist and anti-establishment. They included proto-fascists like Rolf Gardiner, and socialists (H G Wells), and were motivated by a cocktail of ideas including a 'pro-Nordic spirit' and Kropotkin's call for intensive land settlements. Bramwell correctly notes (p122) that 'this cross fertilisation between apparently disparate people is common among ecological thinkers', and we will consider it further in relation to communes in Chapter 3.

As the Nazis gained power, taking on some very green ideas such as organic farming and gardening, the anti-capitalist Bruderhof communes, founded in 1920, were closed down. The communards left Germany to form communes in America and in England (Wiltshire, Shropshire and Buckinghamshire (Mercer 1984)). While their hierarchical and patriarchal organisation was un-green, they did incorporate green elements of openness, communal ownership of goods, pacifism, simplicity and unity.

The anarchist communes of Spain are more relevant. They were formed by villagers during the Civil War who took over the land, abolished money and lived ascetically. Their tradition continued into the post-war Mondragon Owenite cooperatives, which thrive today and are often eulogised by green writers (e.g. Sale 1980, Pepper 1984). Once again, it is in social, economic and political organisation that they come closest to a green utopia, minimising hierarchy, maximising participative democracy, and having a conception of production with an environmental consciousness. Mondragon, for instance, will not participate in any 'defence' related industries.

Spanish communes, and the more socialist kibbutzim, are termed 'communities of work' by Fromm (1956). Their accent is less on acquiring wealth than on working together for collective and personal fulfilment. Among organisational devices to minimise power concentration are consensus decisions, elected and rotating managers and officials, elected courts and neighbour groups of a few families. There is (in Mondragon) a size limit for cooperatives, and a cooperative financial, educational and social service infrastructure. Fromm considers the last as important for communities of work, together with a conviction that 'no man shall be entirely divorced from the soil'. The kibbutzim seem to embody all these features, but their position in relation to green principles is ambiguous. Apart from the sexism reported in some of them, it could be argued that they were born of an inherently anti-ecological attitude to nature – as a object to be dominated, conquered and exploited to further the Zionist cause.

The sixties

The hippy counterculture of the 1960s is frequently seen as a major progenitor of seventies and eighties environmentalism (e.g. by Nash 1974). And Rigby (1974a, p65) saw his 1960s British communes as a counterpart of that counterculture, i.e. that 'island of deviant meaning within the sea of society'. He describes how, in the sixties, a generation gap opened up where youth did not find their parents' role models or values attractive and they were worried at the unpredictability of their own future, faced with issues like the bomb and ecological catastrophe. Rigby's and Abrams and McCulloch's detailed accounts of sixties and early seventies communes bear out Bramwell's contention that the commune and ecological movements were linked in more than the obvious ways of caring about pollution and self-sufficiency. Sixties communes were often compatible with green values, the green critique of conventional society, and green views about social relations. But these accounts also suggest no *central* concern about the environment.

This lack of ecological emphasis was hardly surprising if communes are seen as reactive to broad social concerns and as the product of the society of which they are part, rather than as a vanguard for social change and therefore one step ahead of the wider society (whether the latter perspective is true is the question being examined in this book). In the sixties there was little wider environmental concern to react to: nowadays there is. Hence on the basis of the reactive model we would expect communards now to be centrally motivated by such concern.

Abrams and McCulloch (1976, p4) saw at least seven social issues of the sixties and early seventies to which communes were relevant: youth's rejection of the established order; rejection of the nuclear family, because in it people transgress other people's freedom; feminism; the notion of play being as important as work; the need for people to construct and express their individual identity; the need to restore a sense of community to society; and the possibility of radical social change, not by revolution but by detouring round conventional politics and power structures. None of these were inspired by environmental concerns, though, as discussed, they are more or less indirectly relevant to a green society. So too were the elements of sixties communes that were inherited from the more distant past. Bramwell lists anarchism; the belief in individual values; and the tendency towards spiritualism. Rigby adds high moral principles (from the ascetics); self-awareness through yogic method and recognition of the unity of all things (from mystics); belief in exemplary action to change the world non-coercively, emphasising education's role (from utopian socialists); individual autonomy; and belief in social change and liberation via individual change and liberation (from anarcho-pacifism).

Rigby's account of their critique of conventional society does make it sound very like a green critique. There was dissatisfaction with its giantism, materialism, competitive individualism, lack of concern for fellows, routine and mechanical daily lifestyle from which individuality, creativity and a sense of individual control have been shorn, lack of opportunity, for many, to develop talents, and entrapment into stereotyped roles, acceptance of authority, and a predetermined sequence of life events centred round career and nuclear family. In short these communards, like today's greens, had a deep, almost Marxian sense of alienation. Rigby's profile of the 'typical' communitarian's world view emphasises all these things, along with a basic faith in human nature and ultimate ability to change society. Politically, he thinks, they were either libertarian/anarchist/pacifist or revolutionary socialist. Though there was no overarching concern about environmental things, ecological catastrophe was seen as the main threat to social order, and there was some tendency to Eastern mysticism and elements of paganism – i.e. nature worship.

Abrams and McCulloch recognised links with other social protest movements – for women's liberation and nuclear disarmament – that are today natural allies for most greens. They also described communitarian values of great green relevance, not least a belief in the organic unity of humans and nature, a concern for peaceful, intuitive, loving and sharing relationships, and an anti-rationalism. This last – a profound belief that the analytical and emotional sides of life are out of balance – led to an aversion to theory and to theoretical structures based on rational systematic thought in favour of anarchistic spontaneity. In practice, this meant rejecting systematic and consistent ways of solving problems in favour of letting things happen and dealing with them as seemed appropriate at the time – 'what happens, happens', and there are limits to the desirability of trying to control events. This may or may not constitute a green approach today. Studied chaos used to characterise many early pressure group and Green Party meetings, but this is less common as the movement gains conventional respectability and political power.

Other practices which Abrams and McCulloch document do relate to a green society, such as income sharing, affirming the value of domestic work and sharing it, creating a mutual aid system for practical skills, and trying to abolish the distinction between work and leisure – creating a 'play culture' (see Table 2 for some features of 1960s communes). All these feature strongly in green economic theory (Ekins 1986).

Table 2: Comparing communes of the sixties and eighties (in the USA)
Source: McLaughlin and Davidson (1985)

In their excellent book 'Builders of the Dawn', American authors Corinne McLaughlin *and* Gordon Davidson *came up with these generalised comparisons based on their personal experiences between communes now and then.*

1960s	1980s
● Freedom and "doing your own thing" most important value; "laying a trip" on someone is a cardinal sin	● Cooperation with others and "the good of the whole" important; everyone needs to contribute his/her share; erratic behaviour less acceptable
● Few rules, restrictions, or expectations; largely unstructured; "work only if you feel like it"; spontaneity highly valued	● Agreed-upon rules and expectations; fairly structured work and financial requirements
● Mainly alternative lifestyle and values – drugs, rock and roll, "free sex"	● Variation in lifestyle in different communities – ranging from alternative to middle class professional
● Primarily negative orientation – reaction to a society seen as bad and harmful	● Primarily positive orientation – building a new society, new institutions and/or bridging with best in society
● Retreat or withdrawal orientation	● Service-to-others orientation
● More transient membership; communes dissolve easily; "crash pads" very prevalent	● More committed membership and long-lasting communities
● Non-exclusive; usually anyone with same lifestyle can join	● More restrictive about membership – must be harmonious with group and committed to group's purpose
● "Bad Karma" to turn any visitors away	● Open to visitors by prior arrangement only
● Visitors not always requested to contribute money or labor; no formal guest programs	● Visitors usually requested to contribute money and/or labor; more structured guest programs
● "Free sex;" emphasis on learning to lose one's inhibitions; sometimes group sex practiced	● Sexuality somewhat more restrained but looser than conventional standards; celibacy in some groups
● "Male chauvinist" attitudes; clear male/female roles	● "Women's liberation" prevalent; breakdown of traditional roles
● Mostly single members and non-exclusive couples	● Often a majority of monogamous couples and families

- Little emphasis on personal growth techniques and therapeutic tools

- Return to a romanticized rural past; rejection of technology; few communication links with society

- Return to innocence of childhood; rejection of responsibility

- No formal ideology, except belief in "going with the flow" – whatever happens is meant to happen

- Personal liberation most important

- "Hanging out" very valued and "living in the now"

- Usually anti-intellectual; body and feelings more emphasized than mind

- Emphasis on "dropping the ego" – transcending ego needs

- Anti-political (except for intentionally political communes organized around a specific ideology)

- "Tribal" orientation – strong emphasis on the group; togetherness emphasized; often over-crowding; privacy was "bourgeois"

- Order and cleanliness regarded as "uptight" and "bourgeois"

- Little true self-sufficiency; often food stamps and contributions from parents essential for survival

- More psychologically sophisticated; personal growth techniques in most communities

- Closeness to nature highly valued, but appropriate technology also welcomed; more communication links with society (telephone, TV, radio, some computers)

- Generally more mature and responsible adult attitudes; valuing some balance of playfulness, although sometimes too serious

- Well-developed belief system – usually spiritual and/or political

- Creating a new social and/or economic order is as important as personal liberation

- More of work-orientation, with accomplishment more highly valued and some retreat time available. Sometimes too "workaholic"

- Wholeness most important in most groups – integration of mind/feelings/body/spirit

- More acceptable of the role of ego in personal development; necessity for ego first to be strong before truly going beyond it

- Some political involvement in most groups; "planetary consciousness" important – awareness of earth itself as a being

- More of a balance between individual and group needs; private space more respected

- Order and cleanliness valued in most groups

- Self-sufficiency in food and energy increasing, but emphasis on interdependence with local area (with some outside donations if non-profit)

THE FUTURE

Why communes?

Though communes and decentralised small communities frequently feature in green utopian visions, the rationale for their presence is sometimes assumed and not spelt out. Goldsmith's (1972) *Blueprint for Survival*, however, extensively justifies establishing a network of self-sufficient self-regulating communities (by 2075AD), albeit coloured by the traditional conservatism of its instigator. Bahro's (1986) advocacy of communes as 'the main way to uproot the exterminist peril' is justified from a more socialist perspective, though emphasising the spiritual and moral aspects and therefore mirroring Goldsmith's (1988) preoccupations. One can read these and other communes/small community advocates on a strictly ecologically pragmatic basis, but it soon becomes clear that concern for moral and spiritual welfare and social justice rate as high as, if not higher than, ecological soundness.

Ecologically, *Blueprint* argues that to deploy people in small communities is to minimise their environmental impact because the 'actual urban superstructure required per inhabitant' goes up dramatically as the size of a town increases beyond a certain threshold. And industrial 'economies of scale' usually become environmental diseconomies. But hugely polluting manufacture can become environmentally friendly if it is decentralised and scattered in with the communities, so that no longer will people have to choose between 'jobs or beauty'. (This is not China's experience; see Elsom 1987.) And *Blueprint* reckons that communes and small communities are the best structures for achieving the green ideal of regional and local self-sufficiency. Nicholson-Lord (1987, p215) says that small farming saves land, and that labour-intensive agriculture produces more food per acre than capital intensive farming. And if Britons switched to a 'green' meatless diet based on fruit, vegetables and fibre, this would save 36 million acres of land. In Britain the average person needs 1.6 acres-worth of food, which could be reduced to 0.6 acres if the diet were vegetarian. Indeed, 'Only two per cent of the land now farmed would be needed if intensive gardening for food was practised'. Nicholson-Lord does not, however, discuss whether labour intensive agriculture would involve much drudgery.

The second pragmatic argument is to do with compensating people for the losses, chiefly material, which they would suffer with the onset of a green society. *Blueprint* (paras 260-3) argues:

> It would be sensible to promote the social conditions in which public opinion and full public participation in decision making became as far as possible the means whereby communities are ordered . . . [because] the long transitional stage that we and our children must go through will impose a heavy burden on our moral courage and will require great restraint.

This sounds ominous, especially when we are told that legislation and the operation of the police force will be needed to enforce restraint. But these externally imposed methods, reasons *Blueprint*, will not be as effective as voluntary restraint, worked out as the 'general will' by individuals in small directly democratic structures. Here, then, small communities are a device for social control, 'the form of social organisation in which internal/systemic controls operate best'. Perhaps a drawback of this lies in the apparent assumption that genuine participatory democracy would necessarily lead to willing acceptance of the ascetic ecological imperative, but that is by the way. The argument becomes more attractive when it emphasises the positive quality-of-life aspects of small ecological communities. There are probably lots of quite materialistic people who would opt for the simpler life if it involved being closer to a less spoilt and polluted nature (witness the common habit of stockbrokers and captains of industry who take early retirement to go and work a country smallholding). As well as that, the small community dynamic 'is an essential source of stimulation and pleasure for the individual. Indeed it is probable that only in a small community can a man or woman be an individual' – by contrast with the alienating 'self-conscious individualism' of large societies. To this alternative satisfaction can be added the rewards of intimate fellowship, intense relationships, and the sense of belonging to the group.

> Such rewards should provide ample compensation for the decreasing emphasis on consumption . . . so that resources may be conserved and pollution minimised . . . Rapid accumulation [of material goods] will no longer be a realisable, or indeed socially acceptable, goal and alternative satisfactions will have to be sought. We believe a major potential source of these satisfactions to be the rich and varied interchanges and responsibilities of community life, and that these are possible only when such communities are on a human scale. (Para 263).

Bahro thinks, even more metaphysically, that the function of commune life will not be primarily economic, though it will produce food, jobs and welfare. Rather, communes are conducive to a new 'Benedictine' order, furnishing the 'real alternative to the Industrial Goliath'. They foster a spiritual culture not linked to a monolithic God but to God as male/female and in us all. This God is beauty, happiness, nature, creativity and all the finer parts of our spirit. Here Bahro echoes deep ecology rather as the Findhorn community conceives it: the divine being as a universal mind and energy source, the living force immanent in all things (see Rigby 1974b, and Caddy 1988). For Bahro such mysticism, plus the extended family, an all-pervasive feminine element and uninhibited sensuality and sexuality are the major alternative satisfactions. They feature strongly, too, in Callenbach's anarchistic, socialist – and sometimes fascist – fiction, *Ecotopia*.

Young (1990 pp152-3) also stresses the environmental significance of communal life, as the vehicle for the extended family.

> Central to the ethical system of all peoples whose relationship with the land has remained close is the attachment of great importance to kinship and the obligations which go with it. These involve primary obligations to particular ancestors . . . the duty to honour them by using the land wisely for the continuous fulfilment of obligations to particular members of contemporary society. This of itself is a guarantee that the method of use will be sustainable so that resources can be passed on, undiminished in value, to children in the future . . . Translated into the context of modern industrial civilisation, this makes the extended family an excellent basic unit of a sustainable society.

Communes and the green millennium

Green millennial writing features communes as components of 'ecotopia' at various levels. For one, it paints with a broad brush the vision of a small-scale decentralised society of which communes may form a significant but not exclusive part. Another level is more specific about the commune and its pivotal role, but is still futuristic; while a third level cites existing communes as evidence that the New Age is already upon us.

The small-scale decentralised society
Some visions of this are comprehensive and start from green premises like the need for self-sufficiency. Others cover less ground and do not perhaps focus so much on ecology, but spring from, say, religious or economic concerns.

Of the former, *Blueprint*'s programme was highly ambitious, detailed and specific about when its 25 proposed reforms should be implemented. To meet its target date of 2075 for a basic network of self-sufficient, self-regulating, ecologically sound communes, 22 of the reforms should have been completed by 1990, but in that year only five could be said actually to have been started. *Blueprint* suggested that Britain should be organised into neighbourhoods of 500 people, set into communities of 5,000, in regions of 500,000. Each region would be politically represented nationally, while the nation should be represented in a global forum. This (pre-European-unity) arrangement would facilitate the twin green ideals of community feeling and global awareness – 'think globally: act locally'. All *Blueprint*'s social and economic arrangements stemmed from the imperatives of minimum ecological disruption, maximum conservation of energy and materials and reducing the population level by about half.

Kirkpatrick Sale (1980) echoed Schumacher's call for 'highly self-sufficient local communities' in his comprehensive review of the elements of a 'human scale' society, where avoiding social alienation was as important as the environmental imperative. He advocated a worker-owned and -controlled system, where it is important for economic efficiency to build a sense of community and where the sense of control over economic life in turn fosters community spirit in the wider social life. Community ownership of economic activities and communal living go hand in hand, especially if wealth is distributed according to need, as Sale favoured, or to work contributed, or absolutely equally. He said that this is only feasible on small scales, so favouring a commune form like the kibbutz, whose general assemblies own and control property, its distribution, the allocation of labour and the fruits of labour. In such communes, ideally of 500 to 1,000 people, members could identify economically with others and create a coherent economy adjusted harmoniously to the ecosystem. They would constitute a close knit, stable, balanced and predictable community where people appreciated their own interdependence and the importance of the natural environment. Minimal economic self-sufficiency for a local community, Sale calculated, might require from 5,000 to 10,000 people. From the resultant 2,000 to 4,000 strong workforce could be provided the 1,000 workers who would have to run one plant in each of thirteen basic manufacturing industries. All this follows from statistics which, claimed Sale, showed that in 1980 sixty-five per cent of all US manufacturing plants operated with fewer than twenty people – an argument reminiscent of Kropotkin's, eighty years earlier, in support of his claim that it was economically feasible to decentralise industry. Unlike Kropotkin, Sale saw a role for a free market to regulate inter-communal relationships.

Sale also echoed Fromm's (1956) call to counteract the growing alienation of a prosperous, materialistic post-war society with economic decentralisation and meaningful participation. The 'robot' society of the fifties where, Fromm asserted, 'Everybody is happy – except that he does not feel, does not reason, does not love' would lead again to war. The time was ripe, more so than in the nineteenth century, to set up communes where people shared profits, work and experience and owned their work community. Workers must be in groups small enough to enable an individual to relate to the whole, to give a lifetime's energy to something with meaning for the individual, by dint of being able to influence what is done and having a sense of unity with fellows.

Gorz (1985) also tackles the problems of alienation and loss of individual and communal autonomy, primarily through economic structures. Alienation necessarily follows from a social existence that people have not 'freely created through voluntary cooperation with everybody else'. In green fashion, Gorz sees socialism and capitalism equally at fault for creating large production units. By contrast, a truly autonomous society would be 'exclusively composed of small enterprises, self-managed by their members in free cooperation . . . little islands of perfection'. And autonomous production would be handicraft production where the individual or 'convivial' group controls the means of production, labour process, and nature and quality of the product. But Gorz does not propose a whole society built on such principles. Too easily it could become institutionalised drudgery without the benefits of some high technology, like microprocessors which are potentially liberatory (cf Toffler 1981), that requires division of labour nationally or internationally. Other modern essentials like electricity or railways must also be planned nationwide. Yet self-management is not possible in communities of more than a few hundred people. Gorz concludes that self-management must therefore be limited: it does not solve everything. But there is an important role in his utopia for communes and producer cooperatives, following principles of self-reliance and ecological harmony (Gorz 1980, p42).

James Robertson's (1983) vision of a 'sane, humane, ecological' Britain in 2050 does not feature communes but clusters of houses owned in common by 20 to 25 residents, covering six acres, with a 'minifarm' and sharing deep freeze units, food processing equipment, laundry, repair and maintenance workshops and transport. Clusters meet monthly to decide domestic and external questions: they seem almost exclusively peopled by middle class professionals, reflecting perhaps the nature of many existing housing cooperatives. But it is a recognisably green vision of sustainable local economies, where all are committed to developing their personal potential 'as part of planet earth'. Robertson's chief interest is in governmental, rather than economic or political, structures. Another rather similar vision sees a religious and moral revival in the twenty-first century. Robert van der Weyer's (1986) *Wickwyn* features the looser idea of community rather than communes in a repopulated countryside of Britain where (nuclear) families have their own houses, cultivate small gardens and farms, produce goods in workshops, cooperate in daily work, communally own land and buildings, eat communally twice a week, worship together and decide policy by consensus. The ecological balance theme in this utopia is muted but decidedly present.

Communes emphasised

'Dare to form communes!' exhorts Bahro (1986, p86). These autonomous basic units of social life are

> the only chance in the long term of tearing up the roots of the East-West conflict and above all of our opposition to the Third World . . . the path of reconciliation with the Third World might consist in our becoming Third World ourselves.

His anti-capitalist, anti-colonialist green future would be one of withdrawal from the world market to form self-sufficient local, provincial and national economies, with markets for exchanging activities between base communities of at most 3,000 people: a market economy for basic needs, built from the bottom up. He says, 'I think these commune-type things are, so to speak, the germ cells of a new society' (p112). In them, people will be reunified with their 'conditions of reproduction', which include the natural world. And what is rational in the commune will be defined according to 'what are the best conditions for a human being to be as happy as possible'. In this way Bahro places communes at the centre of the fulfilment of green principles and lifestyles.

Bookchin (1982) does the same. In his anarchist green utopia communes will be networked into bioregional confederations and 'artistically tailored' to their natural surroundings. Their squares will be interlaced by streams, their places of assembly surrounded by groves, and their physical contours respectfully and tastefully landscaped. Their soils will be nurtured caringly to foster plant variety for humans, domestic animals and wildlife. They will form a society decentralised, scaled to human dimensions and obeying nature's 'laws of return' by recycling organic wastes and materials for craft and industry. Solar, wind, hydraulic and methane-producing installations will be subtly integrated into a variegated pattern for producing power. Agriculture, aquaculture, stockraising and hunting (sic) would be regarded as crafts: all kinds of useful things will come principally through craft production, emphasising quality and permanence and diminishing the need for mechanised mass production.

The members of these basic elements of an ecological society, the 'free' communes (i.e. not necessarily founded on blood relationships), will deal with each other in face-to-face relationships. Through them, the 'fetishization of needs' will give way to freedom to choose needs, quantity will give way to quality, mean-spirited egotism to generosity and indifference to love. Physically onerous tasks will be reworked into collective enterprises, more festive than laborious. People will choose either to share and jointly operate industries like small-scale foundries, machine shops and electronic utilities or to return to more traditional but technically exciting means of producing goods. The exact principles of future communities cannot be laid out: this will be for the future communitarians to do. But this is a pretty complete vision and Bookchin insists that it has *all* got to be realised – some of the elements on their own will not make an ecological society. For him, greens will uncompromisingly be 'heirs of a strong natural thrust towards association' having 'a maternally biased need to associate, to care for our own kind, to collaborate'. Greenness and anarchism are synonymous.

And so are greenness and socialism, according to Ulrich. He talks about a socialism which avoids all the undemocratic, inhumane and ecologically destructive effects of 'actually existing socialism' (as found in the USSR and Eastern Europe when he was writing in 1979). Socialists should not, he declares, abandon production in some back-to-nature romanticism, but they should recognise that scale and size of production should be reduced. He envisages that the perfect geographical form for achieving size-sensitive socialism will be the commune, incorporating production units of not more than fifteen people. Communes will be relatively autonomous in work, education 'and the other life processes'. They will not be totally self-sufficient, and will supply delegates to a council, supplying delegates to a higher council and so forth. However, they will be independent from any industrial network, especially a world market.

> By producing as many essentials of life as possible within the commune itself (above all food) the members would not only assure themselves of a quasi-independent existence . . . they would also, by being able to largely eliminate exchange in the market and by adopting the rotation principle in the allotment of work, be able to abolish alienated work, the commodity character of labour power and the division between mental and manual labour in some vital areas. They would in this way also be able to develop a rich personality.(Sarkar 1983 pp167-8).

All of these features are essential to purist visions of socialism of the sort espoused, for instance, by the Socialist Party of Great Britain. Networks of kindred-by-choice families form an integral part of this communal vision, as does small-scale soft technology.

From a different political perspective, planner Peter Hall (1983) makes communes a central feature of his vision of Europe after 2000. This is definitely a green and Bookchin-like vision with homes producing and conserving their own energy, with less, more economical travel (by small cars and airships), more electronic communication, and work in small units, often in a local community:

> The group of people living together and manning these varied workplaces could be described as an extended, non-blood-related family or *commune group*. It will contain a nucleus of nuclear families which dissolve and combine for different purposes, plus a number of more transient members.

People will combine hand and brain and work-share in craft rather than mass production. Cities will continue to decentralise into the countryside, and 'rational', mechanised agriculture will continue to give way before a new concern for natural regeneration of the land.

The New Age is here

Hall is extrapolating trends which he believes already exist, and there are other examples of this among green writers who are convinced that the 'New Age' is well on its way. This age will be based on all the principles and practices described in Chapter 1, and existing communes, together with other aspects of alternative lifestyles, are offered as evidence of what Capra (1982) calls this 'rising culture'. New Age-ism is couched in somewhat vague and inaccessible language and concepts, but its essence lies in replacing a dualistic world view (e.g. humans and nature separate) by a holistic one, emphasising the unity of everything in the cosmos. The former is represented by the Piscean symbol of two fishes swimming in opposite directions, but we are leaving Pisces and entering the Age of Aquarius, whose keynotes are unity-in-diversity, cooperation and global consciousness. The change is towards an environmental conservation/peace/feminist ethic and lifestyle based not only on rational but also on mystical, spiritual thinking.

Such thinking sees all components in the universe linked as part of an energy flow. Matter is energy: so is prayer, and love, which is God. God is not one God, above and separate from humans, but all deities and both sexes, and beauty, love, spirituality and so forth. Energy is the spirit of God, which flows through the whole planet, which is alive. So life is one vast interconnecting unity and the universe is not a mechanism but an affair of the mind, working out as huge harmony. This perspective is not 'new', but owes much to the modern concept of Gaia (Lovelock 1979), and to the medieval one of the Great Chain of Being (Lovejoy 1974), and to nineteenth-century interpretations of the doctrines of monism and vitalism, particularly by Haeckel, the founder of ecology (Bramwell 1989).

A key element of New Ageism is the coming of the millennium, not through traditional political forces but through autonomous changes in consciousness initially among scattered members of the 'alternative movement', embracing anything from meditation groups to Greenpeace to organic farmers, health food devotees and, importantly, existing communes. These people will eventually coalesce to form an irresistible social force impelling the world finally to the New Age – if we are lucky, that is, for

> There are those who are lifting to the light and are being prepared to set aside ego, will and desire and who are taking part in dedicating life to wholeness, and there are those who, through free will, are stopping it happening. On the highest level it's a vast cosmic battlefield. In spiritual terms the forces of good and evil are locked in a fight for man's soul. (Trevelyan 1987).

This apocalyptic view of history is shared by other New Age greens like Capra, or Hazel Henderson (1981), who sees it in terms of a coming 'solar age', when there will be spontaneous devolution away from centralised capital-intensive production towards alternative lifestyles, including communes. Allaby's (1975) rather simple view of history is as the

> story of a never-ending alternation between . . . civilisation, or the kind of life associated with city cultures . . . [and] non-centralisation or dispersal, within which people develop independently, free from the rigidity of city life. Today we are at the point of change between one civilisation and another.

Communes, he thinks, as part of the dispersal phase, are a traditional form of organisation that has worked successfully for many generations.

For Sale (pp48-52), the rise in 'communal and communitarian arrangements' is part of a general rise in permissiveness, liberal and feminine values and a new concern for the natural world and health food: part, in fact, of five 'pulses of our era' – feminism, naturalism, localism, populism and individualism. They reflect a 'real and powerful trend' to which the

> entire societal pendulum may be swinging . . . A new period of human history in the not-too-distant future in which small communities and self-sustaining cities, locally rooted and ecologically sound, cooperatively managed and democratically based . . . might evolve a society built to the human scale.

Nicholson-Lord, a *Times* journalist, is no less sanguine about existing communes as part of environmentalism. They are, he feels, a popular force for social reform, providing the political and philosophical inspiration for 'many thousands of ordinary people' who are eager to help remake their cities. It all amounts to a 'new vision of our place in the world'. He cites Lightmoor, the community-in-the-making of twelve households on 23 acres in Telford New Town, which is to be cooperatively run, and will be designed and built by its residents to facilitate energy saving and recycling. This

> collection of level-headed people dissatisfied with urban life may serve as the symbol of a potential rural renaissance . . . Behind it, for example, lie the dozens of communes, cooperatives and radical social ventures which, particularly since the 1970s, have sought to revive communal identity through a new relationship with nature. (Nicholson-Lord 1987, p216).

Not to be outdone, a *Guardian* journalist argues that a disparate ad hoc alliance has arisen of 'unemployed people and their helpers'.

This has generated 'a new sense of community' (Schwarz and Schwarz 1987). Urban self-help groups, workers' coops, city farms and rural communes are described, all as part of self-help 'decolonised' communities. They have in common cooperative economic relations, appropriate technology, radical politics, organic agriculture, holistic health and attention to spirituality and personal relations. They are all part of this New Age paradigm shift, it is argued: a 'breaking through' to an ecologically sound society. The Schwarzes describe Crabapple and Lower Shaw communes, subjects of this research, in such a context.

Other communes studied here, Lifespan, Glaneirw, People in Common, Laurieston and CAT, are described by Osmond and Graham (1984) in their survey of the alternative movement. Communes, they say, are the most difficult, challenging, controversial and idealistic components of the movement's prescriptions for an alternative society. They are more fundamental than worker coops, but after being hit by recession in the late 1970s, they have gained fresh impetus – the 1980s communes movement is 'tougher, more disciplined, structured and organised than its counterpart of the 1970s'. Like the Schwarzes, these commentators see communes as part of the breakthrough to the New Age. Or, as Kanter (1973 pxi) puts it, they are part of 'communal values and experiences' that have for the past centuries been repressed by urban industrialised societies. But 'now these values return on an unprecedented scale, as hundreds and thousands of communes . . . spring up across the globe'.

This kind of sweeping, wild optimism fits ill with the reality of Reagan-Thatcherite Bush–Major Anglo-America, but it seems to be the hallmark of many commentators on the New Age/green movement and the role of communes in it. The communes and communards described later should help us to see just how realistic their views are. One of them is quoted in Osmond and Graham, describing how communes might help to change wider society. Though the communal perspectives are 'ultimately revolutionary in their implications . . . the method of the communes, like so much in the alternative movement is – through example – to stimulate evolutionary change'. The strengths and weaknesses of such an approach to social change is an important aspect of this work and the questions it asks, and we now go on to examine the essence of the arguments on this controversial matter.

CHAPTER 3
Social change and the politics of community and communes

> If we can create a single valid community... then children will run away from school to join it, soldiers will desert their regiments to serve it, artists will sacrifice everything but their art to contribute to it, businessmen will topple their money gods to worship it, and the entire world will be at war – but this time with all of humanity on the same side – against poverty, famine, disease, hate, fear. (Quoted by Rigby 1974a from 'Centre Nucleus', a New Age community in London in 1966).

> There is a persistent belief not only that the world needs to be changed, but that it can be changed; that a new type of person expressing an authentic fusion of the self and the social can be created through the love and work of communal life, and that once such people have been created, they will serve as compelling examples for others to imitate. (Abrams and McCulloch 1976, p106).

These quotations illustrate that it is not only theorists but also practising communards in the past who have had a vision of a new society, and that they thought they could play a leading part in changing society at large. A major aim of this book is to examine these ideas specifically in relation to the question of social change towards an ideal green society. It will be important to know the view of the communards on how this change will come, and on whether and how they can play a role in it. This will shed light on the potential effectiveness and importance of the communes and it will tell us something about the politics of the communards themselves.

Jeremy Seabrook (1990 p62) declares that 'new initiatives, experiments in living practical alternatives' are green in inspiration, and that their aims of self-reliance and sharing are essentially socialist aims. Indeed, it is often assumed that communes are socialist experiments and/or are peopled by those on the political left, but this does not necessarily follow. In this chapter we will see how the ideas of community and communes can inform socialist or liberal or conservative philosophies. We will, too, briefly examine views on social change from a theoretical perspective, and also see how the sixties communards saw their role, if any, in effecting it. And we will touch on what communards would need to do in changing or influencing wider society, and what problems may lie in their path.

Many of the questions to be considered are relevant to the current debate in and around the wider green movement between reds and greens (Ashton 1985). In conventional political terms, reds (or 'red-greens') are to the left of the spectrum: mainstream greens (or 'green-greens') are substantially in the liberal centre (Table 1). Their disagreements are less about ends than means, though in one respect there is a fairly major difference over ends. Reds place more emphasis on the social rather than 'natural' in their very definition of what are environmental problems. To them, poverty, crime, homelessness, housing, transport, inner cities are all unambiguously environmental problems: the miners' dispute in 1984 was, for example, an environmental dispute (see Weston 1986). Otherwise, most of the differences occur in their respective approaches to social change, as we shall examine below.

SOME BASIC POSITIONS ON SOCIAL CHANGE

These fall into four broad areas of debate; (a) whether social change will come mainly through changing economic and social organisation and structure or through changing the ways that individuals behave; (b) whether it is material economic activity or ideas and consciousness which are most consequential in shaping society; (c) whether the collective approach, perhaps involving revolutionary political mass movements, is desirable, or the less conventionally political approach of individuals and small groups setting examples for others to follow; (d) whether struggle and conflict or consensus and accommodation are more potent forces in social change. All of these issues are related; in each case those on the 'far' left would probably support the first position; liberals, the second.

(a) Structuralism

The view that values, attitudes, activities and relationships are conditioned, if not wholly determined, by the organisation and structure of society is a structuralist perspective. It contains the notion that when people associate together in economic and social life then 'expected' patterns of conduct evolve, which stem from common ways of perceiving and evaluating the world. There is a collective consensus of basic common values – a consensus view, or 'conventional wisdom'. This constrains people's behaviour and makes them unlikely to go beyond the bounds of the established norms, or what appears to be 'common' sense (which is, however, common only for that particular society). The feeling that society exists over and above individual people is implicit in structuralist theories: a collective essence which amounts to more than just the sum of all the individuals in it. If this is your view, the implication, if you want to change society, is that you must change this collective consciousness – either directly (for example through education) or through the economic structures to which it corresponds.

Other, non-structuralist theories may put stress on the individual, seeing society more as the sum of how its members behave and not as a structure that is partly transcendent of these members. So the understanding of society comes down to understanding how and why individuals behave and relate to one another. This might come in various ways: through understanding, for example, the meanings and the symbolism behind what people do, or people's socialisation process from childhood in and outside the family, or what has been called the 'situational logic' behind people's actions – how and why behaviour is likely to be logical given the culture in which it occurs. The psychology of perception and behaviour is important in all such approaches, and study methods involve trying to see the world as the subjects of study understand and perceive it. Hence the attempt to change society comes down to the attempt to change the perceptions of individuals through argument, persuasion and example: unless, that is, one attempts the 'behaviourist' approach advocated by B F Skinner (1948) in the mythical commune of *Walden II*, where physical and moral inducements and disincentives were used to inculcate desired behaviour as a kind of automatic response in children. The prime importance attached in all this to the individual as the 'basic building block' of society, and the view that social change is thought to come about by changing the nature of the individual blocks, is compatible with liberal political philosophy, which holds the individual as supremely important (see next section, on social change).

(b) Materialism and idealism

An old question relates to all this. Which is the most important determinant of society as it is and might be; the *material* circumstances or the prevailing *ideas*? An extreme idealist might claim that the world can be changed by thinking about it. If people decide, for instance, that it is a good *idea* to start behaving cooperatively, non-aggressively and benignly towards nature, then they can do so. If you want to change society in these directions, then you need to change attitudes and values, particularly those in the minds of people who run the institutions where we learn our values and ideologies – media and education, for instance. An extreme materialist would argue the converse – that what we *do* determines what we think. In particular, the economic organisation of society leads to particular social and economic relations between the people engaged in producing things. This in turn determines most people's ideas. Thus in days of slavery the beneficiaries – the slave owners – thought it obvious that they were more noble than their slaves; people who do well in a particular economic situation generally come to see it as being judicious and 'natural'. So if people compete with each other (for jobs, resources, markets) and exploit nature (because this is inherent in the economic system) then these competitive, exploitative relationships will incline most people to *believe* that competition or nature exploitation are good, or 'natural', hence unavoidable – especially if media and education constantly tell them so. Only under different material circumstances will radically different sets of values and ideologies become widespread as distinct from being just minority views.

Marx's 'historical materialism' was something of a compromise between idealism and materialism. It said that ideas and consciousness can shape the world. So the promotion of new ideas can change it, provided also that people act on them – and that it is recognised that the material (economic) features of a particular society in a particular period must set limits on how much ideas, even backed by social action, can significantly reshape society. Even this compromise still implies that most of the appeal to people's reason and good nature, by argument and by example, will not get the majority to be cooperative or benign to nature, unless at the same time the economic mode of production changes to one which by its nature should function cooperatively and caringly for the environment. In other words, the system must be changed to one where people no longer have economic vested interests in being competitive and exploitative.

In a more idealistic view of social change, Weber argued that a new set of religious ideals was influential in the change from feudalism to capitalism. Thus, Calvinism preached that hard work and material success in this world proved that one was to be saved in the next, and such an idea had a fundamental affinity with new, capitalistic forms of economic behaviour. Hence the Protestant ethic was more favoured by economic interests than belief systems that were antagonistic to capitalistic behaviour (e.g. Hinduism, Catholicism). This issue, of the relative stress on idealism or materialism, will be potentially important for greens and any others attempting to change society, for if they decide they have to change the economic system, then they are going to have to confront the political power of those who benefit from the present economic arrangements.

(c) Collective or individual?

This power is so formidable that it might only be resisted by people acting *en masse* in conventional political ways, ranging from parliamentary politics to extra-parliamentary pressure group action or, more likely, revolution – withdrawing labour and/or seizing the instruments of power. These routes favour *collective* approaches, by contrast with the view that all political change starts with the *individual*. According to the latter perspective, it is no good expending energy to get the masses to take political power if you yourself have not changed the way you think and live. This is because 'the personal is political' – a favourite green and feminist adage which means that all our thoughts and actions as individuals (e.g. in choosing the food we eat) have political ramifications. In a way this could be regarded as a collectivist view, because it emphasises how individuals are part of wider society. Yet in practice this aspect of the adage is usually neglected in favour of the implicit suggestion that it is the *individual self* that has the pivotal role in social change. The individualist approach also mistrusts mass revolution, arguing that it usually involves violence and oppression, the very things that revolution probably intended to conquer in the first place (though in the late-eighties revolutionary changes in Eastern Europe there was little violence). And it mistrusts party politics, arguing that the search for political power irrevocably corrupts politicians, and that political parties always have to compromise their ideals. Individualism places faith, instead, in a continuous process of individuals changing their values and lifestyles, which should then produce a new aggregate society. Once again this has close affinities with liberal philosophy.

In Britain, collective action for social change is most readily associated with the trades union and labour movements. But it could also imply the kind of local community politics that is seen more effectively on the European mainland and was, according to Papadakis (1984), the precursor of the German Green Party. In Britain, this community radicalism was strongly associated with the Liberal Party in the sixties, though in the eighties it was socialist local authorities who worked with and on behalf of local community groups in an empowering capacity (and this is still the case with Labour authorities in, for example, Sheffield and Bradford). While some greens strongly advocate the community-based collective politics (Wall 1990), relatively few are happy about working through trades unions. Seabrook (1990), as a socialist, rightly identifies the early struggles of the unions as *environmental* struggles – for better housing, working conditions and sanitation. But he then takes on the typical perspective of a liberal green in his rejection of the movement now. What remains of their collectivisation, he thinks, is directed only at screwing more out of capitalist employers with whom they have a common interest of growth based on exploitation of nature. Seabrook also bemoans the eclipse of the culture of collectivism in our society by the liberal myth of individualism (a myth because in its expression in mass consumerism people's real individuality is totally submerged).

(d) Consensus and conflict

Rejecting mass action often goes hand in hand with rejecting a conflict model of social change. Proponents of such models will argue about the inevitability of conflict in any radical social change process. Groups which want to change society will have to face up to the fact that there will be conflict between those who have power and do not want to give it up, and those who seek power. Hence there may be conflict between 'ruling class' and 'employee class', or between men and women, or between different race/ethnic groups, or geographical core regions and peripheries, and so on. One important conflict model is that of Marxism, which argues that although society may be structured into classes or groups in various ways, *two* classes particularly are significant in social change. Despite the complications of the rise of the middle classes and widespread share ownership, it is still broadly possible in advanced capitalism to think in terms of those who effectively own and control the means of production (including natural resources), distribution and exchange, and those who do not, but have only their labour to sell. This conflict perspective sees social change arising from the struggle between these groups. And since this is the struggle that has been the main concern of socialists and the labour movement, it would follow that new energies for social change – that come through green concerns, for instance – should be directed through these traditional channels. And, therefore, anyone who wants to change society should show a consciousness of how their new concerns relate to the class struggle – the 'old' politics of poverty and wealth, left and right.

Many regard this approach as simplistic and/or as denying the idea that we live in a democratic, pluralist society. This is composed of a plurality of groups, all related in a system, and when one group is particularly alienated or disadvantaged the system will adjust – not through revolutionary conflict but through appeal to the law, or through government responding to pressure group protest, or firms responding to consumer pressure, and so on – to lessen that group's grievances. Thus a new 'consensus' is reached and the system remains stable, though changing and evolving. Hence social change requires changing the consensus by a new interest group (say, the green movement or Charter 88), articulating new concerns and vigorously promoting its own interests. Again, the consensus model is consistent with the liberal belief in society as a pluralist democracy. The difference between it and a (socialist) conflict perspective was illustrated by Professor John Griffith's letter to *The Guardian* (June 1990) about the Charter 88 campaigners' desire for a written constitution that enshrines the right of individuals to free speech and access to information, to protest and form pressure groups, and so on. Griffiths said:

> I have been a member of the Labour Party longer than most, maybe all, of the Charter 88 signatories . . . 'What we need', they say, 'is forthright proclamation that the relative weakness of a *culture* of liberty in Britain is a shame and a scandal'. No it isn't. What we need is hard-nosed legislation that will drastically *interfere* with the liberties of those who use corporate power to make large profits and promote unemployment, who hold monopolies in public utilities, who prostitute the press, who pollute the atmosphere, who destroy the countryside, who create the poverty of inner cities, who exploit the homeless. Their silly Charter is a trivial irrelevance.

As this letter also suggests, it is likely that if one takes a structuralist and materialist perspective on society and social change, one will also think of huge economic and political forces that would want to block social change because they derive advantage from the structure of society as it is. Hence one might also believe that some form of conflict is inevitable and has to be faced up to, and that collective solidarity and organisation is more essential than the efforts and examples of individuals in order to win such a conflict. Hence structuralist, materialist, collectivist and conflict perspectives tend to go together.

COMMUNES IN SOCIAL CHANGE

Literature on recent communes suggests that up to now the communards' perspective on social change has been idealist, based on individualism and believing in or seeking consensus and naive in its rejection of conflict. This is so, that is, where communards have been interested in the prospect of social change at all: in fact this has not always been any very significant part of their motivation in forming and joining communes.

Self-seeking

'Most individual members of most communes are, quite simply but in a profound way, in it for themselves', say Abrams and McCulloch of their late sixties/early seventies examples. Their 'primary reality' was collective self-seeking, and Rigby also identified self-realisation at the centre of the 'underground's' spectrum, of which communes were a part. There was a rejection of conventional values and a search for self-fulfilment in the face of alienation. The impulse to communal living, say Abrams and McCulloch, sprang from personal estrangement and feelings of threatened and frustrated individuality. This need for individual identity was often the uppermost issue, and it came from 'the artificial antithesis between the self and the social which is at the heart of Western capitalism'. Even the communes, which were part of a counterculture, had imported a central feature of the culture it opposed, namely the demand for personal autonomy, which is a moral imperative deriving from the advance of industry and culture since the Enlightenment. But there was also an awareness, lacking in conventional society, that personal autonomy is bound up with relating to others. This fusion of the self and the social was thought to come about through the right sort of living and working. There was much talk about the conduct and state of personal relations and work, which could lead to endless soul searching. Hammering out personal relations could involve slow and hard taming of the rampant self-awareness and self-seeking that brought people together, and life was often at a high emotional pitch. Love, say Abrams and McCulloch cynically, resulted when two people's selfishness pulled in the same direction: for communes were an escape for the petty bourgeois from the alienation of industrialism, but they did not want to escape alone.

Rigby also observed that a lack of personal or fulfilling family relationships in conventional society – resulting from its alienating urbanisation, bureaucratisation and centralisation of power which makes individuals feel like cogs in a machine – was why some, especially the young, joined communes. His and Abrams and McCulloch's subjects sought freedom mainly through self-development, and security through strong emotional and psychological bonds with others. Their most frequent reason for joining was discontent with the conventional family and a desire to set up an alternative. However, excessively dependent members, like single mothers, were not welcomed. The communards might or might not also be 'activists' who wanted to change their local community and society through the commune.

Even Shenker's (1986) 'intentional communities', where there was a communal authority and purpose that transcended the individual, also had the same theme running through them of collective escape from alienating conventional society and a collective search for self-identity. As Lumley-Smith (1978) sees it, this 'obsession with personal freedom' is a fundamental weakness of modern communes. It is the antithesis of freedom in the sense of 'service' to a higher cause. Hence communes are seen primarily as a place where members realise themselves, without submitting to any leadership or discipline. This makes them 'irrelevant to society as a whole', offering no serious solution for an ecological future.

Young (1990 p36) makes a similar point. The environmental responsibility of tribal society is not an abstract idea: it is intimately related to ties of kinship and communality which deeply permeate all social life. However, in the West:

> It is difficult for bonds of power such as this to develop in the context of a voluntary democratic community held together by intellectual ties alone, especially when the motivation for communal life is not so much the welfare of society but, as it often is, the rediscovery of self.

Changing society

This judgement may be correct, but it does not follow that self-seeking is totally irrelevant to changing society at large. First, it does not have to lead to complete divorcing from the society which is to be changed, and this is important, because if communes are to demonstrate the viability of a green lifestyle to conventional society they must be visible to that society. Abrams and McCulloch believe that although their communards were idealistic, with unfocussed political ideas, their withdrawal from the rest of the world was only partial. This was precisely because they were aware of their 'exemplary' role in the vanguard of change for the whole society.

And, as Ashton (1985 p18) has noted:

> From Christianity to Gandhism, Owenite socialism to contemporary communes and GLC [Greater London Council] economic initiatives, the 'exemplary' project and moral stand have been deployed to effect social change. This form of practice is not to be undervalued. It is an important ingredient in any strategy for social change.

Second, as Rigby discovered, the counterculture strongly believed that its activities were revolutionary, and not just private, apolitical forms of social deviance. Their argument went that one cannot get freedom for all society without first getting it for oneself. 'The revolution must start with one's own head and in one's daily life', says Rigby (1974a, p80), illustrating the communards' anarchist approach to social change, and he quotes one who might well be writing in today's green journals:

> It is not difficult to see that it is the individual who is the source of energy and life in society, that society has no volition or life apart from that of its individual members, that the ecological problems which now face us are created by individual acts from minute to minute all over the world . . . These same problems can only be solved in so far as the individual can change his modus vivendi so that he no longer contributes to their causes.

As well as echoing anarchism, this view of the individual and society evokes the liberal view articulated by Prime Minister Margaret Thatcher in 1987: 'There is no society, there are only individuals and the family'. It is also the essence of the green anarchist and green liberal dictum, 'the personal is political' upon which we commented earlier.

Rigby's communards thought that more and more people generally were rejecting conventional values, a view not borne out by subsequent history in the seventies. Communes were seen as 'the one great hope' for the majority, and parliamentary politics, the vote and the pressure group were universally dismissed as irrelevant, immoral and ineffective. Rigby thought that the social change theme was common among all his communards, whether they were mainly motivated by notions of changing society or by reasons connected foremost with self. There was a common utopian goal: a non-exploitative society of love, cooperation and individual fulfilment, got through exemplary and non-violent personal action based on the power of love. And there was common emphasis on value changes and the personal example mode of social change:

> You are changing society every day as you live your life – by living and acting the way I do, I influence people, and if they in turn influence others then it spreads. (Rigby, p15).

Rigby linked this individualist and partly idealistic (because it needs the spread of different values as well as practices) approach to the utopian socialist as well as the anarchist tradition. Robert Owen thought that the key lever for social change was the consciousness of individuals and that the problems of social change revolved round the 'question of awareness, of gradually trying to make others more aware' (Rigby, p35). Rigby's communards firmly rejected class conflict as a motor of social change, again in common with Owen. They saw the working class as ignorant of the chains binding them: poverty was not the main problem of modern society, but lack of personal identity and purpose to life. People, they thought, took to materialism to compensate for the lack of these things, and because they were unaware of alternatives.

Such angst was as typical of the youth of the affluent middle classes in the sixties as it is typical of many greens today. And it will be interesting to see if the communards still are middle class – alienated, as Abrams and McCulloch put it, from capital and also having little understanding of labour. Thus lacking class consciousness, they thought, communards had little potential for effecting widespread change.

It has to be said that there are big flaws in the individualist-idealist-exemplary-consensus approach to social change. For instance, supposing that the green/communard example were to spread, it would pose a huge challenge to capitalism, and capital would fight back with all the power it wields to maintain the hegemony that it enjoys today. Without the alliance of a mass political movement which at least has a potential revolutionary consciousness (realisable only if people stand together in effective solidarity), together with the material means to achieve its end through the withdrawal of labour and other cooperative strategies, it is hard to see how any present minority can win radical changes which oppose capital. And the present spread of new ideas and lifestyles may, in fact, be severely restricted. Green consumerism is one thing, but it can only be practised by that world minority that has any substantial consumer power, and it does not anyway convey the green message of consuming less – 'Let's all buy for a better world', the slogan of *New Consumer* (issue 1, October 1989), is a contradiction indeed for greens. As for cooperation and loving, the transformation of consciousness towards competition and violence under Thatcherism seems far more powerful than any countercultural values in the nineties. And placing so much of the onus for change on the individual as opposed to the collective makes for guilt if individuals fail to live by their high standards. This feeling will be counter-revolutionary if it leads to disillusionment and withdrawal from the fight, as seems likely (Pepper and Hallam 1989).

Murray Bookchin, an advocate of creating a green society via some form of communes, puts the case for a historical materialist view of social change (1982, p346):

> No movement for freedom can even communicate its goals, much less succeed in attaining them, unless historic forces are at work to alter unconscious hierarchical values and sensibilities. Ideas reach only people who are ready to hear them. No individual, newspaper or book can undo a character structure shaped by the prevailing society unless that society itself is beleaguered by crisis. Thus ideas, as Marx shrewdly observed, really make us conscious of what we already know unconsciously.

Bahro, a socialist, argues a non-socialist, non-materialist view. He wants (1986, p98) an 'accumulation of spiritual forces, the association of people who create a common field of energy which confronts the old world with a new pole of attraction'. This association will eventually exceed a 'critical mass' and 'then acquire under certain circumstances a transformative influence over the whole society. The only purpose of commune-type communities today would be to develop the spiritual foundation [for a] biophite culture'. In the process of this 'deep change in subjectivity' (p104) the individual must, through 'therapy with a spiritual perspective' (William Reich's approach) become 'Christ' by achieving 'complete access to his own nucleus'.

How today's communards react to this debate on social change will bear on their potential for moving society in a green direction.

Lessening the potential for social change

The literature suggests four potential barriers to communes succeeding as agents for social change. First, they may lack a wider audience for their example, through not relating fully enough to conventional society. Second, they may lose clarity about what they stand for. Third, even if there is agreement on important principles for an alternative society, communards may not live by them, so the example fails. This may stem, fourth, from the tension between the needs of individual discovery and fulfilment (the private) and those of group functioning and coherence (the public). This tension is potentially most serious because it can break up the whole commune.

A wider audience

Rigby pointed out that the communards' counter-definitions of social norms and values, and the 'alternative realities' of their lifestyles, were potentially revolutionary. But clearly there had to be a wider audience, who saw them as living examples of their counter-definitions, for that potential to be realised. There was little audience in the late sixties because, thought Rigby, there were not enough communes and too many were on the point of collapse. Furthermore, what audience there was was young, educated and middle class. There was a failure to reach people en masse as part of a strategy of institutional and cultural change from the bottom up: failure to connect with movements for workers' control, for women's liberation, for tenants' control, for free (libertarian) education and for the rights of claimants. This is a key issue which Abrams and McCulloch also pursued, pointing out that one of the communes' major links with outside groups for social change was with the Campaign for Nuclear Disarmament, which they said was drawn from the educated middle class employed in non-profit organisations in welfare, education and the creative professions – exactly the constituency of the radical green movement identified later by Cotgrove (1982). Abrams and McCulloch's communards aimed to solve social problems as *they* saw them. Therefore they were the problems of the 'petty bourgeois' rather than of the working class (spiritual alienation, not material lack) – hence their difficulty in relating to that class. Indeed, thought these authors, the very aim of providing rich personal relations within the commune militated against outside political activity. It encouraged a revolution in private life leading to personal salvation but not social change.

Ideological clarity
If people at large are to be converted to a new ideology, then the communards who are converting should, presumably, have a clear definition of that ideology, of which they are a living example. However, Shenker's (1986, pp242-3) intentional communes, where one would expect a clear sense of purpose beyond daily living, sometimes lacked this clarity, either at the beginning or later on in their evolution. This could actually be an advantage, in that daily practices come under less scrutinising for 'ideological soundness', but it does perhaps decrease revolutionary potential and 'image' in the eyes of the outside world. Shenker also points out that the ideology could become taken for granted by members in order to reduce the strain entailed by questioning every action or deviation from ideological purity – which led them to accommodate to pragmatic 'economic, social, personal, organisational and environmental demands'.

Principle and practice
It may be pragmatism, or deeper reasons, which causes such deviation from principles in daily practice. Few of us can live by what we believe in for most of the time, especially if it puts us in constant opposition to dominant social beliefs. But if we proclaim the principles of an alternative value system, as communards might, our failure to live by them often affirms a view among our audience that there must be something wrong with the values themselves. So our failure may be understandable, but it is nonetheless 'counter-revolutionary'. Shenker (p244) highlights the problems for communes seeking technological efficiency and economic success: to do so may 'vitiate the "we feeling" of the community' and create a labour surplus which marginalises some members. In the case of the Hutterites and kibbutzim, searching for economic efficiency conflicted with some of their basic principles – for example, the former opposed commercial practices.

Abrams and McCulloch's communards often talked about doing things and sharing tasks, but some did not feel that others pulled their weight. Perhaps, these authors conclude, there should have been more emphasis on working together and less talk about love. Rigby (1990) describes how, in the search for anarchist structurelessness, de facto leaders may emerge; how, in the attempt to eliminate sexism, sexual role stereotyping occurs; and how the collective ownership principle leads to individuals who do not take care of communal property. All these practical violations of principle stem from a deeper clash between the public and private domains.

Public and private
Shenker (p247) puts this tension thus:

> To sustain collective efforts towards the attainment of supra-individual goals, the individual needs to be treated, and needs to see himself, as a means to an end. For the community to persist over a lengthy period the individual must, up to a point, subordinate himself to the satisfaction of collective, functional needs.

So commune survival depends on sustaining members' *self-interest*, balanced with mutual attentiveness. Abrams and McCulloch pointed out the delicacy of this balance which, when it fails, leads to breakup of the commune – unless, that is, communal attention can be diverted to higher goals than the personal. Religious or quasi-religious purposes would give the commune a life beyond that of individual members. However, the sixties communes were founded on the general Western liberal philosophy which developed over the past 300 years, of 'possessive individualism'. This means the 'individual as the proprietor of his own person or capacities' with freedom from any but self-interested and contractual relations with others. Sixties communards felt that if they could attain possessive individualism by removing the problems of self-identity which existed for people in wider society, then the demonstration of this to the public would lead to social change. But there were contradictions, for full self-realisation by some communards (usually core members) led to stunting of others (usually fringe members) in this respect. Also, communes were forcing-houses for self-realisation, but those who achieved it very often then found others intolerable. Abrams and McCulloch (p199) concluded that there needed to be a more directly instrumental and explicitly revolutionary political commitment in many communes, for as things stood communes were 'a movement of those petty bourgeois for whom the self is all that matters'; and because of this 'the only fundamental obstacle to successful communal living is the sort of people who want to live communally'!

Certainly this would be an obstacle to communes becoming part of a widespread revolutionary movement, for such a movement's revolutionary potential would depend on solidarity – collective identity – as for example does the labour movement. Sixties communes, say Abrams and McCulloch, were an attempt by those petty bourgeois who had belatedly discovered their true situation in material society to follow the example of the working classes and construct some power through combination. The attempt failed because communards were not in practice prepared to sacrifice enough of their possessive individualism to achieve collectivity. They did not see that the cause of their alienation from their own true individual identity in wider society had been, specifically, *capitalism*. They blamed it instead on vague generalities like the 'incomprehensibility of complex society' or the 'obliteration of spontaneity by routine' or the 'fragmentation of whole man by the division of labour'. Hence they were not prepared to see themselves as 'proletarian' in a revolutionary sense, and part of a class struggle. These are very much the criticisms which 'red-greens' level at 'green-greens' today. The former adopt a socialist approach to social change, like Abrams and McCulloch, and the latter a liberal approach, and the disagreements hinge around the problems of individualism and collectivism, and the analysis of why people are alienated from themselves, from each other, and from nature.

THE POLITICS OF COMMUNAL UTOPIAS

These fundamental political differences extend also to the question of what kind of future society communards may envisage. They may all believe that communes should figure strongly in it, but the notion of communes and community can have conservative, liberal or socialist connotations.

Gemeinschaft and *gesellschaft*

The differences referred to above, between individualism and collectivism, underlie a basic political difference between, on the one hand, socialist and traditional conservative approaches to community and, on the other, the liberal concept of community. This

Table 3: Society and community

GESELLSCHAFT	GEMEINSCHAFT
Society (sum of the individuals in it)	Community (more than the sum of the individuals in it)
(i) Relationships based on division of labour and contracts between isolated individuals consulting their own self-interest; relations become mutually beneficial.	Solidarity between individuals based on affection, kinship or membership of the community. Unalienated organic face-to-face relationships.
(ii) Atomistic relationships based on individual interests and rights – all individuals have equal rights, e.g. to property, possession of which carries further rights.	Involving religion, hierarchy, status inequality, as binding forces in the organic society. Medieval society was this kind of organic totality.

contrast comes through in the distinction introduced by sociologist Ferdinand Tonnies in 1887 between the ideal types of *gemeinschaft* and *gesellschaft* (see Table 3).

Broadly speaking, socialists favour *gemeinschaft* communal relationships, though they would reject part (ii) of the definition of this concept, whereas the liberal notion of community embraces *gesellschaft*. Traditional conservatism would embrace *gemeinschaft* completely as defined. The latter also conveys the idea of 'total community' which Kanter (1972, p72) calls 'the submission of private states to social control, exchanging former identity for one defined and formulated by the community'. It incorporates Rousseau's view that

> The general will which should dominate all public life and determine all public decisions was not the sum of individual wills. It was something qualitatively different: an expression of man's social, universal nature, of his status as a human being, living with others and concerned for them, an expression of his membership of a collective and not of his egoistic pursuit of personal advantage. Man, this meant, expressed himself most fully, was most properly human, precisely in a community (Kamenka 1982, p8).

Socialism and community

Kamenka believes that collectivism in the socialist tradition embodies precisely this sense of community. The socialist communitarian also thinks that property should be social rather than private, labour has dignity, humans are fundamentally equal, and austerity, modesty and devotion to the public good are virtuous. Furthermore, society should be fundamentally reorganised to make it cooperative rather than competitive. Egalitarian communities were part of the common ground shared by early socialists, be they romantically inclined to the pre-industrial past, or biased towards a technological future. In fact the ultimate goal of nineteenth-century socialism was the utopian commune, though after the middle of the century this became less of a mainstream concern. However, it was important in Marxism, for in Marx's desired future of 'truly human communism', private property, the town-country division, the state, the law and classes would all be replaced by self-regulating communities of many-sided, all-round men and women working cooperatively for the common good and expressing themselves fully as creative human beings. Marx had come, says Kamenka (p13), to the Rousseauan-anarchist view of human nature as capable of living in spontaneous, cooperative fellowship with others and seeing the common interest as one's own. But alienation, derived from the material relations of production, prevented this from actually happening. Socialists argue for an unhierarchical and secular *gemeinschaft*, which Marx called *gemeinwesen* (ultimate communism). The short-lived Paris Commune of 1871 was a model. It embraced federalism, decentralisation, participatory democracy, social justice, and a rapid improvement in workers' living conditions. Still, today, this is the preferred model among many Western intellectual socialists, who dislike the socialism of the centralised state. Some red-greens, like Bahro, reject the state altogether in favour of anarchist self-sufficient communes interacting through barter. Others like Gorz, Ryle, and Frankel (1987) believe that there must be some state presence to mediate between communes and represent supra-communal interests.

But away from theory, in the actual history of socialism, trades unions and mass political parties have been central, and the utopian socialist decentralised communal living tradition has been marginal because, says Kamenka, the latter did not connect with the mass of people. It put too much stock in the independent power of moral example, had no conception of class struggle, but instead appealed to the 'world at large', and rejected conflict politics and revolution in favour of pacifist, incremental small experiments. But, Kamenka (p24) believes, the world cannot be restructured piecemeal by well-intentioned people who are not of the working class:

> Those who seek an undifferentiated community as the ultimate goal of socialism know full well that it will have to created, like the medieval *gemeinschaft*, by force and fraud, by censorship, indoctrination and the ruthless suppression of contrary opinions.

These criticisms are very similar to Abrams and McCulloch's of sixties communards. The revolutionary conclusion is one that not only those communards rejected; today's mainstream greens, as well as democratic socialists, also shy away from it.

Traditional conservatism

In this view of an ideal society the notion of 'natural' laws binding people together in an organic (slow-changing) unity is strong: as is the idea of an organic unity between people and nature. The latter comes out in the concept of intimate links between people – in a nation, region or local community or commune – and 'their' soil and landscape. The close bonds between them are represented in the *gemeinschaft* concept and in a romantic vision of medieval, pre-industrial society and, again, in national, regional and local chauvinism (most extremely, in Nazism's 'Blood and Soil').

As Cotgrove (1983) describes it, there is a unity based on sentiments that grow out of the community, locality and shared physical life. The general will of the community is the source of authority, yet it is a naturally hierarchical community, and so that will is expressed by and through the leaders. Conservative utopian environmentalism (e.g. Goldsmith 1988) says that there is a need to re-establish these values of small-scale 'traditional' (pre-industrial) communities, and to conserve nature, landscapes and the holistic relationships between them and their people. Such relationships go beyond rational explanation, but are appropriately expressed in nature mysticism, creative art, folk legend, 'traditional' pagan ritual, festivals, and the idea of a community of comrades with shared values, goals and emotions (Mosse 1982). This also is a version of community which fed into the idea of 'volk' – the national community – that became part of the German Youth Movement from 1900 and nourished National Socialism in the 1930s. It also fed the back-to-the-land and communes movements in Europe during the thirties, forties and fifties; and could have echoes in the deep ecology-based quasi-mystical communes of the eighties. Rolf Gardiner, for instance, whom Bramwell (1989) describes as a 'right-wing proto fascist', attempted to make his Springhead estate a cooperative self-sufficient commune. He was enthusiastic about many things – personal spiritual rebirth, holistic thinking, organic farming – which characterise deep ecology today, as were many of his high Tory friends.

Bramwell reminds us that the idea of giving land back to the people – the farmer or labourer – *seems* left-oriented, because it involves substantial wealth redistribution.

But to support the peasant, the yeoman or the agricultural labourer was an emotionally conservative position, usually backed by a deep sense of specifically English patriotism.

It will be interesting to see if any spirit of back-to-the-land/yeoman repossession exists in communes today and, if so, whether it really carries overtones of right-wing communitarianism.

Liberal communitarianism

Cotgrove (1983) draws the same link between anarchist liberatory communes (opposed to almost everything the traditional conservative community concept stands for) and the liberation-of-the-individual theme which Rigby and Abrams and McCulloch identify among their subject communards. Like them, Cotgrove places such individualism in the liberal tradition.

Liberals will bow to the collective if they get something out of it for themselves. But they see human nature as essentially *autonomous* – having a set of standards or principles which are unique to the *self*. So they will not (as conservatives or socialists sometimes do) blindly accept collective mores as part of tradition, without questioning them via their own critical rational judgement.

This is all in keeping with the *gesellschaft* concept, but incompatible with the notion of total community or self-in-others. Any concession to the society, in the form of cooperation and communality, is based on strict reciprocity and mutuality, so it relates to Proudhon's anarchism rather than Rousseau's or Kropotkin's. Mutuality can be seen as a fully participatory relationship where each party respects and values the other as full partner. It is an autonomous relationship, because people monitor their own behaviour towards others and adjust it accordingly (and, presumably, conditionally: depending on the reaction of the other, such adjusted behaviour may not be maintained, or may be further revised). The focus is very much, therefore, in the mutuality commune, on relationships themselves rather than on the grander enterprise, where 'total community' – loss-of-self in others and the enterprise – is more appropriate. It is only possible in a face-to-face community of, say, six to eighteen people where individuals can know all the other members well.

As discussed above, the type of communal relationships – their basic political nature – may affect the potential of a commune for effecting social change: Abrams and McCulloch certainly think so. Something more akin to a socialist or conservative conception could avoid the over-individualism which they see as ultimately counter-revolutionary: part of the problem rather than its cure. And the view of what constitutes the best way to effect social change will also be relevant to a commune's effectiveness. If it is an individualist, exemplary and 'apolitical' (in the sense of class politics) model, then it will have to answer some of the potential criticisms outlined above. Again, if the communards' political position owes more to liberalism or conservatism than to socialist-anarchism, then it may be doubtful whether it can relate to a truly 'green' society, because the green vision is ultimately based on cooperation, anti-capitalism, egalitarianism, small-scale decentralist non-hierarchical organisation, common ownership of the means of production, and harmony with nature. As Gould (1988) says: 'The relevance of this paradigm to the left-right division is obvious. Greens are better placed on the left'. Or we might add that despite tendencies to liberalism and conservatism, perhaps they *should* be on the left.

These three chapters have reviewed such questions, along with the definition of a green society and lifestyle, in abstract or related to past communes. They form the context for the following report of the research which was done in order to establish the present relationship of communes to a green society of the future. We now go on to that research.

CHAPTER 4

Decline of green evangelism

TO FOUND A GREEN SOCIETY

> We had this naive belief in how easy it might be to find an alternative – 'the wind is free'. But so is oil . . . it isn't that simple; it doesn't work out that way. (CAT member).*

Were the communes which we examined set up in order to help change wider society [1.1-2]?† And, if so, did their founders see them as a route to an *ecologically* sound society [1.3, 1.6]? Did founder-members intend to be a vanguard for the rest of us, setting a personal example like many of the movements outlined in Chapter 2? Alternatively, were 'self-seeking' motives uppermost – motives of individual and group self-realisation; a petty-bourgeois escape from alienation, as the sixties movement was described in Chapter 3? The broad answer seems that these communes started as the former, but have drifted towards the latter.

As Table 4 shows, seven of the twelve were established between 1972 and 1975 and a further two in 1978: all hot on the heels of the first post-war period, 1967-74, of high media attention to, and public concern about, global environmental issues. Of the others, ZAP comes in the second period of such concern (1985 on), while Monkton Wyld started in between. Sixties Findhorn was an early example of deep ecology ideas in action. Given this timing, we would expect, and do find, that most accounts of these communes' founding are replete with the language of green values, and that their founders nearly all wanted to change wider society rather than just escaping from it. Nine out of twelve groups had strong green ideologies and intentions, six being inspired by back-to-the-land/self-sufficiency examples, both factual (John Seymour's 'Centre for

---

*Unless indicated differently, all quotations in the text from now on are direct quotations from interviewees.

†Throughout, numbers in square brackets refer to the questionnaire schedule – see Appendices 1 and 2.

69

Living') and fictional (BBC-TV's 'The Good Life'). And education was seen as a big factor in changing society – only three groups did not originally intend to operate as educational centres, even if that intention was lost early on. Five of the nine, Laurieston, Monkton Wyld, CAT, LSF and Findhorn, are thriving educational centres today, of which the last three became communes 'by accident' rather than original intent.

A long-standing communard who remembers the seventies well listed four major motivations among founder members:

> (i) Many educated women, tied down by children, wanted more than the nuclear family offered (see Phillips 1990).
>
> (ii) Mistrust of the conventional educational system.
>
> (iii) Disgust with consumer society.
>
> (iv) Environmental concern.

In descending order, these have increasingly obvious relevance to green issues though 'second order'/social concerns like (i)-(iii) may in the long term be more important for greens than direct environmental concern.

CAT epitomised this strong green ideology. Its founders were 'acutely aware of the environmental crisis: they saw it in urgent, apocalyptic terms', said one member. Another said, 'they were worried about limits to growth and exponential curves; the philosophy was "sustainability, trust, fulfilment"'. They were utopian, arcadian socialists at heart, though their money was put up by a 'green' industrialist ex-Guards officer and old Etonian! Although the alternative movement had largely seen technology as the enemy, this particular group did not. It started CAT on an old 40-acre Welsh slate quarry as a demonstration centre for alternative technology – particularly in energy, gardening and building. It wanted to show ordinary people what the implications of their lifestyles were – how, for example, using electrical appliances contributed to pollution.

Little about these intentions was written down: 'There was an element of let-it-all-hang-out; part of the anarchist legacy of early days'. But as the workers began to form an on-site community, the purpose of demonstrating ecological lifestyles became important – 'most important' according to one member who believes that CAT neglects this aspect today.

This is true of most other ecologically oriented founding groups. They wanted not only first order green practices, but also second order aspects of lifestyle – communality, non-hierarchy, consensus and anti-sexism (see Appendix 2) in particular. It is difficult from this distance in time to disentangle the two 'orders'; as it is difficult to pin down types and strengths of motivation. Though most groups had several principles in common, one of them seems to have been that it was valid (within the boundaries of an 'alternative' world view) for each individual to think and do their own thing. Unlike some other purposive communes (religious communities, for example), there had to be great freedom to interpret aims and methods and develop individual interests, notwithstanding a strong sense of common purpose and even political ideology.

Canon Frome founders, many of whom came from Postlip Hall, were 'definitely Good Lifers of the late seventies'. Typically their complementary intents were to 'live together, ecologically soundly' and, as an extended family with collective childcare, and retaining the identity of individual families, to practise non-hierarchy and consensus. 'We saw ourselves as role models, living out early seventies environmentalism'. There was an (overdone) evangelising intent, for the founders called a meeting of locals and told them they were bringing the 'alternative culture' to the area. This, we were told, did not go down too well! As with the previous back-to-the-land movements, there was colonising intent. Rural regeneration was to be achieved, based on labour-intensive organic farming, crafts, and education. A former school building was used for the Frome Society, which was pivotal and intended as a base for environmental courses for local people and other groups.

Redfield, Laurieston, Crabapple, LSF, and Glaneirw were similar. They were, largely, founded by ex-urbanite (especially London) people – as a Lauriestonian put it, 'privileged middle-classes with a sense of awareness that they could do what they wanted, and the money to do it'. Phillips (1990) says that for such people,

> collective living was both a political statement and a practical solution . . . It was a challenge to the whole concept of the modern family [and] a collective household provides a practical means of sharing tasks, avoiding overconsumption and combining childcare with the massive programme of meetings and events which filled the evenings and weekends.

Lower Shaw was a farmhouse saved from obliteration by the spread of suburban Swindon through the intervention of a Swindon

Table 4: **The communes examined in this book** [1.1]

Commune	No of over 18s*	No of under 18s*	Year started*	Situation*	Present professed ideological focus*	Income sharing?
CAT	10	9	1974	rural	ecological	pays wages
Z to A Project	5	1	1986	urban	anarchist	yes
Canon Frome	27	20	1978	rural	ecological	no
People in Common	4	2	1973	urban (now semi-rural)	eclectic	yes
Crabapple	7	5	1975	rural	ecological	yes
Laurieston	20	10	1972	rural	mixed	no
Redfield	22	13	1978	rural	mixed	no
Monkton Wyld	9	6	1983	rural	mixed	yes
Lower Shaw Farm	6	7	1975	suburban	ecological	yes
Lifespan	9	1	1974	rural	various	yes
Glaneirw	4	3	1975	rural	mixed	yes
Findhorn	200	ND	1962	rural	spiritual	no

*Apart from Findhorn, most of these data are drawn from the communes' self-description in Ansell et al (1989).

councillor who wanted it as a centre to run courses on self-sufficiency, organic farming and 'alternative education' involving yoga, massage, alternative medicine and vegetarian food. But the others were decaying large country mansions, which could be picked up cheaply at the time, Laurieston, costing £25,000, developed its People Centre, running courses as a 'public service, disseminating information relevant to our chosen lifestyle' – a lifestyle described in the written guidelines as based on 'green

Organic farming/gardening	Founded with some evangelical intent?	Was green ideology strong?	If so, main aspect	Educational centre originally planned?	Education centre now?
yes (2½ acres)	yes	yes	alternative technology	yes	yes
yes (allotments)	yes	yes	green economics	yes	no
yes (35 acres)	yes	yes	BL/SS	yes	no
yes (Mill gardens) (3 acres)	yes	no	diffuse	no	no
yes (40 acres)	no	yes	BL/SS	no	no
yes (120 acres)	yes	yes	BL/SS	yes	yes
yes (8 acres)	yes	yes	BL/SS	yes	no
yes (10 acres)	yes	no	diffuse	yes	yes
yes	yes	yes	BL/SS	yes	yes
yes (2.5 acres)	yes	no	diffuse	yes	no
yes (40 acres)	no	yes	BL/SS	no	no
yes	no	yes	spiritual/deep ecology	yes	yes

BL/SS = Back-to-the-land/Self sufficiency.

politics' and comprising self-reliance, ecology, healthy diet, non-violence, non-discrimination, spirituality, therapy, outside politics, personal fulfilment, cooperative living and feminism. Excepting the last item, which was sometimes ignored (Canon Frome did not challenge sexism), this list forms a model of most of the communes researched here. While Glaneirw was described as an escape for 'middle management dropping out into the country', most of the rest were, like Redfield, to a major degree 'founded as a route to an ecological society'.

Crabapple members did not want to evangelise, but they were 'ecologically and politically highly motivated'. They initially went as far as espousing *Walden II* principles and practices. Based on behavioural psychology – a 'scientific technology of human conduct' – these would, according to Skinner's 1976 introduction to his novel, answer the question: 'How are people to be induced to use new forms of energy, to eat grain rather than meat, and to limit the size of their families?' Among the answers which Crabapple tried were some behavioural conditioning of children (mainly rewards for desired behaviour), banning couple relationships, and a work credit system whereby people who did the most unpalatable jobs accumulated most 'credits' entitling them to take holidays. These ideas were soon abandoned as impracticable; for instance, people could not afford to take the holidays they became entitled to! They were among what a Redfield member called many 'grand green ideas and plans which have not been realised' by the seventies communes.

Education centres and renewable energy devices seem to be foremost among those green things that did not come about with the passing of time. That they are still favourites among the green dreams of first-generation communards was demonstrated by ZAP members, who were all under 25 in 1987 (see Table 6) when the Birmingham commune was founded as the 'New University Project'. Its patrons included Henryk Skolimowski, Sally Willington and other prominent advocates of green economics. For nearly two years its members led courses that talked of setting up green networks for organic food production and distribution, and of generating energy *à la* CAT. But now, although one member enthusiastically manages urban allotments, the renamed project is practically centred on the more immediately anarchist than green objective of enabling people collectively to buy houses which individually they could not come near to affording.

Paradoxically ZAP, a 1980s commune, has many 1960s-style characteristics, while Findhorn, which started in 1962, is well described by the 'eighties' features laid out in Table 2. The well-documented history of Findhorn (e.g. Hawken 1975) makes it clear that although its initiators and early followers were not motivated by political ecology, their brand of spiritualism incorporated some very basic 'green' philosophies. Their ideas of organic unity and harmony between humans and nature, animism (one of our interviewees communes with the plant spirits, as did Dorothy McClean in the sixties), and the 'planetary village', as well as their individualistic

Table 5: **Major tenets of the Findhorn consensus**

1. The new (Aquarian) age is on its way – a technological and cooperative age.
2. Findhorn is a 'light centre' where people transform themselves and tap into the 'new type of energy' of the Aquarian Age. (Light centres work towards the good of the planet; 'light' is a life-giving force that pervades all beings and inanimate objects in the universe.)
3. We are more than just material, but part of a greater spiritual reality, which is caring and intelligent.
4. Everything has purpose, love and unity (three principles behind all great religions).
5. Everything is part of a whole – not separate ('planetary consciousness').
6. All people are members of the same biotic community, or 'planetary village'. There is a oneness behind all divisions.
7. Everything, including all daily tasks, should be done with 'love'.
8. 'Love' includes spiritual commitment and a sense of purpose. It involves being a perfectionist in everything because everything and everyone has god (a divine spirit which is love) in them and therefore is good.
9. 'Love' involves working cooperatively in groups, by consensus. Findhorn's 'sacred culture' features groups attuning to a common goal.
10. The process by which you do things is as important as the end product. The process should bring life and spirit into everything and always be open and honest.
11. The individual is where all social change starts.
12. Individuals must love themselves and discover themselves, particularly their emotional and spiritual potential, and the blocks to achieving it. These processes, together with intense emotional crises, lead to spiritual growth and transformation.
13. As transformed individuals we can all be light centres.
14. Individuals are fullfilled by working together and being subsumed in the community – but their individualism must not be subsumed in the group identity.

approach to social change (see Chapters 5 and 6) are particularly compatible with the principles of deep ecology (see Fox 1984, Devall and Sessions 1985 and Naess 1988). Other aspects of Findhorn's organisation – hierarchy and sexism, for instance – have been less so (see Francis 1985). But a purpose evolved which included evangelising 'green' ideas. Findhorn became what was described to us as a 'social laboratory' – experimenting with bringing spiritualism and love into everyday activities – and a 'demonstration centre' of communalism, spiritual and holistic education, and New Age culture, all dedicated to awareness and appreciation of 'all the kingdoms – animal, mineral, vegetable and human'. The resolute spiritual ideology and purpose which developed early on seemed to us to be still evident, despite one veteran Findhornian's assertion that 'I have difficulties with the word "purpose": I really don't know what it means'.

The motive of contributing to a future green society was less prominent in the formation of PIC, Monkton Wyld and Lifespan. Individuals in PIC were strongly influenced by *Blueprint for Survival*, but the overall purpose among its founders was to 'provide an alternative to the capitalist way of life'. PIC grew out of the squatting movement, and its practical priority (like ZAP, our other urban commune) was to produce low cost housing. Beyond this there was no other *group* aim save 'non-exploitative living' (green enough but unspecific). Each individual's separate concerns were equally paramount – but creating an anarchist-socialist society formed the underlying ideological bond. Social change was an important theme in the initial educational plans at Lifespan and Monkton Wyld. Lifespan's plan was for its converted railway cottages on moorland near Sheffield to become a craft-centred education centre following the principles of A S Neil's Summerhill school. There would be 'ecological study' which, according to a leaflet describing the project (April 1974) 'would grow out of the ground' through the agricultural and recycling methods developed by the community. 'Alternative to the nuclear family', 'outside patriarchy' and 'against the nuclear state' were other phrases that the founders often used. Although 'self-sufficiency', 'solar energy', 'anti-pollution' and 'proper use of ecological resources' were further phrases, and organic gardening and a wholefood shop were early institutions, when the education idea fell through it was cooperative living that became the main motivation – collectivity, cooperation and control over one's own life: important 'second' rather than 'first-order' green principles.

Monkton Wyld grew from the ashes of what had been a progressive boarding school (part of the Dartington movement) from 1940-80; then for two years an alternative education centre for the local community. Its founders wanted to maintain this function and provide courses and facilities for other groups – on self-knowledge and development, relationships, healing, yoga, tai-chi, rebirthing and Reichian therapy. They stood for a mix of things, among which specifically green principles figured, but not prominently. *The* important thing was liberal progressive non-hierarchical cooperative education, emphasising a message about people taking charge of their own lives. One member had come from Findhorn, and spirituality became a significant sub-theme.

What comes through, repeatedly and universally, about these first-generation communards is their huge level of energy and commitment as well as idealism and political motivation. In four (CAT, PIC,

ZAP and Redfield) the political ideology of anarchist-socialism seems to have been part of the cementing force: in two others (Findhorn, Monkton Wyld) it was spiritualism. But whatever, most of the members had positive ideas about changing wider society, and they wanted to help to create an ecological society, imagining that they could make a major contribution by their actions.

As Harper (1986) puts it:

> The early Quarry was basically a fundamentalist enterprise. It was all good frontier stuff in them days – caravans and tents, old tin sheds with leaky roofs, begged and borrowed equipment, very little money, turbulent relationships, lentils and adrenalin. But the pure vision was tested daily by the mud and rain and the need to succeed; and after work the debates raged in the candle-light. Should a JCB be used to excavate foundations, or should it all be done by hand? Should compost toilets be provided for the public, or would only WCs be acceptable? Should we have wages or put everything back in the common pot? What about plastics? Could the restaurant use tinned tomatoes in its pizzas?

RUNNING OUT OF STEAM

A decade or more later, nearly all of these communes had changed greatly [1.7]. While, as we show later, there are still ideologically committed and evangelical individuals in them, as a whole nearly all the communes have lost ideological intensity and focus, while the commitment to wider social change is now muted. Almost alone, Findhorn perhaps remains as intense as it was; while it has shifted focus towards relations between people rather than with plants, it has a clear sense of mission and an increased conviction about its central role in the coming of a New Age. At the other end of the time scale, it is too early to tell with ZAP, though there have already been many personnel changes, and a change of purpose noted above.

Each of the remaining communes approaches environmental issues with less sense of urgency. They have seen the crisis expected in the seventies developing gradually rather than apocalyptically in the eighties. CAT's overall aim of demonstrating soft technology gathers pace, but not without some agonising among members; partly because, as some put it, 'we have less to show in the way of innovations; we were at the forefront but others have overtaken us – everyone's into AT now'. Ideological coherency has diminished too; 'a lot of the standard left-wing baggage has been dropped', and 'CAT is an exhibition of political bias which draws back softly from the politics' (meaning that the bias is no longer obvious) were indicative statements. Similar things were said of Redfield and Canon Frome, where the 'broad socialist' approach of the founders has been vying with a more liberal individualistic view (see Table 1).

The outward missionary zeal of the Frome Society waned early. The evangelising quietly

> ran out of steam . . . We were a bunch of do-gooders bringing 'the word' of rural regeneration but we didn't appreciate the extent to which people in the countryside already knew what they were about.

Loss of communality here is evident: Canon Fromers now eat together formally but once a week. More spectacularly, Laurieston ceased as a commune in 1987: it is now a housing coop and 'work collective' focused around the farm, garden and People Centre. While one member thought that there is now no remaining common bond or ideology, others insisted on the integrity of their very ecologically-oriented constitution. However, the former believed that this gave a more committed impression than the lived reality, which was not green. 'The maintenance fortnight is what bonds people now – and in summer, lying on the lawn'. Another thought, more positively, that the Laurieston 'guidelines' written in 1988 attempted to 'salvage a distinct ideology and character – they are an achievement'.

We came across a similar difference of opinion at CAT. Peter Harper wrote in 1986's *Quarry Newsletter* that revisionism had taken over from fundamentalism at the Quarry, and:

> There seems to be a general waning of fundamentalism in the movement as a whole, and it is true also for the Quarry. We come here for a job, and we are all chosen and later judged primarily on the quality of our work. Community matters are not recognised nor accorded respect by the general body of opinion . . . Even with the on-siters themselves there is little sense of common purpose or community spirit . . . Nobody seems interested in contributing much to community life . . . As a lapsed fundamentalist myself, and with nothing to be proud of in my own achievements, I nevertheless mourn this fall from grace . . . Sadly, but inevitably, I see a time of revisionism ahead . . . The Quarry will become more efficient, harmonious, consistent, respectable and boring. It will be a successful institution, not a community.

He met a barrage of refutations from fellow communards in the same Newsletter and the then Director, Peter Raine, wrote:

> ... he [Harper] gives me the impression that the Quarry as a whole has fallen from grace over the past few years, and that we have buried our early ideals beneath a heap of pragmatism. I simply don't believe that he is right. At the heart of his article is a suggestion that we have improved what we do – displays, courses and so on – at the expense of how we do it – collective working and community living. I think we have improved what we do but I don't agree that the quality of our life together – both in and out of work – has suffered ... Peter ... is judging our standards of living together against a standard that never existed in the first place, except through rose coloured glasses.

While the current Director, Roger Kelly, said at the 1988 Quarry AGM:

> The Quarry exists as a *revolutionary* force. It seeks to bring about *radical* changes in the individual and society – change towards an evolving understanding of this planet in its ecological complexity, and a transaction of that understanding into new ways of thinking. (Reported in Hay 1989, emphases added).

And in advertising literature written in 1990 to promote 'alternative investment' in the Centre this was reinforced. 'In many ways the Centre for Alternative Technology is a model of what a green world could be like', said an advert in Friends of the Earth's *Earth Matters*, while Roger Kelly, this time in a letter to Alternative Technology Association members, said that 'the Centre for Alternative Technology has been [since 1975] a working model for positive solutions to the environmental problems faced by people and nations all over the world'.

Despite such insistences on CAT's remaining fundamentalism, the weight of our evidence suggests that Harper is fairly accurate in describing a trend in communes generally.

But then, given the 'problem' of frequent personnel changes which all communes have, ideological coherence and unity of purpose is almost bound to dissipate and change. To get newcomers to agree to a set of ideological 'guidelines', as at Laurieston, is quite unusual. Rather more common now, when members are hard to get, is the Redfield entry criterion, where the

> level [of ideological commitment] might not be the level you started off with. It comes down to [accepting] anyone whose views and behaviour aren't outrageous – the question of whether you get on with people is the paramount one.

However, none of this means that an extreme ideological entropy has replaced earlier coherence. For in most places we heard about a 'subculture determining who comes and goes' as at CAT, where it is more important to be part of the 'tribe' than to have impeccable ideological credentials. At Monkton Wyld it was described as 'no common spiritual or political binding, but we're linked by an under-the-surface thing which we don't acknowledge'. The 'thing' frequently amounts negatively to 'Thatcher bashing: the main political bias' (Redfield); or positively to being 'left-green', as at LSF where we were reminded of the obvious:

> If people didn't have similar ideals they wouldn't get on – we all have the same vision of the future but maybe different ideas on how to get there.

In fact there was a wide tendency to claim great diversity of opinions and world views on behalf of the commune as a whole, but this frequently was not evident to an outside observer. At PIC, where a most significant change of direction from urban location to semi-rural converted mill got under way in 1989, a 'wide' ideological cross section was claimed, but actually described as 'green/anarchist/labour', thus really accounting for a small minority of the British people.

More unsettling to us, however, was the feeling we had at Findhorn that people had been almost brainwashed into a common view during their period of being 'student members' (see Table 5 for the main elements of this consensus). Our guide told us: 'People are not taught here: if you talked to 200 people they'd say 200 things'. We did not talk to so many but all those we did interview in fact used the same key phrases in seemingly Pavlovian responses to certain questions, in a manner reminiscent of American fundamentalist religious sects.

This is not to say that Findhorn has been without similar disagreements over changes in practical emphases to those in the other communes, such as the shift from emphasising the natural to the social world mentioned above, increased educational activity and self-advancement, and less driving of people in the way of Peter Caddy's original manic 'work is love in action' ethic. Numbers of Findhorn Foundation members have fluctuated from 350 in the late seventies ('we were undiscriminating about membership, including hippy dropouts – people who wouldn't work. And our prices were too low') to 120 in the early eighties, when some departments closed. Now there are about 200, as there were in the early seventies. Physical growth has included acquiring the camping site on which the initiators first parked their caravan, and buying the very hotel from which Peter Caddy was originally sacked, while a spinoff community has grown in Forres, and Foundation members and associates ply 'alternative' trades throughout the surrounding area. In stark contrast to our other subjects of study, Findhorn's mild asceticism is set amidst the underlying wealth of £1.6m worth of assets and debts of only £0.25m.

Hence, this study did not repeat McLaughlin and Davidson's (1985) American findings that whereas sixties communes had no formal ideology and went with the flow, eighties communes had well-developed belief systems – spiritual or political.

THE PROCESS OF CHANGE

Splitting into factions

The processes of changing ideological and practical direction and losing ideological intensity have not necessarily been smooth or gradual. They often started with the appearance of internal factions, representing divisions over the aims themselves or how they should be achieved. A common divide was between pragmatists and hardliners (replicating the realist/fundamentalist split in the green movement). At CAT, for instance, some fundamentalists opposed a visit by Prince Philip; they wanted to abandon the Quarry's upper-class connections with which it was initiated. On other occasions practical measures to make life more convenient by, for instance, removing obstacles to driving a Land Rover around the site, were opposed by 'purists' wanting, it was suggested, things to remain difficult. At CAT also, early difficult anarchist ideas about spontaneous organisation were abandoned by pragmatists:

> Anarchism didn't imply no structure at all. But this [in early days] was idiot anarchism; it was naive. You get this in anarchist communes today – they have no idea of the power that could be theirs, because they have this illusion it will work out spontaneously. It's still anarchist here; we don't have a leader but we have structures – it takes a long time to become mature in the culture of collective living.

At Canon Frome one of the more recent members denied any broad ideological shift, but said that by contrast with the 'oldies', the 'newies' were no longer 'big in principle; small in practice, but the reverse – more selective, more eclectic, with smaller ambitions and bigger achievements'.

Pragmatism, too, showed in splits between meat eaters and vegetarians, or the latter and vegans. The last were excluded from Redfield on the grounds that they would be too much trouble to cater for. At Laurieston, meat eating was vigorously defended as part of 'country living old style' – meat was what was growable and available from the surrounding land. By contrast those who just liked 'living in the country' bought their lentils from town, infringing self-sustainability.

Another common divide of major significance here concerned the approach to social relationships and social change, which will be discussed further in Chapter 6. Opposing schools of thought appeared at Canon Frome, Monkton Wyld, Redfield and LSF. On one side were those who emphasised the individual, and 'personal growth' through therapy, holistic medicine and personal health. The other side emphasised the community, and collective political action. This led to a 'major rift' at Redfield and a 'stormy period' at LSF. At the former, some had proclaimed, 'the individual is dead, long live the party': others that 'Redfield isn't about the place – we don't want *people* sacrificed to the *community*'.

Don't talk about it

'I haven't much time for talk – I'd rather see what the community does', said a Monkton Wyld person:

> Some people are doctrinaire – they talk about 'taking responsibility', then walk out and leave their dirty teacup on the side. The talk's a load of boloney. It's what we do that's more important. This place doesn't have a message: messages are dangerous. It's a tolerant place.

In these communes as in any daily personal living-together relationship, so, in these communes what people *do*, not say, is what soon becomes more important. This partly explains why, in all of them except Findhorn, where there were weekly 'attunement meetings', questions of overall purpose and ideology were rarely addressed by the group [1.12]. This may surprise romantic outsiders who might see communes as seething hotbeds of revolutionary theory. Another reason is that given by Shenker (see Chapter 3): if you do not discuss ideology and purpose it is less likely that daily practice will be continually scrutinised for ideological purity, resulting in the kinds of factional division described above. Hence, from Canon Frome:

> One of the things that keeps this place going is the lack of intensity, of scrutinising navels . . . We try to steer clear of dissent: we don't tolerate it.

While some thought that aims and principles were not discussed enough, a Lauriestonian's view that 'there isn't much to be gained from trying to talk about what we're doing' was common. Discussion was nearly always about practical things – ideology and purpose being either assumed, not explicitly worked out, or only rarely or ineffectually dealt with as side issues. They made many uncomfortable: 'I don't go in for analysing a lot', said a Lifespanner. 'There can be suspicion about ideas and talking', thought a Crabapple member. 'Every now and then we do talk about fundamental principles, but it's considered slightly bad form to raise them', a CAT worker said: 'We're so busy keeping the ship afloat that we haven't time to discuss things'.

The down side of this apparently sensible approach also came through – in the very enjoyment which many interviewees showed on being invited to talk about their ideologies and beliefs. The Crabapple person summed up the problem:

> It's like being in a relationship – you're so busy having a good time that you don't recognise the point at which you've stopped stimulating each other, and you need stimulation. We're caught up in daily living – shut off: too down-to-earth and basic.

A Redfield veteran complained: 'It's very philistine here: you can't have a conversation above the commonplace. To get on you have to suppress sides of your personality, like my interest in the arts'. In this way much of the early ideological intensity and intellectual energy has now been dissipated, at least at group level. Partly, said the Redfield member:

> The ideology is no benefit to anybody. It reduces choices. In earlier days it would be a turn-on, but now we can't get personal satisfaction doing it this way. Even if someone makes a resolution if often lapses. We don't like to nag each other.

And, partly, the daily struggle is more important . . . 'there's been a steady slide towards convenience' at CAT, while at Glaneirw the self-sufficiency aim has now become a more distant ideal because in practising it they 'could not meet the bills'. Here there is no collective goal except to take care of Glaneirw, and much the same was said at Monkton Wyld. Ideas about simplicity here had changed; it was 'spartan' in its early days, but it now was 'comfortable, with no self-sacrifice'. At PIC, though individuals retain the strong anarchist-socialist leanings noted above, the unifying and all-consuming twelve-year group project had been the conversion of a local mill into comfortable living quarters. Practical affairs have also virtually taken over Lifespan, where the sudden expansion of its print business 'has run away with us . . . there's less time to be happy here: there is more stress'. Everyone there had different ideas about the community aim, but ironically they were united in not wanting to live in the rat race. However, now Lifespan is 'not a crusade for a social alternative'.

Phases of development

The growing preoccupation with the practical and with obtaining material sustenance and comfort has been partly born of necessity. For instance it is now more difficult for individuals to draw social security and work on the commune all the time, while the communes have had to avoid financial deficits – so people have had to do more conventional outside work than originally bargained for. And this trend may partly relate to the age structure of, and length of time

Table 6: **Approximate ages of interviewees** [2.2]

under 20 years	1.5%
20–29	15%
30–39	47%
40-49	32%
50-59	3%
60+	1.5%

Table 7: **Length of time in communes** [2.1]

Up to 4 years	42.7%
5–9 years	27.2%
10–17 years	29.8%

Seventy people answered this question, of whom seven had been in other communes before their present one. The most common lengths of service were 10 years, and 2 years (10 people each) while 6 or more people each were in their first, third, fifth and eleventh years.

at, the commune (see Tables 6 and 7). There seems to be a 'bulge' of people in their late thirties and forties, a time of life where material considerations typically begin to outweigh matters of principle and ideology. Also, nearly two-thirds of interviewees were medium- to long-stay (five to seventeen years), and as such they may be expected to have tired of talking about the same ideas and to have developed a daily and yearly routine whose assumptions would be unchallenged.

After all, this is what happens in conventional life, and communards are not immune from such factors. Nor can they remain unaffected by developments in the conventional society which they oppose.

This tendency identified here also partly relates to changes in membership. This was described by an experienced communard, now at Laurieston:

> In general, over time, ideological strength and consistency dissipates in communities. One reason is that the natural structure and life of groups is that people with strong ideas set them up. They then leave because they're the kind of people who are motivated to start things – they want to move on and start something else. And also, if they are strongly idealistic they'll eventually get frustrated because things never turn out as you want.

This kind of sequence occurred at Redfield. The early core members were 'very political': socialists, Marxists and green. They 'ruled the roost' for about four years, and then a second wave of practically oriented and motivated people moved in and took centre stage. The original ideas had 'evaporated' by 1983. Then from 1984 onwards the people who moved in increasingly wanted to address emotional and relationship issues, being of the self-realisation and self-discovery-through-therapy school. Ultimately an unspoken conflict developed between them and the previous waves. At Monkton Wyld the first wave people were described as 'political/want-to-change-the-world', the second wave as 'just nice people', and the third wave as 'specialists' brought in to work as such rather than because of their ideological leanings. Canon Frome had also experienced power conflicts and big upheavals since the mid eighties, which rumbled on for years. Many people came and went around 1984-5, but the core influential group remained. Power centred on a small group of women, and policies were worked out in their kitchens rather than at mass meetings. When eventually the 'newies' pressed for decision by consensus (an original aim), they met rejection and resistance on the grounds that the 'oldies' had tried their suggestions before and found them impracticable. They had power because of their knowledge and experience, but eventually the newies asserted themselves and the oldies were eclipsed and marginalised and most of them left. As a result, Canon Frome life now may be less stressful, but the ideological aspect is more subdued and channelled, as described above.

'A middle class wank'

There seems to have been a double irony at Canon Frome. The first is that the founders had their missionary zeal to change society blunted by the need to spend most of their energy in setting the place up. The second is that their efforts created an especially attractive place to live, which has drawn middle class professionals with far less missionary zeal. A 1989 advert offered for sale one of the living units here in the Herefordshire countryside at £80,000 – a price then affordable only by the affluent.

Canon Frome operates best for someone with professional qualifications who can exercise them part-time: social workers, teachers, designers, who can work two to three days a week for high wages (see Tables 8 and 9). This is probably true of other communes, like Redfield or Laurieston. When the members first came they may have had visions of doing relatively little outside work. What actually happened was described by one member:

> Many thought when they came that they'd give up their jobs and do crafts, but at this level [of accommodation and lifestyle] you can't earn enough, so they continued with normal jobs. Hence it has become the middle class wank that so many people have described [c.f. Abrams and McCulloch, though not in these words!].

Table 8: **An elite?** [2.2]

Proportion of interviewees entering higher education	67%
Getting degrees or equivalent	49%
Dropping out/failing	18%
Getting higher degrees	7%
Describing themselves and their background as 'middle class'	60%
Not describing themselves but clearly identifiable as such	10%
Total 'middle class'	70%

At Canon Frome this has been accompanied by an increase in the trends to material comfort and individual self-realisation referred to above. Similar things have happened elsewhere, so that our Laurieston commentator described communes now as places where 'people live together because it's nice. Ideology comes second, although a common ideological purpose is a great unifying factor'.

Similarly, at Crabapple:

> People don't feel strongly about ideology now – things have become relaxed ... What we're about is making ourselves happier people: to look after the environment we first have to look after ourselves ... and we're cagey about the notion that we're showing something good to the outside world.

At Monkton Wyld we were told that while the original members had wanted to change the world, people were now there for themselves as well as society: 'Unless *you* feel powerful, you can't do anything about *it* [society]'. This summarises a popular view from across the communes – one which a socialist at Redfield put in context:

> Early people [sixties and early seventies] thought that they could change something *out there* – society. But this degenerated in the late seventies and eighties into the 'me generation' – people who saw *themselves* as wrong, and believed that if they could change themselves then society would change.

JOINING: MOTIVATIONS AND BACKGROUNDS

The class issue

Table 9 seems clearly to confirm that communards are a middle class 'elite'. As a Canon Fromer put it, 'Being middle class and having money gives you the confidence to give up affluence and come here'. But both this view and these data should be treated with caution. Most people we met were not conspicuously affluent, while the data we collected were not based on rigorous sociological criteria – neither was our sample random, since our interviewees were self-selected (albeit on the basis of an initial letter which was deliberately vague about our purpose).

Table 9: Major training and/or jobs and/or skills developed before joining the commune

This list of descriptions does not include the skills which respondents may have learned from scratch since joining the commune. Several respondents had more than one major skill/training.

University scientific research (4)	Writer/editor (e.g. for Undercurrents) (3)	Commercial rep. with large firm
Antarctic survey	Technical writer	Hotel management (2)
Industrial/business research	Dancer	Retail management
Electronics/computers development	Actor (fringe theatre)	Airline management
Engineer (2)	Teacher (inc. special needs, childcare, university lecturer) (10)	Small business owner
Builder (2)		Organic gardener
Town planner	Probation officer	Disc jockey/musical technician
Architect (4)	Social worker (2)	Secretary
Design consultant	Doctor	Handyman
Graphic designer	Radiographer	Manual worker
Commercial artist	NHS therapist	Housewife (3)
Painter-artist	Natural therapist (2)	Restaurant worker
Screen printer	Astrological counselling (4)	Hotel worker
Sculptor	Personal growth counselling	Army (subsequent deserter)
Photographer		

Nonetheless the apparent social profile of these communes bore little resemblance to 'average' conventional society (see also Table 8). As many communards had been in higher education as had identified themselves as 'middle class' (i.e. most). On this criterion, they are middle-class professional/intelligentsia rather than middle-class in the purely economic sense. Table 9 shows that their skills – at least the initially acquired ones – lean towards academia, the arts and the 'caring professions' rather than business and commerce: just the kind of middle classes who form the constituency of radical environmentalism, according to Cotgrove (1982). Or as Hays (1987) put it, they are members of the 'humanistic intelligentsia' who are struggling against the world view of the 'technical/managerial intelligentsia' over the environment, peace and so forth. The high proportion of 'drop-outs' from higher education in Table 8 should not deceive. In very many of the cases, discontinuation was the conscious act of obviously highly intelligent and capable people who could have 'walked' conventional degree courses had they persisted. But they could not stand the context of structural violence in which 'education' commonly occurred: hence the emphasis now on themselves running 'alternative' (i.e. non-hierarchical, non-competitive) education courses and creating anarchistic skills and knowledge sharing opportunities for people (ZAP, for instance).

As for why people join communes, Chapter 2 has shown two broad and related categories of motivation. First were the 'positive' reasons. They included getting closer to the land and countryside, and owning it and being self-sufficient. They emphasised 'doing it' – living out alternative economics, social relations and values – in order to furnish a lived example for conventional society to follow. This was often coupled with assertive evangelism: a positive intent to broadcast, and educate for, radical social change usually in a socialist-anarchist-feminist direction. Second were more 'negative' reasons involving rejection of, or being outcast from, or misfit in, conventional society. Materialism, hierarchy, competition, conflict and structural violence, as focused in the nuclear family, sexual stereotyping and role-models, and the career ladder/rat race, have been particular targets of dislike. They led to suppression of the true self and to loneliness, so that self-discovery and self-realisation, companionship and deep relationships were persistent obsessions among communards.

Only about twenty per cent of respondents here said that they had not been dissatisfied or disillusioned with conventional life and society when they joined the communes (Table 10). Of the others' reasons for discontent, only fifteen per cent were directly to do with nature and the ecological crisis, but over a third concerned aspects of society which are particular targets of the green critique, namely 'second' order issues like materialism and consumerism, competition, the nature of work, the nature and scale of cities, and unholistic attitudes. Another third had mainly rejected relationships and roles in conventional society for the most personal reasons – though, again, not irrelevant to the general green critique.

When reasons for joining are analysed (Table 11), a large proportion (a third) specifically concern ecology and nature, though such reasoning may often be after the event since interviewees frequently confessed to little ecological awareness when they joined. Few mentioned only one important reason and it is hard to tell which, if any, might have been paramount at the time. Two experienced communards told us: 'Most people came for individual reasons; not to change society', and 'most people get into communes because of personal crises'. The data in Table 10 could bear this out: nearly 85 per cent of the reasons given could be described as 'personal/ individual', while at best only about a quarter represent the category

Table 10: **Dissatisfaction as a motive for joining communes: the reasons which respondents most emphasised** [2.5, 3.1]

	Number of people giving this reply
Not dissatisfied with conventional society when they joined	15
(inc. never experienced conventional lifestyle after leaving home)	(9)
Dissatisfied with aspects of conventional society on joining, particularly	
Ecological crises and the treatment of nature (inc. animals)	12
'Role traps' and limiting sex relationships in the conventional marriage	14
Materialist/consumerist/competitive lifestyle	12
Emotional/spiritual dissatisfaction inc. difficulty in making relationships	9
Constraints on individual expression/control over own life	5
Work – unuseful, antisocial or boring	3
Cities (esp. the South-east) as unattractive, unhealthy, crowded, physically impure environment	8
Theoretical rather than practical nature of conventional political activism	4
Analytical rather than holistic approach to life (e.g. medicine or science)	3
Various aspects of conventional education (e.g. core curriculum, values taught)	5
'Middle class conventionality'	1
A conventional career	1
Private property	1
Large scale organisation	1
The Army as a way of defending Britain	1

[NB. Some respondents gave more than one particularly dissatisfying aspect of conventional society.]

which most interests us – people who joined communes specifically to change wider society to an ecologically sound one. All this is, perhaps, to overgeneralise. Nonetheless, when we examine particular cases we can discern several fairly distinctive – though not mutually exclusive – types of motivation and background [2.1-6, 2.10].

Ecologically motivated

Among those who joined particularly from a prior concern about

Table 11: **Major reasons given for joining the commune** [2.3, 2.6, 2.10]

(A) Specifically mentioning ecology or nature	Number of people giving this reply
*To be a force for social change to an ecological society, because of the 'environmental crisis'	12
*To help create an ecological society *and* to live communally	5
*Contributing to the spiritual (Aquarian) revolution in order to create an ecological society	2
*To create an ecological society *and* be affirmed as a person	2
*To create a feminist/anarchist/green society *and* because of a broken nuclear family	2
To work, from interest, with alternative technology and to have deep personal relationships	1
To live ecologically – especially healthy food – *and* share childcare	2
To live ecologically – especially healthy food – *and* practice therapy nearby	1
To live soundly with and enjoy nature and countryside	2
The same *and* living communally	1
(B) Not specifically mentioning ecology or nature	
*To live a lifestyle (unspecified) as a political act (to change society)	5
*To live out socialism *and* non-exploitatively as a political act	2
*Contributing to the spiritual (Aquarian) revolution by helping individuals to self-discovery	2
Looking for personal (inc. spiritual) growth and self-realisation	7
To take power/control over own life	3
To live communally and share	5
To have many deep friendships (extended family) not just one, and share childcare	2
To have friends and be with them	2
Because of the breakup of a marriage (single parent)	6
Bored with conventional nuclear family – wanted shared childcare *and* more freedom	2
To be with a partner who was joining	7
To work when wanted and be own boss	3
To be able to do lots of different jobs, not just one	1
To benefit people (inc. self) without having to be qualified	1
To form a workers coop	1
To be a graphic designer *and* have deep friendships	1
To be a gardener and work where there's a sense of community	1
To learn cooperative management techniques and work in a spiritual way	1
Left education and didn't want to go into conventional lifestyle	3
Seemed a natural thing to do, as was brought up in a community environment	3
It was somewhere to live (among like-minded people)	5
Had nothing better to do at the time	3

*These answers specifically mentioned changing wider society.

[N.B. All the reasons which people considered to be important are listed here. Some people defined two or three major reasons.]

the society-environment relationship, some in their forties clearly identified with the 1960s culture and were affected by the apocalyptic environmentalist literature of the time, especially that concerning the population-resources ratio and limits to growth. A second group, in their thirties and younger, espoused self-sufficiency and organic farming (the back-to-the-land urban escapees) and were influenced by the peace movement and pressure groups like Greenpeace and Friends of the Earth. In most of them the motivation of influencing and changing wider society are present.

Of the first group, several acknowledged an early attraction to hippie culture, coupled with radical left politics, e.g. membership of the Communist Party, anti-apartheid groups, and the original Aldermaston marches. One had been in France just after the events of '68. Some wistful talk of 'swingin' London', anti-materialism and the joys of dropping out from architecture degree courses slightly evoked the 'laid back' ambience of that time in our conversations, but on the whole these had been practical people, itching to put theories (especially about alternative technology) to the test, to head off perceived imminent environmental disaster. One CAT member soon lost romantic ideas about hippydom and theoretical revolutionary politics: 'CAT was a loose community of hippies – I tried to organise a workers coop'. Today he does not panic about environmental Armageddon, nor does he despise the benefits of modern 'civilisation'. Over the years he began

> to understand why modern life is as it is – the alternative is too hard – it's boring. You've got to be bred to it [communal/ecological living] through generations. We're too soft. We just can't take it.

A colleague of his, however, came to it from a spiritual, non-political route: 'I'm naive about social issues'. He has not gained enthusiasm for conventional life, but lives in an idyllic Thoreauvian setting on a forested Welsh hillside and works bio-dynamically in the garden at CAT. After private school and a distinguished university career in biology he went on to work for Shell, developing insecticides, but then joined the British Antarctic Survey for eight years, where he became imbued with the bioethic. He developed awareness 'of the planet as a whole. The atmosphere is very different down there, with the bulk of humanity on the other side of the planet from you'.

Another distinguished environmental pedigree belongs to the oldest communard we interviewed, at Redfield. Over 60 now, he was a founder-member of the Conservation Society in 1967, and his conviction for green politics is unabated. We also met four American ex-hippies, still deeply motivated by environmental concern. One had joined Laurieston after planning restrictions in the English village she had moved to prevented her from building a sauna, windmill and non-flushing loo and planting trees on the village green! The other three were Findhornians. One, a veteran of, and profoundly affected by, the Kent State riots, had been an inner city and community development activist in Indianapolis. Another had written a book about nuclear technology, pollution and the lack of 'truth, love and spirituality in the USA' as long ago as 1955, when he left college having had a 'spiritual experience'. He 'had been looking for something like Findhorn for twenty years' when he met the founders in 1975. Because 'the planet is threatened' he works at Findhorn 'to develop global structures above the national level'.

The younger primarily-ecologically-motivated members show a more diffuse set of influences. Only one described himself as having been 'a raving eco-activist'. In the seventies he had written for and edited *Undercurrents*, and had founded a local alternative newspaper in Aylesbury. He joined Redfield in 1984, partly to develop it as an environmental study centre and partly to share resources with others. The latter is very frequently an important element of environmental motivation: 'Living communally is more economical on the environment. You can grow your own food' said an LSF member, describing that commune as an 'oasis of green in Swindon'. All its members embraced a strong ethos of 'environment, consensus and communality', partly stemming from former nurturing work with young and/or disabled children. But they shed romantic illusions quickly: 'I had visions of people dancing and singing together. It would be spiritual and meaningful. It sounds quite twee now' – this after just four months in the commune.

Although such communards are generally too young to have been active in the sixties, the influence of those times may have been transferred to them via their teachers or parents. Several acknowledged stimulation towards alternative ideas from higher education courses in architecture, human ecology, environmental science, economics and Marxist geography. Others acknowledged unusual parents, for instance a British Telecom supervisor and a cleansing supervisor 'very much into green things'; a university classics professor and a laundry manager – both Communist Party members; a mother deputy Mayor of Cambridge – Liberal but formerly Communist; a father who ran a Cyrenians hostel in London. This, however, was not common among the communards we talked to, most having middle class parents with conventional values. And there is the ubiquitous influence of the environmental and associated pressure groups which came to prominence in the eighties. Very many communards have worked for Greenpeace, Friends of the Earth and CND in particular.

Other alternative influences

A small group came to these communes not necessarily through disaffection with conventional life, nor as ecological crusaders, but because of early influences making it seem a natural thing to do, or after a long and varied 'alternative' career. Prominent among the latter is the CAT person who left school at fifteen to become an engineer apprentice at Lucas Aerospace and a shop steward. After sixteen years and the breakdown of a conventional marriage, he left to be a builder and set up a collective house. He had already been heavily influenced by the feminist and anti-Vietnam movements in the sixties. In 1971 he helped to occupy Birmingham University and attempted to start an alternative, free university. In 1976 he started 'Rapid Transformations', a group which, every summer since then, has in a most practical way pursued 'ecstasy and the total transformation of society' by visiting different communes and doing re-roofing work on their buildings.

Another striking alternative route was taken by a PIC member who turned down a conventional job with Lucas after school to be an actor, but was refused admission to drama college because 'I had too many ideas of my own'. After a National Youth Theatre summer school he became a squatter and joined an acting company that played in prisons. Politicised through the prison reform movement, he eventually decided that 'building a community was more important than community theatre'. A few others, radicalised by university courses and green/feminist student politics, travelling and in one case going to prison, joined communes because it seemed 'natural' – the way to have control over their lives and be their own boss. One of these more-or-less 'direct entrants' to alternative and communal lifestyles joined Canon Frome to work in an alternative therapy practice nearby, and because 'it's right to grow your own food – it's healthy'. Despite this, and some general ecological awareness, none of these people joined through ecological motivation, nor do they particularly want to change society.

Disaffected

Then there are those who have become disaffected with quite specific aspects of conventional society – its organisation and world view – such disaffection figuring strongly in their defection to communes. Boredom and frustration with conventional marriage and family life is of course a major theme. For many this contributed to mid-life crises – see below – but many also opted positively for freedom rather than treating the commune as a refuge. Here the values of sharing (including shared children) and 'people working together towards important things' were actively sought.

Disillusionment with hypocrisy impelled a highly lucid and educated communard to leave South Africa and discover his roots in Wales, where he worked on bio-dynamic farms and smallholdings before joining Glaneirw to live out his anarchistic, ecological and bioregional beliefs for a while. His disgust was evoked by the examples of professing socialists in East Europe who flouted human rights, and professing liberals in South Africa like the proprietor of the bookshop where he worked, who supported the ANC yet paid his own employees slave wages.

And there is disaffection with conventional education. For one former higher education lecturer it came after a long college career, where his attempts to introduce student-centred teaching methods had been an uphill struggle. After rejecting sixties radicalism on the grounds that it was mostly 'rabble-rousing nonsense' he eventually rejected the scientific rationalism and conservatism which underpinned higher education, and trod the path to the New Age via self-programmes in humanistic psychology, encounter groups, and astrology as keys to self-understanding. After some broken relationships, and running smallholdings, he finished up in Monkton Wyld.

For ZAP members, disillusionment with education came earlier, while at university. One characterised it as 'screwing my head up – I couldn't cope with the pressure, competitiveness and narrowness. I wanted to explore ideas and university was stopping me'. Another, who had trained as a doctor for six years rebelled over 'useless, irrelevant stuff about biochemical changes. I, however, wanted to broaden my mind and learn how to make bread'. He did, and also developed an interest in alternative medicine which he carried back into the mainstream as a junior hospital doctor in London in 1989 (where he also struck a blow for all junior doctors by suing the Secretary of State for Health in a test case over the long hours which they have to work).

Abandoned careers

Still others abandoned conventional careers after a long time in them – not always with any disaffection, but for the sake of a change in mid-life. A probation officer for twenty years, for instance, was not dissatisfied with the job, but 'wanted a change' and liked the idea of living cooperatively. A fellow member of Canon Frome gave up after six years with Courtaulds' textiles, but 'not from a desire to change the world', and then discovered at the commune that he had a practical talent for joinery. Findhorn has former longstanding professionals from advertising and marketing and airline management, none of whom was actively dissatisfied with these careers. Elsewhere are ex-teachers of five to ten years standing who joined because their partners did, or through meeting and having a relationship with a communard.

Liberation from crisis

Very many more people, however, joined after personal crises, most typically in their conventional marriages and families. Comments about experiences of nuclear families were often particularly damning and bitter, especially from women:

> My twenty years married with a family were wasted. It got duller and duller. I wish I hadn't done it. I wish kids were warned about it at school.

> It was a hopeless marriage. I left my husband and started looking at communes. I decided to stop looking for one man.

> I was very jaded with the nuclear family. It was restricting and inequitable – one partner is more exploited than the other.

This last woman now takes pleasure in living in her own space with her children from a previous marriage. She has a close relationship with someone, but is independent. As a way of escape from the isolation and emotional problems of the nuclear family, communes are not easy options, as other studies have amply shown. It does not always work: 'being here I thought I'd be able to sort myself out but that hasn't happened' was not uncommonly heard. However, as was explained at Redfield: 'A community does have emotional problems but it also offers a wide circle of people, access to land, and is a more open family'. A particularly poignant story of self-liberation came from someone married at nineteen: 'It was a very naive relationship, but I thought it was the end of my problems. I had no sense of control over myself'. At twenty she felt trapped and isolated on a suburban housing estate, not having really wanted marriage or a house. She started reading, off her own bat, and became aware of ecology, feminism and vegetarianism. Her husband moved out so she threw the house open to people who were 'into drugs, anti-police and anti-Nazi', and she had some harrowing experiences at this stage. But now:

> Coming here [Crabapple] was the culmination of years of self-politicisation. All my values were lived out here. For me this was perfection. But I'm no longer idealistic – living day to day is important.

We heard another remarkable story of liberation unconnected with family entrapment. After leaving school with no qualifications, this man had signed on with the Army for three years, but soon wanted to leave. Driven to desert, he ended up serving four months in jail. There he struck up a correspondence with an unknown outsider. The letters soon became deep and thoughtful. In them, the correspondents started to envisage what an ideal society would be like. They came round to decentralist ideas, communalism and a 'cooperative village'. With no prior influence he had identified a need for anarchistic communes, deciding that the 'guidelines that the human race needs are minimal' and that the Army is an 'irrational, expensive and irrelevant way of protecting Britain – there is no need for armies to roam around countries'. Eventually, on release, he contacted communes and lived on-and-off in several.

'Misfits', roamers and travellers

This is but one example of a communard whom conventional society would probably label as a 'misfit' – a potential 'problem'. We encountered very few of these, and in fact they had had interesting and diverse, if unsettled, experiences. Though the above example was motivated by anarchistic ideas, most saw communes primarily as just somewhere to live: but also a place in which to be valued, to play a valuable, hard-working role, and not to be controlled by anything except a voluntary sense of duty to community. 'I've always struggled to fit in with how things are . . . My head's too loose for a conventional life and career', said one drifter from a middle class background, 'but it felt really good and warm here. I felt at home'.

Lack of self-worth was clearly a problem to some. One, for example, had been 22 years in manual jobs and travelling, and as 'a professional dole receiver'. He joined the squatting movement partly because of its anarchistic politics and worked for environmental groups, mainly to get companionship. Eventually he joined a commune hoping to get self-esteem, but had not found it: 'I don't feel a worthwhile person. I don't get on with anyone here – I'm really good at finding fault with people and falling out with them'. Another spoke of his difficulty in making friends: 'I don't feel confident or intelligent', he said, though, if nothing else, he played the violin extremely well. He had dropped out from veterinary school in the early seventies, and had gone on the dole and around major festivals. Then, after dropping out of teacher training and influenced by courses of meditation under Guru Maharaji, he went to the USA to find an Ashram community and spiritual fulfilment; but 'it was too uncivilised: it was near New York and I got mugged'.

Drugs

Very few interviewees mentioned drugs as a major influence, contrary to the popular image of communards. But for one person they had been positively liberating. Thrown out of home at sixteen, he did not believe he had intelligence or creativity, but discovered he had after taking LSD in the Canaries, where he had become a hippy in the early seventies:

> Living naked, long-flowing hair, aware of nature, LSD was a major part of my character formation. I realised I no longer needed to control myself: I could smile. I then discovered this son inside me and decided to come back to England and look for his mother. She was sixteen and living in a squat. I found her making love in this room with lots of other people. After she finished she stared at me. She knew then that she was going to have me – she was fascinated with me.

After adventures in Greece and Wales and another relationship with someone (a 'princess'), he went to prison having run off with his son. Then there was more travelling, and studying Chinese philosophy, before joining a commune where he looks after children. Drugs had, he thought, brought out the yin characteristics in him.

But another communard had her life marred by 'bad trips' on LSD. She had left university in 1971 for hippydom and the drug culture. Two vivid experiences with LSD followed. The chemical had uncovered her psyche and revealed 'things that should stay covered up', including a death preoccupation. On her first bad trip the first few hours had been beautiful, intense, revealing and mind-expanding. But bad hallucinations had followed, of physical things disintegrating. She spent twelve horrific hours, then recovered physically, but her mental health had been marred for sixteen years, suffering periodically from depression and a 'damaged ability to see anything as being important'. Seven years in a commune had temporarily given her a sense of direction and liberation, but she was afraid of losing it again, and lived a day-to-day existence.

Getting guidance

One final class of motivation was unique to Findhorn among these communes – that of a spiritual/mystical revelation or calling which some describe as an attractive force impelling them to go there. Once there they feel at home – it feels 'right', and a 'better place from which to change the world', and they stay. Not all Findhornians describe such experiences but those who do find them powerful:

> I just got guidance to join. My spiritual life in Florida was growing. I got an inner voice like Eileen [Caddy] . . . I did some reading and one day I had an amazing two-minute experience. The steel door in my head opened and I tapped into the universal information and knowledge . . . I had a spiritual group who helped me to realise my purpose. I didn't have to worry about the future. I learned automatic writing. I got attuned to the highest vibrational level, to let love come through.

This Findhornian visited ostensibly to see how cooperative management could work, and she never left. Now she gardens, and communicates with the plant spirits in the process.

Another woman had left her husband in Spain, where they managed a hotel. She had felt a spiritual emptiness which was 'cracked open' in encounter groups in a sister community to Findhorn. This provided motivation, along with the highly religious nature of her second partner. She kept hearing about Findhorn and the two of them impulsively drove to Scotland: 'When we arrived I suddenly recognised it – I'd always known it; I'd been guided here'. From then on her life appears to have developed considerable parallels with that of Eileen Caddy, even to the extent of conniving with her partner in his efforts to take a new lover, and meekly moving out of their caravan when the lover moved in (see Caddy 1988) – all the time professing to be 'guided by God' in such actions.

A more prosaic story came from a disc jockey whose twin motives for joining had been music and ecology. He had wanted to use and develop the considerable recording facilities at the newly-built Universal Hall, and had also been profoundly affected by a visit to his family from Richard St Barbe Baker, the 'man of the trees'. Even this very down-to-earth Findhornian tended to talk in predestination terms: 'I didn't *want* to be here – everything dictated that I had to be here and use my brain to get music at Findhorn'. But there does also seem to have been a more negative side to these stories of positive calling. The self-discovery and discovery of destiny that they recount was often preceded by deep personal crises. They involved not only the usual break-up of family relationships, but also drugs and alcohol abuse. These crises were described in equally graphic terms:

> My psychiatrist called it a psychotic episode. I was totally flooded over with unconscious contents of an extremely unpleasant kind. I became paranoid and schizophrenic: couldn't cope. I felt rejected by God.

Again, there is a parallel with Caddy's experiences, almost a struggle between good and evil, even though Findhornians do not believe in the latter.

The above accounts put the present communards into context, in terms of the relative unimportance for them of ecological matters and creating a green society. Such matters form a large part of the initial motivation of only a minority of the new wave of members. However, this does not necessarily mean that their world views and philosophies of life are incompatible with green principles, as we now see.

IDEOLOGIES

We asked the communards a very open question about their deepest convictions and concerns [2.7], to find out if green issues and principles loomed large among them. As Table 12 shows, over forty per cent did spontaneously raise the treatment of nature and environment in this discussion. From this and other parts of the interviews it was generally possible to judge people's overall ideologies – even if they did not label themselvees, which they often did. The categories in Table 12 seem the most appropriate to describe these ideologies: apart from socialist and anarchist they do not constitute political philosophies alone, though the following discus-

Table 12: **Ideological beliefs** [2.7-9]

Category	Percent of all respondents
Anarchist (a)	16.0 ⎫ 20.4
Anarchist (b)	4.4 ⎭
Feminist	6.0
Green (a)	14.7 ⎫ 22.0
Green (b)	7.3 ⎭
Socialist (a)	14.7 ⎫ 17.7
Socialist (b)	3.0 ⎭
Spiritual New Age (a)	10.3 ⎫ 16.3
Spiritual New Age (b)	6.0 ⎭
Eclectic or professed "apolitical"	17.6
Percentage of all respondents spontaneously mentioning environmental issues and concerns when asked what they felt most strongly about	41.2

NB
1. Each ideological category except 'eclectic' corresponds to *major* beliefs, i.e. the categories are not totally exclusive.
2. 'Liberal' and 'conservative' beliefs are subsumed under the other categories, especially 'green' and 'spiritual' (see Table 1).
3. Where categories are divided, (a) means self-professed, (b) means not self-professed but adjudged by the interviewer.
4. Party membership: only Green and Labour were mentioned.
5. Pressure group membership: Greenpeace, Friends of the Earth, and the Campaign for Nuclear Disarmament were the most common.

sion takes political philosophy under each category: within 'green' and 'spiritual', particularly, are several political shades. However, traditional conservatism, green or otherwise (see Table 1), was not well represented among these communards, neither was their view of community generally a conservative one (Table 3). Socialism of the social democratic/state type was more evident, but mostly it was decentralist and anarchist, so that it was not easy to draw boundaries (for instance, 'I *may* be into anarchism, but I've never read about it', said one socialist). A *green/anarchist/socialist* continuum describes most people's dispositions. The following discussion mainly illustrates some differences of emphasis within this continuum.

Socialism

A dozen or so socialists were distinguishable by their overriding concern for social justice, which over half of them put above environmental worries. The rich-poor gap in Britain was what most concerned them and they saw responsibility for all people's health and welfare lying with the healthy and wealthy, not the sick and poor. Consequently, Labour was favoured over the Green Party, though cynicism and disillusion about the Labour Party was rife, with several past but few present Party members.

Their socialism carried over into some doubt about greens, because they might put 'nature'(non-human) above people. 'I'm at odds with people who define themselves in terms of nature', said one socialist; 'I don't believe in nature' [as a separate category], said another; while a third believed that 'we *should* exploit nature – I can't stand hypocrisy, I like material things'. Relevant here are the answers to a difficult question on what the term 'the environment' meant and evoked [2.13-14]. Part of recent socialist criticisms of greens is based on this issue: the former suspect the latter of a middle-class understanding of what 'nature' is, missing out the social, political, economic and human-constructed world in favour of wildlife and a romantic rural vision, and downplaying the importance of inner city and suburban conditions, which are, however, the conditions of most people's 'environment' (Table 1 and Weston 1986).

Table 13 shows that only a tenth of the communards took a clear socialist position on this (though more might have done if coaxed), with such answers as:

> I'm more concerned about inner city environments: racism rather than aerosols.
>
> The environmental crisis isn't about nature: social and racial oppression are environmental crises.
>
> I'm unclear. To me it's nature and the countryside – but the miners' strike was an environmental issue.
>
> The environment is my use of opportunities to become myself: I'm not a birds-and-bees person.

In their prime concern for social justice, the socialists here were very divided on the role of the state, reflecting their real situation of living in a small-scale commune. Most were pro-state in some way,

Table 13: **What 'The Environment' means** [2.13–14]
(N.B. Only half (39) the respondents answered this question)

Percentage emphasising social/human elements	18
Percentage emphasising non-human elements	33
Percentage emphasising both, or giving vague answers (e.g. 'people and life', 'the planet in a global sense').	49

but against the centralist large-scale version. Its necessity, in order to redistribute wealth and make large-scale decisions, was generally conceded, but an equal or greater need for small-scale community forms was usually voiced – except in one case: 'Small-scale organisations like neighbourhood watch and Steiner schools worry me because they're only appropriate for the well-off, privileged and well educated'.

The socialists also put blame squarely on capitalism, not just for social-environmental problems but for 'distorting the movements opposed to it'; the Body Shop was cited as a perversion of the green movement. However, only one described themselves as revolutionary Marxist ('Benn, Ruddock, Livingstone'). Others saw a role for a market economy and large-scale industry. Neither planning nor small-scale decentralism could do everything, but coops, industrial democracy, a 'people's power forum, as in Cuba' and street-level groups and projects all needed emphasis. Only a few specifically required, in their revised form of industrial market economy, land nationalisation or other methods of common ownership – the Chartist's *cause célèbre* (see Chapter 2) has apparently slipped well down the agenda of grass-roots radicalism here, as it has in the wider Labour movement. We had to look to the anarchists for firmer commitment on this issue.

Anarchism

What people in these communes have attempted, above all, is to take 'control over their own lives'. And in this phrase, which was uttered more often than any other, communards expressed their anarchistic leanings: leanings which also tie in somewhat ambiguously with the liberal political philosophy and view of community (Table 3) as well as the socialist or even conservative view. 'Self-help is the idea. What matters is people taking control and doing it for themselves', we were frequently told, and 'People must have responsibility for their own actions'. Many communards labelled here as 'green', 'feminist' and 'spiritual' said exactly the same, but their interpretation of how it was to be achieved varied – more than one supported Thatcher's free-market-liberalism version of the 'taking responsibility' idea.

Generally the anarchist's rejection of power relations came out in positive ways – in practice as an attempt to forge non-hierarchical relationships in the daily round, in decision making and in sexual relations. Even an angry young anarchist followed

> Everything about the whole fucking world stinks – we've got to turn it upside down basically. For me, power is at the root of most things

with

> But rather than react *against* things I decided to ask what I *myself* could do to build an alternative society.

Hence he tried to live communally and to enable others, by campaigning for animal rights, peace, homosexuals and black people. About a third of the anarchists had squatted in the past for political reasons, not just because they needed accommodation.

After the nuclear family, the state was their main bugbear, seen as the major usurper of people's power. As the nation-state and as government its decision making was too remote, and it was a war machine that had to be fed. And the idea that he or others were 'living off the state' was roundly rejected by the 'professional dole receiver' quoted above:

> I have a basic right to a piece of Britain . . . At my present level of affluence [the dole], *I am subsidising someone else* to take more than their share of resources. I potter round growing vegetables and doing odd jobs. I'm fairly productive and useful, whereas an advertising executive or the ICI Chairman *isn't* useful. So I'm subsidising *them*.

He was, in effect, a 'ragged-trousered philanthropist'.

Social and economic devolution and decentralism were the anarchists' answers to state power, thus the way they lived amounted to a political statement. 'I'm a communalist [voluntary sharing] rather than a communist [imposed sharing]' was how one put it. This meant enthusiasm for collective ownership of land as the key to a more responsible attitude to the environment, and to wealth redistribution:

> I feel wealthy here: I own land, control and influence what should be done and I have a car (shared with six others), tools and a colour TV (shared with 25 others). You can have lots if you share and you don't have to work so hard to get it.

Again, this theme was taken up by non-anarchists: one CAT member, for instance, had calculated that he was materially far wealthier than a middle-management friend who lived in a house in London.

However, anti-materialism was a recurrent anarchist theme. A few had come to their anarchism from a definite spiritual background, rather than a materialist perspective. This spiritualism varied from Christian anarchy to Taoist-inspired; in both cases with a 'planetary, ecological outlook'.

Feminism

This is virtually impossible to treat as a separate category. Although four or five women clearly labelled themselves as feminists, most of the other interviewees, men and women, expressed strong views in support of what are feminist (as well as anarchist) principles of non-hierarchy, non-violence to people and the earth, and non-sexual-stereotyping. The desire for autonomy which characterises all feminism was very prominent in all the ideologies which were described. While such feminism, implicit or explicit, often coupled itself with anarchist, green or spiritual philosophies it tended to reject socialism as synonymous with Labour or old-style Eastern state socialism. One feminist said: 'I feel that if Thatcher had such an appeal then there must be something wrong with socialism. It's like collective living: you can't run things by guilt'.

Green

By applying the criteria outlined in Chapter 1 and Appendix 2 it was possible to distinguish a 'green' group, though again there were few clear boundaries with other ideological tendencies described here, particularly anarchist, spiritual and apolitical/eclectic. However, although most of the communards had views about nature and environment, which we discuss especially in Chapter 5, this group, described below, identified green principles and issues as of *particular* concern to them. They thought similarly about some key matters, though they were more divided over a precise political philosophy.

Most were worried about perceived resource crises and pollution. The world 'cannot go on taking, taking. The way we live isn't sustainable, cutting down tropical rainforest and building bombs'. The West's unequal share of wealth was to blame, and could lead to world conflict, yet in principle 'it's possible to be satisfied [simply], have a good time and keep the planet going'. From there, and a universal concern about food production and quality, people tended to emphasise anarchist or spiritual/deep ecology approaches. Small scale, grass-roots politics, non-hierarchy, consensus, cooperation, craft production and blurring the town-country distinction were constantly reiterated themes. They were sometimes mixed in with deep ecology, blurring the polarised 'deep versus social ecology' debate in the green movement generally. Hence, the communard who strongly advocated anarchist social organisation also said, somewhat apolitically: 'I'm a solitary person. I think more about nature than I do about other people . . . If I do what is morally right the planet will look after me'. Similar thoughts came from a 'green-anarchist-feminist' who belonged to a women's psychic group based on wicca practices. Typically, they were misunderstood and persecuted by local Christians, but she spelled out why paganism and deep ecology are compatible:

> Paganism is a way of feeling how you are part of nature's whole, and getting in touch with yourself. You have weekly meditations deciding what part of yourself to give away. And you take on an animal as part of your personality: it's not based on logical thought.

Others spoke of 'being part of the earth and the earth part of us' or 'an integral part of the planet – I worry about poisoning the planet; I'm really worried about it'. And the essence of deep ecology and its connection with rural communes came in the view that:

> There's an almost religious value in living a certain kind of life – being in tune with nature. People think about political change in terms of themselves and whether it will *feel* different after a revolution. Green things are about morality in politics.

There was no consensus, however, about where in the political spectrum that morality lies. As well as the anarchist preferences noted above, this group included Labour and SDP voters, as well as Green – 'I'm not a political animal but I vote Labour and sympathise with the Greens' was quite typical. Another view, that 'socialism is part of ecological thought', was not, although a few did accept elements of neo-Marxism. By contrast there were also:

> I'm attracted by the personal freedom aspect of the Tories.

> There's nothing in Lightmoor community [near Telford] which Mrs Thatcher wouldn't like.

> Some of the ecological ideas of the National Front are acceptable.

One Green Party activist and veteran communard demonstrated his pragmatism when asked about his blueprint for an ecological

Britain. There would be *no* blueprint in a country of self-sustaining bioregions and communes provided that they all bowed to the imperative of universal laws of ecology. Beyond that, anything arrived at by true local consensus would go. If a community wished to base its lifestyle on child abuse, for instance, this would be for its members to decide, and was not for outsiders to gainsay (see also Chapter 5).

Other green pragmatists declared themselves mixtures of every political philosophy, or that they were 'anti-ideology: things always turn out differently from what you think so if you start off determined to stick to a particular ideology you come unstuck'.

Apolitical/eclectic

Other communards thought this about *all* ideologies, including green. Some were anti 'extremism', saying 'I can see all sides of the arguments, including National Front – I don't knock everything I see', or 'There's no common sense: everyone's pushed to one extreme or the other'. Some were pragmatic; 'I'm not a pursuer of fundamental truths; all beliefs are provisional and not unshakable'.

And there were 'apolitical' people for whom everything revolved around a need to attack problems at a practical level, or who had arrived at their position through clear frustration. The latter spoke of politics as 'not saying what you *are*, but saying what you're *not*', or as

> a male thing. When I was growing up the men around me made me feel stupid by talking in an intellectual-political-philosophical way. And *talking* about changing the world is a game. It's how you live individually that counts.

Indeed, most of our interviewees would have sympathised with this view. An ex-communist now thought political dogma was 'no use – we need more communication and less repression of feelings'. 'I feel things rather than define and think', said one woman when asked about her deepest convictions. 'I don't have ideologies', said another, 'We should try and love one another and live humbly on the earth in relation to the rest of nature. I reject Western values and accept the values of the South American Indians'. This brings us close to our last category, the 'spiritual', among whom some voiced green concerns while others did not. Most of their world view, however, was quite compatible with deep ecology.

Spiritual/New Age

This ideology was best represented at Findhorn, although a sprinkling of communards from elsewhere (who had sometimes visited Findhorn) expressed it strongly. It has several elements. There is an evolutionary view both of human history, which is entering the New Age (Aquarius) of love, cooperation, harmony and spiritual awareness, and in some cases of the human soul evolving to greater heights of consciousness through reincarnation. New Age deep ecology hinges on a revival of the seventeenth century (and earlier) doctrine of monism, a theory that there is only *one* basic thing in the universe, a single reality, whether it be material substance or spiritual 'God' or both. For the Findhornians the common reality of the material and spiritual is *energy*. One ramification of this is that everything is part of a unitary system. Monism is an extreme form of holism (see Chapter 1), of which terms like 'wholeness', 'interdependence' (of people and nature), and 'the planetary culture/village' are deep ecology expressions (see the discussion of deep ecology in Chapter 1).

It follows that matter is seen as a manifestation of energy, or 'spirit' as Findhornians sometimes put it. Spirit is a 'higher frequency vibration' than emotion, but the door to spirituality is through the heart, the feelings, intuition and heightened consciousness via meditation and 'attunement'. Love, too, is a form of energy ('not the lovey-dovey type we feel emotionally'). Knowledge of the world as this whole does *not* come from rational thought, which in the West is based not on monism but dualism. Dualism means a tendency to think in terms of opposites which are also separate from each other. (Hence the two fishes swimming away from each other – the symbol of the 'old age' of Pisces which is drawing to a close.) Dualism places humans separate from nature, masculine from feminine, mind from matter etc. – and it tends also to see one side of such opposites as more important than the other.

Hence Westerners are generally out of balance because they think dualistically, in the classical scientific way. This hinders us from gaining true 'New Age consciousness'. But when people do gain it through meditations and 'peak' emotional experiences that bring revelation and insight, they have a holistic sense of how they are intimately part of the rest of human and non-human existence – the rest of the planet. They now have 'planetary consciousness', appreciating that they are part of this collective consisting of Earth and all its creatures (Gaia). 'God', of whatever religion, is another term for that consciousness, consequently if we have it, *we* are God. God is an immanent (in everything) consciousness, a universal collective mind of which we all can be part. This idea is akin to Hegel's idealistic concept of the universal spirit or geist, which one Findhornian specifically invoked while also repudiating Marx's materialism (see Chapter 3 on idealism and materialism and Chapter 6 on social change).

World history is shaped by this spirit or consciousness: consequently if we want to change society – to influence the course of history – we must open ourselves up to the flow of cosmic energy which represents planetary consciousness. To do this we must first discover ourselves as individuals. Only after finding out what we really are, and loving ourselves, can we *change* ourselves – towards spiritual, loving people. Thus enabled, we can *do* things, such as loving others and the planet, working cooperatively, and spreading the new consciousness. We can also make things happen materially. Collective meditation, for example, can bring down the crime rate in a district. Individual meditation can bring us to communicate with the spirits in plants (devas, which are also part of planetary consciousness), helping us to grow things well (a revival of pagan animism which seemed actually to work spectacularly in the early days of Findhorn – see Hawken 1975 and Chapter 5). Or, if we need (as opposed to merely want) material things or the money (another form of energy) to get them, we can *manifest* them. This does not mean that we can conjure them up out of nothing, but we can indirectly, and in a way of which we are not necessarily conscious, influence events so that what we need becomes available. (While we were at Findhorn, two communards advertised in their bulletin for colleagues to help 'manifest' enough money for them to go on a holiday.) Again, this idea seems to have succeeded, if measured in terms of Findhorn's own wealth.

New Agers think that growing planetary consciousness is already leading to significant world changes in the 1990s. Gorbachev's peace and openness initiatives are seen as part of this inexorable trend. Given all this, politics and economics are irrelevant and meaningless, for the world is more mind than matter. Politics, furthermore, is based on dualistic confrontation rather than holistic 'love'. Findhornians refuse to think in terms of conflict, confrontation, evil, sin or the devil. If you should object to other people's actions, you must build up a sympathetic understanding with them, to influence them by your view, and hope that they too will take on planetary consciousness. This is 'positive thinking'. 'I try to be compassionate and sensitive to things around me and to be more understanding – it makes me less critical of things and relieves me of stress', said one: a remark which sceptics might well reinterpret as 'I find political thinking uncomfortable'. Such sceptics might be outraged at the following typical response to our quuestions about the plight of people in the Third World:

> Third World peoplle arre exploited. They can't control this. But they can control how they *feel*. They can walk around in a *victim* cconsciousness or they can walk around enjoying everything. You go to Srii Lanka and you see the kids happy, happy, happyy. You go to America and they're not happy as a race . . . You can be happy living in cardboard boxes.

Findhornian New Ageism is, thus, ostensibly an individualistic, free will doctrine of self-liberation (for example, from 'negative thoughts') which, it is claimed, is also liberating the world slowly but surely. Other communards we interviewed were often doubtful when they heard we were to visit Findhorn, for they mistrusted this kind of 'apolitical' (in reality, deeply conservative) spiritualism, and the apparent elitism which follows from the high prices that are charged for the self-discovery/therapy courses – an elitism which several Findhornians themselves were uneasy about. But, as we have argued elsewhere (Pepper and Hallam 1989), we think that most greens – including green communards – display elements of the 'Findhorn tendency', especially when it comes to questions of social change, as we shall discuss in Chapter 6. And Findhornians also share the anarchistic desires of communards elsewhere – although perhaps their true political disposition is most closely represented in the multifaceted and thriving small businesses which have been set up in association with the Foundation, and the business mentality and language which their members (especially the American ones) tend to use to express their world view.

Influences

This Findhorn tendency is borne out by the list (Table 14) of books and people which most influenced communards' views on the society-environment relationship [2.12]. Approximately two-thirds fall broadly into the category of calling for a spiritual-moral revival: a change in consciousness away from traditional Western dualistic and materialist thinking, towards holism, achieved not through 'tradi

Table 14: Major influences
(Figures in parentheses indicate number of mentions)

Specific books

- (8) Small is Beautiful (Schumacher)
- (4) Blueprint for Survival (Ecologist)
- (4) Turning Point (Capra)
- (4) Practical Self Sufficiency (Seymour)
- (4) Magic of Findhorn (Hawken)
- (3) Seeing Green (Porritt)
- (2) Awakening Earth (Russell)
- (2) Silent Spring (Carson)
- (1) Population: Resources: Environment (Ehrlichs)
- (1) Costs of Economic Growth (Mishan)
- (1) Person/Planet (Roszak)
- (1) Lifetide (Watson)
- (1) Fear of Freedom (Fromm)
- (1) Guide for the Perplexed (Schumacher)
- (1) Good Work (Schumacher)
- (1) Anarchy in Action (Ward)
- (1) Post-Scarcity Anarchism (Bookchin)
- (1) News from Nowhere (Morris)
- (1) Jesus, Gandhi and the Nuclear Age (Douglas)
- (1) Woman on the Edge of Time (Piercy)
- (1) Wisdom of Insecurity (Watts)
- (1) Modern Man in Search of a Soul (Jung)
- (1) Secret Life of Plants (Tompkins)

Authors (no titles mentioned)

- (2) Kropotkin
- (2) Colin Ward
- (2) Buckminster-Fuller
- (1) William Godwin
- (1) Herbert Marcuse
- (1) Patrick Rivers
- (1) Martin Cecil
- (1) Theodore Roszak
- (1) Eric Fromm
- (1) E.P. Thompson
- (1) Jill Tweedie
- (1) Margaret Mead
- (1) Alvin Toffler
- (1) Rudolf Steiner

Other publications

Resurgence
The Leveller
Peace News
Undercurrents
The Ecologist
Christian Ecology Group Publications
Greenpeace leaflets

People met or heard in public meetings

Kit Pedlar
Fritz Schumacher
Eve Balfour
Earl of Bradford
Richard St. Barbe Baker

T.V. programmes

'Doomwatch' with Kit Pedlar
'Due to Lack of Interest, Tomorrow Has Been Cancelled'
- (5) Unspecified environmental programmes

Others

- (2) Polytechnic/university course
- (2) Visit to Findhorn
- (2) Soil Association Meetings
- Quaker summer schools
- Events in France 1968 (eyewitness)
- Spiritual programme of Alcoholics Anonymous

Courses of study on:

Gandhi/anarchism
Kibbutzim
Taoism
Zen philosophy
Astrology
Paganism

tional' left-right politics but by individuals transforming themselves. Few 'political' or social ecology, rather than deep ecology, books are chosen, although the anarchism of Bookchin and Colin Ward are present. There is also a slight 'old-fashioned' feel about the list (most books were published in the seventies), perhaps reflecting the limited time which the daily communal round gives for reading. While this does not imply that older books are not extremely relevant, it does suggest that communards may neglect some of the newer and more complex political developments in the green debate.

WHAT'S WRONG WITH THE OUTSIDE WORLD?

As another indication of the 'greenness' or otherwise of these communards, we asked them about their critique of conventional society [3.1]. As our account below shows, it agreed closely with the 'standard' radical green critique we described in Chapter 1.

Society [3.4]

The most frequent criticism from these people who were trying to live frugal lifestyles was that conventional society is hopelessly over-materialistic. Though only two communes (Findhorn and Monkton Wyld) had overtly spiritual approaches, nearly a fifth of our respondents bemoaned the lack of value which society places on spiritual matters. 'Money is a religion today, but it must change', and 'The quest for material things doesn't bring satisfaction but problems like Chernobyl', were typical comments. However there was also a significant minority from two of the more private communes (Laurieston and Monkton Wyld) who did not reject materialism out of hand. For example, we heard that:

> This commune is a rich environment – a half-way house from capitalism, which is why it works. I don't want a new car every two years but I do want a reliable car . . . Our level of materialism in the West can't be sustained globally, but it's not a bad ambition.

An equally important concern was with forms of alienation, particularly, in anarchistic vein, resulting from people's lack of power and control over their own lives. Correspondingly, hierarchies, bureaucracies, the military-industrial complex and, in two cases, religion were attacked as forms of oppression. Not uncommonly the welfare state was included in with the oppressive structures: though socialists did not do this, more liberal greens and anarchists did. Perhaps, however, only anarchism could reconcile this concern for loss of individual identity with an almost equal set of worries about loss of community and extended family, and *too much* individualism and privateness. Anarchism might attack individualism as self-interest, but applaud it as self-fulfilment, where that partly involves relating to others in a non-material, non-monetary way. Hence another target of opprobrium was conventional social relationships between people, especially in the nuclear family and between men and women. They were seen as unequal, oppressive power relationships where people did not really listen to each other. Among a wide range of other concerns, the more directly 'green' ones of lack of holism (specifically in medicine) and unsustainable lifestyles were well to the fore.

Few Findhornians responded to this section of the interview schedule. Where they were prepared to identify bad aspects of society they added that things were rapidly changing for the better. But they also refused to 'condemn, judge or disapprove' on the grounds that 'this is a lack of love in me: everyone has a right to the way they are', and 'I get angry when I see pain and misery, but I work hard at not doing so. If I can't do anything about it then it doesn't serve by getting emotional about it'.

Economics and work [3.3, 3.5]

Following the force of criticisms about society in general, when it came to economics, we found that wealth maldistribution, excessive consumerism, growth and waste, and production for profit rather than 'real needs' or quality of life were the most common targets of disapproval.

> Economics isn't about social responsibility, but greed and profits.
>
> Basic needs get perverted by the power interests of a few.
>
> Economics is about the abstraction of money rather than real needs: this is an out-of-balance malignancy.

These observations were typical. They condemned 'economics' rather than capitalist economics, although competition and multinational corporations or 'big business' were blamed most often. On the other hand little was said about small businesses. Their role if any in the destructive system went unconsidered, or there was indifference to the proposition that it was in the nature of capitalist economics that small often tends to become large or otherwise extinct. Since most communards depend on small businesses this was hardly surprising. As Elkington and Burke (1987) put it, quoting Rosabeth Kantner, 'A lot of sixties phenomena – the collectives, the alternative institutions, the small enterprises – were entrepreneurial activities'. However, our communards did point to the cooperative nature of their businesses, and the view that *they* were producing for need. The idea that 'business' itself 'destroys society – it reduces us to digits', which one person proposed, would probably have been denied by most, since *their* businesses, they felt, involved what the Findhornians called 'love' and spiritual values. No more than half a dozen came out against capitalism in any form. Most popularly it was the imagined abstract motive of 'greed', rather than the system itself that inspires it, which was denounced.

But the nature of work under capitalism – which communal working practises tried to correct – was often roundly condemned for its overspecialisation and division of labour and the way it makes people cogs in a machine. It was thought boring, undignified and alienating. Anarchists, particularly, went further, attacking the work ethic itself (though many communards seemed to display that ethic *par excellence*).

> People should not feel they must work to justify their existence.

> Work and education are defined according to institutions and frameworks. People who aren't in these are [wrongly] regarded as not educated or working.

> People are valued according to their material contribution, but it is absurd to pay people more for doing one thing rather than another.

In one way or another, many communards supported these sentiments. Whether they called themselves anarchists or green or whatever, most followed the 'green economics' line unswervingly (Ekins 1986) – down to paying people for work in the informal economy, the concept of the social wage, and the call for independent, not dependent, Third World development. Yet few mentioned the key question of ownership of the means of production, especially land, though the idea that communes are specifically a way for the majority of people to own land was popular.

Technology [3.7, 3.11]

Given how trenchant the above criticisms were, the view of technology was surprisingly bland. There was virtually no trace of romantic anti-technologism – the kind of view that 'technology has alienated us from the Earth' being a rare one. More commonly 'alternative/intermediate/appropriate' technology was favoured rather than high technology. But many benefits of conventional technology were also applauded. It was generally seen as neutral or even 'convivial' (after Illich), but abused by those in control of it – used to make profit or control people. A more radical view, that some technology, far from being neutral, is inherently bad or exploitative (see Albury and Schwartz 1982) was seldom encountered, though on the other hand nearly all the communards made their opposition to nuclear technology very clear. By about three to one, communards supported the technocentric idea that technology would be able to find ways out of any environmental predicament – the 'technofix'. However, again, that fix would often be seen in the form of alternative and local technology that requires radically different social and economic organisation. The computer occupies an ambiguous position here, and this is how most communards see it, as do greens in general.

Education [3.6]

Again, relatively little really incisive criticism was voiced on this topic, except in two of the communes with a special educational focus – ZAP and Monkton Wyld. Here there was opposition to compulsoriness, compartmentalisation of knowledge, boring irrelevance, assessment, grading, the hidden curriculum which moulds people into roles where they exploit others or are exploited, hierarchical organisation, stifling of free expression, of creativeness and of children's sense that they have control over their own lives – all anarchistic criticisms which Thoreau voiced a hundred and fifty years ago. Little, it seems, has changed!

Elsewhere this torrent of criticism dwindled to a steady trickle aimed against sexism, the core curriculum (centralised control), neglect of subjective expression in children, and unchallenging, regurgitative, undemocratic learning. The common 'academic' bias, as against the practical, was also disliked. Just occasionally there had been good experiences, particularly of Dartington and Stantonbury Campus (Milton Keynes) schools, and of some higher education courses (see above).

Why? [3.10]

A clue to the communards' position on social change – particularly how much change for the good they think is possible and likely – came from their answers to the question '*why* do these things [the faults of conventional society] occur?'. There is not as much optimism about the state of 'human nature' (and therefore the potential for change) as one might expect from individuals who believe in their *own* potential for change. Greed, selfishness, competitiveness and tendency to error were most commonly invoked. And explanations for these commonly came down to the level of the individual where a person's inherent nature is unpleasant, rather than to socio-economic structures, though structuralism was evident too (see Chapter 3).

> Me and you are the cause. I'm greedy and so is the world. I'm here to straighten myself out, which is necessary before the world gets straighter. Governments must get it wrong because they are composed of human beings and full of error. Somewhere *inside* they and I are making the wrong decisions. [Author's emphasis].

This reflects the essential psyche of many communards, it seems, as does this:

> We're sick. I'm sick and I know other people are. We go on killing and maiming people. I don't know why we are as we are – why our culture is as it is. We've got out of balance. I can't think of any other reason apart from original sin. It's beyond me, we're not in control over where we are.

After so many explanations like this from mild people who obviously were not inherent maimers and killers, the Findhornians' insistence that there is no such thing as original sin came as a welcome relief. Predictably, they saw the lack of spirituality in people as a reflection that society has not yet reached the right stage of evolution. They also suggested that a sense of insecurity had entered earlier in history, making humans forget their 'interconnectedness'. This theme was taken up by people elsewhere. It was a 'vicious circle which started from people being too poor'. They had become frightened of lack of enough, and fearful of being exploited and invaded, so they had done those things to others.

Just a few were prepared to attribute this to the development of specific modes of production – particularly capitalism. They saw consumerism as a feature of this system, with its attachment of the notions of self-gratification and self-fulfilment to material things. One Lauriestonian proclaimed that this is what material things bring: 'People want the quality of their lives to be good, and this involves money and getting a car'. But this view was rare. Almost as rare, however, was the idea that private ownership, especially of land, was the major cause of society's ills; although one person said, 'Multinationals are not taking into account the needs of the land. I'd like to do away with multinationals'.

Explanations based less on economics and more on history revolved around the Enlightenment, the development of classical science and the development by Descartes and others of a philosophy of separation from nature, reinforced by a Judaeo-Christian message of dominance over it. Scientific reductionism and the mechanical view of nature, together with a love affair with machines, were blamed too – a reflection, perhaps, of wide readership of some green literature (such as Capra's *The Turning Point*). This sense of history also extended to the industrial revolution, and the idea that too-rapid technological change had overtaken people. It tended towards technological determinism: 'It wasn't planned; it just happened following technological developments'.

Without saying why they had developed, several communards saw power structures as the chief problem. Once in place they led to built-in reinforcement mechanisms that discouraged the majority from recognising either their own inherent power, or the possibility of social change. This argument ran as follows:

> People are asleep and they never wake up. Society is constructed to keep them asleep. Asleep people are not problems.
>
> The problem is that only one way of life is presented as possible and is thought possible.
>
> The Government, who control education, want people to be subservient. They want a whole nation full of subservient workers. The nuclear family is a form of social control.

These perspectives on causation, with their relative emphasis on individuals and their values, and on the nature of human nature, but with a more minor subset of explanations invoking structures of political power and sometimes economics, conform to a typically green understanding of why things are wrong.

One Green Party member invoked virtually all of them, together with 'overpopulation': 'Malthus' views are coming true'. Marx's, by contrast, were regarded as relevant to the past but 'ludicrous' in application to the future, for 'capitalism may be a cause of environmental problems but communism is just as bad'. The Marxian view of the relationship between ideas and social structures had value, but the 'economic structure is but a reflection of mass psychology', said this green, shying away from placing too much importance on the historical development of the economic mode of production. Such a pot-pourri of causes was because 'There's no one explanation: it's spiritual, material and psychological – its the hubris of mankind'.

This chapter has shown that the communes we visited are less oriented to social change and green ideals and practices now than they were when founded. There has, overall, been a loss of ideological coherence and evangelising energy. The present communards have joined more for reasons to do with their individual situation than with a desire to change society or live a 'green' lifestyle – although such desires are there with a minority. Ideological beliefs are particularly consistent with a green anarchist and/or deep ecology perspective, as are the criticisms which the communards make generally of society and their analyses of what is wrong. We will discuss their specific views of the society-nature relationship [3.9] in the next chapter, which focuses on attitudes to nature and environment, on how much green principles are translated into practice, and on what difficulties and obstacles stand in the way.

CHAPTER 5

How green are the communes? Ecological values and practices

This chapter asks whether communards are by and large 'ecocentrics', in other words radical greens, in thought and deed (see Chapter 1 and Appendix 2). It presents what they described as their beliefs and feelings towards nature, and what environmental problems most worry them. It also tells us what they do in 'living green' – or, rather, *try* to do. For just as we all find it difficult to practice what we believe, so do these communards, sometimes. Not least difficult are the very processes of living together, trying to share, to relate harmoniously and peacefully, and to achieve high quality of life at low material levels – all important 'second order' elements of a green society.

This account of belief systems about nature and environment, of attempts at ecological 'soundness' and of some of the realities and complexities of social relations, will give some insight into other issues raised in Chapters 1 to 3. For instance, we may be able to see what historical phase of communal living most parallels this phase, and we may determine what view of community (i.e. *gemeinschaft* or *gesellschaft*) most of the communards hold. Such considerations feed into the discussion in Chapter 6 where, having asked if communes conform to green ideology and practice, we go on to consider various factors affecting their potential to encourage and be part of wider social change to a green future, a potential which many outsiders maintain is there.

CONVENTIONAL ATTITUDES TO NATURE [3.9]

The communards roundly condemned the way that conventional Western society thinks about and behaves towards nature. It was described as violent, destructive, ungrateful, exploitative, oppressive and domineering. Trying to control nature was, of itself, often regarded as wrong. 'We hunt and shoot it – just can't leave it alone'. 'We' destroy its beauty and resources, and the latter are running out.

> We treat nature as a fount into which we dip; we take and then throw rubbish back – it's a frontier mentality.
>
> It's live now, pay later – there is no long-term view on behalf of future generations.

Such comments echo strongly the mainstream green critique and, again true to green idealism, they see our attitudes and values as the first and foremost causes of environmental ills. 'The way you treat the environment stems from the way you *see* it', said one communard, thus speaking for many.

People 'do not value nature enough and are arrogant towards it', was a common complaint. 'We think we're the most important thing on the planet and nature is dispensable'. Some attributed this attitude to an alienation from nature which arose through a historically specific period and process – that of 'industrialism'. Industrialism now gives us the power (technology) to 'completely destroy' our environment, yet our 'mental adaptation' to this new situation over the past two hundred years has been minimal.

> Society is alienated from plants. You can hear them crying out under the conditions of artificial cultivation [this from Findhorn].
>
> We treat nature as an object – as dead material having no effect on us. We don't realise how interrelated we are.
>
> Nature is seen as a day in the country. People don't understand the connection between it and our daily lives.
>
> People are too removed from nature. So much of what we get is packaged, selected and purchased for us. We get nature's provisions in artificial dollops, i.e. from garden centres.

An astrologer's view from Glaneirw regarded alienation from nature as a legacy of the development of rational thought and the metaphor of science as a machine (i.e. during the scientific revolution of the 'Enlightenment'). This analysis seems to reflect the impact of the green critique developed by such mainstream writers as Capra, Schumacher and Skolimowski, as does the solution to the problem which was most commonly raised – that of education. Lack of understanding of our 'real' relationship (that of interdependence) was usually seen as a fatal problem – particularly, of course, by those involved in education ventures. CAT members typified this view:

> People are quite into nature conservation, but they don't understand the indirect connections between themselves and nature, i.e. what happens when they flick on a light switch . . . Few people consciously degrade the environment when they're really aware of what it means . . . unawareness of the planet is the problem . . . lack of planetary consciousness.

Just a few people blamed economics and the fact that 'it's too easy to make money out of nature. Life-damaging initiatives (Concorde or the Channel Tunnel) are profitable, but life-enhancing things are done on a shoestring, or voluntarily'. This fact, which Galbraith recognised in *The Affluent Society*, explains why, in reality, people often harm nature in full knowledge of what they are doing.

While one communard bemoaned the lack of romanticism in the common view of nature, another thought 'Our approach is *too* sentimental; we are interested in fluffy mammals, but not habitats as a whole'. A third saw lack of holism as ultimately fatal to us: 'If we keep messing with Gaia, she'll throw us out – nuclear weapons and AIDS are all part of Gaia'. This interpretation of the Gaia hypothesis is not unknown in green thinking. It conveys – almost with relish – a disdain for humanity (at least in any numbers) which smacks of romantic ecocentrism and is rather unpleasant to humanists, socialists, liberals and technocentrics alike.

AVERTING ENVIRONMENTAL CRISIS: THE APPROPRIATE VALUES [4.0a, 1-3]

The crisis

Nearly half of our interviewees strongly believed that these 'wrong' values and attitudes to nature, just described, have led to an environmental crisis. Few disagreed (see Table 15).

The catalogue of elements which comprise this 'crisis' contained no surprises. Pollution topped the list – in general, and of water and air (including acid rain), in particular. There were also many concerns about global warming and ozone depletion, which were correctly linked with deforestation and desertification. These, the particular worries of the late-eighties environmentalists, were mixed with early-seventies fears about resources running out, but only one respondent anticipated nuclear war, the early-eighties preoccupation (though several foresaw danger from the nuclear power industry).

The apocalyptic language which particularly marked early-seventies environmentalism was also evident:

> If we don't stop treating nature as we do things will be terrible.
>
> We're making an awful mess of the world.
>
> Everything is out of control.
>
> The earth is in serious danger.
>
> Nature's being raped and plundered.

Such comments were mingled with insistent demands for action now. This perspective – of disaster at a global scale – was sometimes argued and rationalised: for instance mismanagement of Third World land at the end of a chain of causes and effects initiated through economic development of the West. But it was also strongly and clearly just *felt*: in ways sometimes graphically described, people were worried that things are out of control:

> I feel that tentacles of harmful activities are reaching out from the south-east of England, and we are being pushed towards the Irish sea [from a Lauriestonian, living near the rim of that sea].

Such bleakness became nihilism in a Canon Fromer:

> I'd like to think of my family and DNA going on, but if they're dead in a puff of smoke what difference does it make? Once the Earth has gone it doesn't matter – this is a priceless piece of knowledge. If my kids were Ethiopians I wouldn't be wild about their surviving – be quite a good idea if they snuffed it. It's hard to know how we're to avoid World War Three – it ought to be Asia and Africa versus the rest.

What was generally lacking was the more socialist view (see Chapter 4) that sees any 'crisis' essentially in social, not 'natural', terms, though there were two exceptions, from Canon Frome and Lifespan:

> There isn't a crisis – what does that *mean*? The inner city has gone beyond crisis to devastation, while crises like Ethiopia are *political*: not to do with nature and weather.
>
> The crisis is in the polarisation of *people* . . .

However, this kind of perspective was more evident over the particular issues of economic growth, resources and population. For every respondent who believed that the world is overpopulated ('The whole world, including this country, is *incredibly* overpopulated, and this leads to crime'), about three did not. Many emphasised maldistribution of resources in relation to people, particularly blaming high levels of Western consumption and advocating wealth redistribution. Others worried about economic growth and 'overconsumption' rather than too many people. They generally agreed that 'economic growth can't continue'; 'We're in a finite system'; 'uncontrolled growth is a cancer'; and 'the present way of life is unsustainable', although a few counselled caution. Stopping world industrialisation would harm poor people: one does not *have* to live 'like a peasant': there is room for growth in miniaturised and low-energy technology; and there is room for growth in services (this last, predictably, from a commune whose members mostly work in the caring professions). Just one respondent specifically confronted the *system* of economic organisation rather than 'economics' in general:

> Yes, there's going to be a resource crisis. A total breakdown of life in the city. They'll be in a totally unsustainable system. The only way to survive will be to prey on other people – mugging and robbing for food. This won't be because of a total lack of resources, but the breakdown of *capitalism*, which can't keep on endlessly expanding.

The bioethic and animal rights

Table 15 shows strong general support for the bioethic – the idea that nature has intrinsic value and a right to existence of itself (see Chapter 1). Some of it was unqualified:

> I absolutely believe in the bioethic. Humans are hopeless, they can't even live in harmony with nature.

> The wellbeing of the planet comes before an affluent lifestyle.

> We must respect nature: it is alive. Like primitive cultures we must ask permission before exploiting it.

> If man blew himself off the face of the Earth, morally I wouldn't object.

Table 15: **Beliefs about nature**

(First-order ecocentric principles: see Appendix 2. Figures refer to the number of interviewees expressing strong support for (or rejecting) the following principles and beliefs)

There is an environmental crisis	33
(There is not	4)
Humans are part of, and are globally interdependent with, nature; we should be its steward	27
(Disagree	1)
Bioethic – respect/worship/moral obligation to nature	22
(Rejecting the bioethic	10)
There are limits to growth	21
(There are not	2)
Nature is a self-regulating system – Gaia – and/or is female	16
(Disagree	14)
Anti-urban/pro-countryside	13
(Pro-city	5)
We should promote diversity in nature	2
We should promote stable ecosystems	2

But there were also qualifications, particularly from those who saw that to believe in 'nature's rights' must imply 'animal rights'. They came from communes in or near an upland farming economy, where grass grows best, sheep and cattle are therefore appropriate and 'the meat follows from the milk'. Such communes consume animals and their products (though they are not the only ones) and communards stoutly defended the practice – partly because it contributes to self-sufficiency, and partly because:

The defence of animal life is not mirrored in nature. Animals don't think it wrong to kill animals. Providing food for people is a basic principle, not defending animal life. If you carried this to its ultimate we'd pick berries.

Such arguments emphasised that killing animals is part of nature's cycle. It does not equate with exploitation if agribusiness techniques are shunned and, possibly, if those that eat meat are prepared to do the killing themselves (they generally are in communes). Furthermore, it does not infringe the bioethic, if interpreted in defence of species rather than just preservation of individuals.

Occasionally vegetarianism or veganism was attacked as 'holier-than-thou', or as hypocrisy or attention-seeking. To drink expensive soya milk, for instance, is not only elitist, it may use Third World products as substitutes for something indigenous to the local area. And: 'There's too much fuss about getting a diet together. Diet's the new thing: a way of giving attention to yourself and getting it from others'.

While some emphasised how respect for nature might connect intimately with respect for people, others felt that it militates against the human species:

> I put my own species first – I'd rather kill a cow than see a human starve.

> 'Yes' to respect but 'no' to worship of nature – I like to be on my own in nature, but this isn't healthy: it's to do with shunning people.

> Nature is valuable because it gives us pleasure – it's not got intrinsic value. And I'd forego this pleasure for less hardship in the world. I care more about Eskimo communities than whales.

Two other communards who support green causes rejected the bioethic on the grounds that 'value' and 'rights' are human constructs:

> I'm not interested in guilt about nature. At the end of the day it doesn't matter if this world disappears in a puff of smoke, because I don't have any consciousness after my death.

> ... there can't be an intrinsic value for nature. You can't place value outside a social framework – i.e. your *own* framework. It's all in our heads – it's our creation.

Both legally and existentially these are compelling arguments, but most communards rejected them for the more conventionally green view.

Mother Earth

> I'm struggling to try and see nature and the planet as a living organism. To get back the more ancient view. To change consciousness from mechanistic to organic.

> I like the idea of Mother Earth: it's good symbolism.

General support for the first view did not always extend to the second. The idea of Earth as a living organism, which humans are a relatively unimportant part of, was very common. Human pollution and control of the planet is but transient, part of the system's 'adolescence'. Gaia will adapt and survive, but possibly without humans. (Here, Russell's *Awakening Earth* was often mentioned.)

However, though Gaia is the Greek term for 'Mother' Earth, some of these Gaians surprisingly had never linked feminism with nature, or did not like the idea of so doing: 'The Mother Earth image is dangerous – it suggests that, in our patriarchal culture, nature is but passive'; 'Nature as female is as much a stereotype as God being male'. Our interviewees did not like the dualistic masculine-feminine split. However, this did not preclude positive discrimination towards feminine *values* to achieve a holistic balance with masculine ones, a sentiment which could shade into the anti-intellectualism which Abrams and McCulloch noted among their communards: 'We need holism [feminine] and less theorising and intellectualising [masculine]'.

Anti-urbanism

It also shaded into a distinctly romantic pastoral idealism, not surprising for a group which has generally chosen to live in the country, but remarkable for the rawness with which it was expressed:

> I go into unspoilt countryside once a week. This contact energises me: it's therapeutic. I like wild country and mountains. It's about survival; feeling the wind and the ravages of weather.
>
> I love the countryside and don't like cities . . . I sometimes feel cosmic about nature.
>
> People weren't meant to live in large conurbations like Milton Keynes.
>
> Country dwellers are morally better than urban ones.
>
> There's little crime in villages, but you become anonymous in cities.
>
> Cities are identical to cancer cells. Like the latter, cities and the people in them take no notice of the whole organism [i.e. Gaia].

Such sentiments hark back to Muir, Emerson, Thoreau, Carlyle and other romantics and to the sixties counterculture. They are deeply ecocentric, but they often display a (subconscious?) anti-people bias which suggests the rural commune as a place of escape from an environment of masses of people. They contrast with another 'anti-urban', but explicitly pro-people, view that sees social alienation in the city, but also cultural and economic advantages there. To retain the second but minimise the first, anarchist planning is favoured. This view also came across in a few interviews; 'We could have *everyone* living in the countryside: a house in every field. You can free a lot of land for this by getting rid of the meat production which is excessive now'.

Holism, deep ecology, monism and the New Age

The deep ecology idea that humans are intimately part of nature and totally interdependent with it was the strongest and most common view (Table 15) of the society-nature relationship. One or two people had reservations, warning that humans are positively different from and either above or equal to nature, or that 'If you get too much into this big picture you forget "smaller" issues like racism and inner cities', or (correctly) that seeing society as an organism or part of it leans towards right-wing conservatism and legitimation of meritocracy.

But, from most, holism was evident in some form, such as 'Everything is connected to everything else', with the corollary that society should cooperate with and steward nature, leaving it alone as much as possible. Dualism was firmly rejected: 'The concept of nature as something outside oneself is handing over our responsibility for it to a bigger power. That's wrong'.

There were also many 'New Age' responses where, as described in Chapter 4, holism stretches towards monism, emphasising how *completely* intimately humans are part of nature: part of the same collective 'planetary' consciousness as the whole universe, of the same material cosmic energy flow, of the same Chain of Being:

> I don't believe in 'nature'. *We* are our environment. TV nature programmes encourage us to believe nature's 'out there', but this is unsatisfactory voyeurism.

> LSD showed me I was a tool in the process of drawing spirit into matter. It transformed my feelings about nature – as something to love, worship and recognise with my emotions. It helped me to feel a unity with nature and experience it as part of a whole and part of myself.

> My relationship to the planet as a whole has become very strong. I think about it as much as I do my relationships with my family. It is helped by living in a beautiful spot across the valley. I feel a strong sense of something good and relaxing . . . the same feeling of love for the planet as I have for my wife and children. *And* I believe I feel a response . . . when I raise my consciousness of nature, which I'm trying to do. I love the rain now – in it I feel heightened consciousness . . . there is a planetary force that turns things your way. Once I was open to this . . . things (like a new car) constantly manifested themselves.

This last was from a CAT gardener. Gardeners at Findhorn similarly expressed heightened consciousness of 'the nature realms: the unseen forces of nature':

> Working in the garden, I see that there's an energy that brings something from spirit to form – that helps things grow. All thought is energy, so I can think, 'I want abundance', and things will grow (I can also think 'I want a red car'). The nature spirits bring this about. They take the energy, which is vibration, and made it denser. As it gets denser it turns into form.

Here is a clear statement of New Age animism (owing something also to modern physics), which is also pantheism. The latter because this spiritual energy is described by the term 'God', and so 'God' specifically is the spirit which is in everything. So the plant spirits or 'devas' are also 'God'. This gardener described her communion with the devas.

> Animals and nature are my family . . . My higher self and the garden spirits are the same, we're all energy anyway. I manifested them and co-created with them: they are co-workers. Through growing and meditating in the garden, and drawing them, I made contact with the deva of the garden – an energy overlooking it – and with the nature spirits in charge of each individual plant, bringing life-force to it and making it grow. Over each individual plant spirit is the deva of all those same plants everywhere (e.g. cabbages) . . . I was told to open myself to the deva of each plant and find out what they wanted . . . I tell the radish deva 'Welcome: I'm open to you, come and work with me'.

The vegetables she grew were not of the proportions celebrated in early Findhorn legend, but they were produced after she had been gardening for only six months with no prior expertise.

Her reference to 'life-force' evoked one more element of the New Age conception of nature: the belief in vitalism. Popular before the twentieth century, this proposed that living things cannot be explained merely in terms of their constituent parts, but that an unanalysable life force suffuses them. Sometimes this was extended to the notion that such a force was in *everything*, albeit of a lower intensity in those things which we think of as 'inanimate'.

Some New Agers appear to believe this too. An astrological communard from Glaneirw said:

> I'm just another portion of life. There's no overall spirit except the common collective consciousness of not just humans but animals, plants, pieces of wood, stone . . . Life is in everything, communication occurs within it . . . I stopped being a vegetarian because I experienced the discomfort plants went through.

A Findhornian who did not herself profess a deep relationship with nature put it this way:

> There's consciousness in everything, for example in a stone. There's love in a stone. Love attracts things together. It makes subatomic particles stick together. There's an essential unity and interconnectedness in all – the planet is one living organism. I'm not separate from nature. I came from the Earth.

SOCIAL IMPLICATIONS

The belief systems described above overwhelmingly suggest green radicalism. Many communards clearly have 'deep ecology' green attitudes to nature. But when they were asked about the implications of such attitudes for social organisation [4.0b], they had generally far less strong and clear ideas. Some avoided answering on the grounds that they had no idea of what the implications are. More often they felt that there are social implications, but could not express them.

Those few (about half-a-dozen) who could find the words put the connection in three ways. First and foremost, it is a matter of relationships. People must relate well to and feel good about *themselves* before they can take care of the environment:

> If we did what made us more profoundly satisfied then the Earth would start healing up. If you love and communicate with other humans then you won't mess the Earth up. Stay outside and feel healthy rather than working in a factory. Follow your intuition and self-interest and have fun. That's the best thing for the Earth and for us. It's as simple as that; it's not mystical at all.

> Relationships between people are important. It's to do with health, whole people and vision. If you are sorted out emotionally you won't be an exploiter.

> The environmental crisis must be dealt with by loving, sharing, and other aspects of an Aquarian lifestyle – by being in touch with your core.

These answers and others like them did not spell out specifically why better personal relationships would make us treat the environment better. Two communards did however. Cooperation, they said, between people leads to lower material consumption; or, conversely, the lower material standards which will have to come because of the environmental crisis will be compensated for by higher quality of life, including better human relationships. This is the all-important pragmatic connection between social and ecological wellbeing which *Blueprint* spelled out twenty years ago.

This leads to the second social implication – that people should live in small communities, hence closer to the land and less alienated from it. This, plus closeness to what you produce from nature in labour-intensive hand and craft work, will 'lead to understanding, which creates less likelihood of disturbing nature'. Third, collective living is implied. Groups share resources, using less. And a collective and consensual approach should also be a better framework in which people relate to nature because it encourages holism. In collectivism people tend to value each other *and* nature: 'It's shallow to save the whale and not people'. Another respondent put it that while individuals maximise material gains, groups optimise them, and the latter is what leads to long-term environmental stability (c.f. Hardin's *Tragedy of the Commons*). A third held that overindividualism is a problem for nature. But if you can live in a group with other people then you can also cooperate with nature. These communards clearly have a theoretical idea of community which accords with *gemeinschaft* (Table 3), as does ecocentrism generally. Though many could not express this in words, by implication from the lifestyle they had chosen, this probably goes for most of our interviewees.

Other observations on the social features which should follow from the attitudes to nature described above conformed closely to the ecocentric 'second order' list in Appendix 2, as has already been implied in the description of the critique of conventional society. Most reference was made to the needs for feminist principles, and balancing yin and yang, for fundamental changes in human relationships, and for small-scale organisation. There was, too, particular support for less consumerism, industrialism, giantism and high technology, for self-actualisation, for self-reliant communities and countries, and for the concepts of community and extended family. Most of the other items on this list were also mentioned, if only once, except for holistic economics, low impact technology, population control, education for change, and, interestingly, social justice and the state as an enemy.

Green utopia or distopia: right, left or centre?

This lack of the social justice theme suggests no strong socialist consensus among communards (Table 12). Their concept of community, supported at least in theory, suggests either an underlying socialism *or* conservatism. Such ambiguity reinforces the impression of ideological incoherence – within broad limits – suggested in Chapter 4. It was conveyed graphically by one particular communard, who was a veteran of the movement and also a Green Party luminary. He had a very clear but eclectic image of his future 'ideal' society. It would be both green and communal, and it had strong elements of liberalism (individual freedom) combined vigorously with dashes of anarcho-communism, eco-fascism, and a non-ecocentric belief in the supremacy of 'objective' science.

The ideal green society will be marked, he told us, by big increases in personal freedom, and an end of state domination. Most things will be allowed, but not for money-making. While capitalism is a form of enoblement whereby labour creates things, in the ideal green society this will be done locally by the community using its own labour for its own priorities.

The only things which will not be allowed will be those which do not fit in with the ecological imperative. People will be permitted, but not encouraged, to bugger their children if they want to, though 'if the local community went in the direction of heavy exploitation you might have to do something about it'. However, 'you can't repress people on some beautiful idea of what morality happens to be'. There are no social imperatives. People, choosing for themselves, can set up communities of buggers, rapists or cannibals. However there are ecological imperatives which will form some heavy restraints on freedom. An absolute ecological code will be enforced by an ecological police. What they enforce will not be ideologies but scientifically verifiable truths. Science is the fount of ecological wisdom because it is objective.

> When you want to know what to do you look for facts and information . . . Science is a field where propositions are testable and replicable . . . If you want to scoff at science you would go back to the world where the Earth was thought to be flat . . . Debunking nuclear scientists is a form of Luddism unfortunately. The process of destabilising belief in science is going on in the green movement, via religion and mysticism.

Indeed it is, abetted by such events as Chernobyl, which is why we believe that many of our interviewees with green leanings would not support most of this remarkable but highly individual vision, although elements might be to their taste. At this stage, perhaps, it would be politic to leave the realm of speculative ideas and turn to the question of how much communards try to live them out.

LIVING GREEN: THE ECOLOGICAL PROFILE

We asked communards how their attitudes to nature, environment and related issues of social organisation translated into practice through individual or group action [5.1-2]. No leading questions were asked, so that Table 16 represents what activities the communards themselves highlighted. The absence of any category from Appendix 2 in the description of specific communes in this table does not therefore necessarily mean that it is not practised, but simply that for one reason or another it was not raised by respondents. It should also be realised that where practices are entered this does not imply that they are unerringly observed or that what is intended always follows, a point we shall discuss later.

Clearly the communes have notionally a strong ecological profile. Sharing and recycling resources (including clothes) and using less – especially energy – feature consistently, as do non-polluting practices and home production of crafts and (invariably organic) food. Minimal or shared car use, alternative technology and medicine, soft energy, using food coops or exchanging labour between country and city; all these had few mentions, however. While the minority of communes are vegetarian or vegan, all of them have high dietary and health and consumer consciousness.

The Appendix 2 list is not exhaustive. Seven communes added to the list tree or hedge planting, coppice renovation or woodland or lake/marsh conservation and management. Five emphasised that their animals were free-range (though all were). Other 'sound' agricultural practices include folding sheep after cattle to control pests (artificial fertilisers or pesticides are rejected in favour of natural means), urine collection and its application to the land, using much labour instead of few machines, and minimum-maintenance farming.

General awareness of the effects of lifestyle on the environment and of world resource inequality was translated into support for environmental and peace groups, 'gardening with faith', running environmental education courses, bringing nature into the classroom (Monkton Wyld) and celebrating the relationship with nature at solstice, equinox and harvest.

While most communes are doing less than their members would like to see, a few are expanding their list of environmentally sound practices. They include PIC, on its new rural site, CAT, with its ambitious expansion plan for more houses, for a water-driven cable railway and for an expanded education programme, and Findhorn. Findhorn's July 1989 newsletter, *Angels and Mortals*, described a rolling programme to improve its poor environmental record by replacing all its caravans with ecologically sound (insulated, sewage recycling) houses, building a wind park, planting thousands of trees, and using recycled paper and ecologically sound cleansers. The programme had already started, and was supplemented by an 'environmental excellence audit' of the Foundation's many activities.

The following more detailed account of ecological practices also partly draws (with permission) on Fiona Hay's (1989) survey of ecological practices in eight communes – six covered here, plus Birchwood Hall near Malvern and Shindig in Edinburgh.

Organic cultivation and self-sufficiency

As Table 16 shows, cultivation is a central feature of all the communes, whether large-scale as at Laurieston (120 acres – see Table 4) or small, as at Shindig, which has a small tenement garden in Edinburgh's centre. For the urban communards of Shindig, cultivating their own food is not central. But ZAP runs six allotments, the products of which supply the Project's wholefood cafe in Birmingham.

For all communes, *organic* cultivation is a central concern. Many members had been influenced by green iiideas which stressed the undesirabilitty of chemicals and machines in cultivation, and the desirabilityoflaboourinntensiveness–asgoodforthesoiland(more to the point) good for the soul of the labourer. The food produced is also more healthy, it is said, than the products of agribusiness, and this answers a major concern of late-eighties environmentalism. In both respects, then, organic agriculture soothes the phobias of the urban intellectuals who form the backbone of these communes. It was also part of the self-sufficiency craze which characterised early-seventies environmentalism and infused most of these communes (John Seymour's influence was strong in Canon Frome and Redfield, for instance).

However self-sufficiency has not been achieved. Lifespan, Canon Frome, Lower Shaw and Redfield are between 30 and 50 per cent self-sufficient in vegetables during summer and autumn, for example, while Monkton Wyld is so for half the year and Glaneirw for all year, except in oats and flour (it grows wheat). But self-sufficiency is not as important as it was to green thinkers and doers, and communards generally reflect this change in emphasis. They do not hold

Table 16: Ecologically sound practices
(for explanation see text, Chapter 5 and Appendix 2)

	FIND	CAT*	CF*	RF*	MW	LSF*	PIC	CRAB*	LAUR	LSP*	GLAN	ZAP
1. Sharing resources	X	X	X	X	X	X	X	X	X	X	X	X
2. Recycling resources	X	X	X		X	X		X	X	X	X	X
3. Vegetarian/vegan	X				X	X				X		X
(3a. Food consciousness)	X	X	X	X	X	X	X	X	X	X		X
4. Home produced foods/crafts	X	X	X	X	X	X	X	X	X		X	X
5. Soft energy		X							X			
6. Cutting energy use		X	X	X			X	X		X		X
7. De-emphasise cars							X	X		X	X	X
8. Non-polluting practices		X	X		X	X	X	X		X		X
9. De-emphasise consumerism		X		X			X				X	X
10. Food coops		X								X		
11. Alternative technology		X							X			
12. Alternative medicine			X	X	X	X				X	X	X
13. Organic garden/farm	X	X	X	X	X	X	X	X	X	X	X	X

*studied by Hay (1989)

self-sufficiency as particularly desirable, for it could encourage inwardness and discourage external interdependence: 'We don't want to be self-sufficient, we want to be part of the world', said a Findhornian.

As for the 'virtues' of hard labour, these seem to have become part of a routine of self-exploitation on occasions, especially where livestock is involved: for instance at Crabapple or Canon Frome or Laurieston, where some individuals have to be up and milking at six or seven in the morning from one end of the year to another. Communards who did want more produce stressed that this factor of labour was the limiting one. At Redfield, CAT, Monkton Wyld and elsewhere, volunteer labour from outside is used, for instance from the 'Working Weekends on Organic Farms' network.

Livestock is a contentious issue, creating divisions among groups. While Canon Frome needs livestock for their manure, others do not. Findhorn, for instance, satisfies the plant spirits through a diet of greens, seaweed and kitchen wastes. At Crabapple, Canon Frome and Laurieston some communards argue along classic ecocentric lines that to use livestock for food is inefficient: up to ten times as much land is needed to produce a given amount of calories, by comparison with growing crops for direct consumption. This argument incurs the scorn, referred to earlier, of those in a western location who argue that here livestock production is traditional, most in sympathy with soil and climate, and essential for any degree of self-reliance. Nonetheless there can be arguments over the exact proportions of land used. At Canon Frome nearly ninety per cent of the land is used for livestock, and only two acres for direct-consumption crops.

The issue is bound up with vegetarianism and animal rights. Our Monkton Wyld interviews suggested that this would have been a non-livestock commune were it not for the visitors who attend courses. They are often meat-eaters, and to impose a vegetarian/vegan diet would alienate them. This does not seem to matter at CAT, however, where normally carnivorous visitors consistently eulogise the vegetarian food – Egon Ronay having been among their number. It is the *residents* at CAT who eat meat – but very occasionally, and it is home grown, free-range, humanely treated and killed by the eaters. This is the pattern for most communes, who thus deviate but slightly from hard-line ecocentrism. Morally based vegetarians cause problems of separate catering at Redfield, and so are excluded, as they are at Canon Frome (see below).

The centrality of organic cultivation and a degree of self-sufficiency at such places as Canon Frome, Laurieston, Crabapple, Glaneirw, Monkton Wyld, Redfield, CAT, LSF and Findhorn strongly suggests affinities with some back-to-the-land movements described in Chapter 3, especially when bio-dynamic principles are invoked. These imply a mystical relationship between cultivator and cultivated, and we met gardeners and farmers at Findhorn, Glaneirw, CAT and Monkton Wyld who felt this relationship. The mix of organic cultivation, vegetarianism, mysticism and self-sufficiency featured strongly in many utopian and romantic socialist and anarchist communes which were part of the 'early green' home colonies/back-to-the-land movement of the 1880s and nineties. But perhaps the strongest parallels are with that movement as it developed in Britain and more especially Germany in the 1920s and thirties.

Recycling

Commitment to recycling and re-using resources is at least nominally strong for both ecological and economic reasons. All communes separate out domestic 'wastes' to an extent, especially paper and card, food and perhaps bottles and cans; the last two depend particularly on the local availability of collection points. Waste food is used religiously to supplement animal feed where appropriate, or as compost. At Crabapple, Canon Frome and CAT human sewage is used for fertiliser. The first puts it on to the land via a septic tank, notwithstanding potential contamination by heavy metals. The second removes these, and pathogens, by a trickling filter plant, then puts the sewage deep into the soil at the rate of half a field a year. At CAT they can use the sewage from their visitors – over 50,000 a year. Their public lavatories flow into a septic tank and the sewage is stored for up to a year, then composted with straw or bracken. The end result is an odourless, dry, crumbly compost rich in nutrients and organic matter. In 1989 CAT built a partly self-contained complex for visiting schoolchildren. It consists of log cabins, a reservoir from which they get some power and water, and, downslope, a series of sewage reed filter beds. The water from these goes with its nutrients to vegetable plots further downslope. There are sewage plants at Redfield, Lifespan and Monkton Wyld, too, but not for fertilising. At the last, the local water board places restrictions on use.

Many communes support local wastepaper recycling schemes organised by green pressure groups, and use local bottle banks.

ZAP's thoughtfulness is far-reaching. Not only do its members use recycled lavatory and other paper, they re-use envelopes, use scrap paper fully, avoid buying packaging, and separate out food, glass and tin, though they try to boycott tins in the first place on account of the conditions under which Bolivian tin miners work.

Buying second-hand clothes is also a very common form of recycling, mainly through economic necessity, as is scavenging materials from local waste dumps. At Glaneirw a profitable business serving the local area has been built around restoring Rayburn stoves. Their green-style commitment to the local economy is emphasised by using a local blacksmith to make stove parts, rather than ordering from suppliers seventy miles away.

Energy

For a group of people generally committed to energy conservation and using renewable sources for the sake of the environment, energy is a problem area. CAT was established to be a shining example of both principles, which it largely is: the building programme of the late eighties and early nineties incorporates highly workable conservation features, as distinct from more experimental earlier buildings with their quadruple glazing, thick walls, or walls consisting entirely of solar panels. The site, through wind, sun and water, generates just enough energy to keep its visitors and residents in a frugal but not ascetic lifestyle. Happily, compact disc players and hi-fis are seen as virtual necessities, but electric hair dryers draw opprobrium. The communards are unusually thoughtful about the implications of everything they do for energy supply. They have to be, for if they are not they will sit in the dark to eat their evening meal. That, however, is cooked on imported bottled gas, but the extension of such use for more than back-up purposes is often a subject of principled debate, as is the matter of whether the site should connect to the National Electricity Grid – a development which is now planned, but as donor rather than receiver of supplies.

Elsewhere, only Laurieston generates its own energy, from a small hydro-electric plant. Notwithstanding its forthcoming wind, solar and insulation projects, Findhorn is at time of writing woefully unsound in its energy practices from a green point of view.

However all communards spoke of a commitment to energy frugality. They will put on several layers of clothes rather than use an electric or gas fire, though rural communes all have their wood-burning stoves supplied from local sources. Many woods are owned by the communes themselves and are rigorously scavenged for dead wood or sustainably cropped.

Ethical and environmental buying

Many of the 'green consumer' products that now fill supermarket shelves have been on the shelves of commune kitchens for years, and they continue to be. Organic foods, biodegradable cleansers and 'ethical' coffee and tea (from Third World producer coops) – or substitutes such as herbal teas and chicory or barley drinks; these are universal. But we have already seen that communards are, foremost, opposed to consumerism. Consequently electric gadgets, cosmetics and overpackaged goods, for instance, are not as common as in conventional households.

But the green consumer philosophy, that the individual can effect social change through purchasing power, was widely supported by our interviewees. And, as Fiona Hay says, communards generally seem to have a high awareness of green and/or health issues, so that they are knowledgeable on the links between manufacturing processes and sources and the end products. This allows them to discriminate in what they do buy. However such awareness has limits, and few will boycott tin products, or chocolate and other tropical cash crops, as ZAP has done, for ethical reasons. In fact deeper economic or political boycotts, such as a refusal to consume cash crops, do not seem popular, except for the 'easy' case of South African goods. Partly this is to avoid endless debates. But in Findhorn's case,

> that's not the level we operate at. What you should do is bless the fruit of the planet and help people to appreciate that they are part of the planet. Then apartheid would disappear.

Sharing and non-materialism

Sharing resources and functions like eating make for reduced environmental impact. But generally this reasoning is less important than economic necessity, or the ideology of sharing itself. Virtually all communards declared that sharing was the major practice by which they were environmentally sound, and this is the major way that their environmentalism distinguishes them from green non-communal households. They share land, washing machines, TVs, cooking and food, cars, income (sometimes), and many other things

– though how much this happens varies according to different intentions and abilities to practise principles. Both of these factors are discussed below; they make a crucial difference in the case of car sharing, for instance. Lifespan shares one car between eleven people and PIC used to share two between fifteen. But the grounds of Laurieston or CAT, by contrast, are nowadays littered with cars. Ecologically sound action in this critical area is hampered because communards are influenced by the mores of wider society, including the infatuation with mobility and what Mrs Thatcher called 'the great car economy' (see below), and for the practical reason that most of them live in the country, where cars are virtually essential. Hence urban communes like Shindig can score highly: they have far less need for motor vehicles for most of the time, and can use bicycles. Indeed all communards are pro-bike, and most either have car-sharing schemes or (as with Canon Frome) try to, but unsuccessfully.

At Canon Frome shared food production and purchase was described as a 'true communistic system. Each puts in according to ability and draws out according to need'. The system makes for less waste, and it generally works (as it does for Findhorn) – except, that is, in the case of meat, which has to be allocated because some people tend to forget their communal essence when contemplating a succulent roast dinner.

FALLING SHORT

The above account paints a picture of strongly green communes in both theory and practice, but as far as the latter is concerned the paint often wears thin. There are some practical difficulties in living green [6.1-3], but, more important, the spirit's willingness often runs up against weak flesh and there are many gaps between intentions and outcomes [6.4]. Failure to live up to principles can produce guilt, but it is arguable whether guilt helps or hinders the attempt at living green.

Poverty

Surprisingly few people mentioned limitations of lack of money on the group's potential to be green. Nevertheless this was a possible factor in energy matters. For rural communes the sheer size of their country houses is a problem. There is never enough money to have them properly insulated, while lack of both cash and labour for maintenance and decoration can often make them drab environments. This is usually why new energy projects involving wind or solar power have not come about, although it may be said that soft energy generation methods and equipment such as those demonstrated at CAT are commonly very cheap. Old radiators and glass panels, for instance, can be made into solar panels, provided there is sufficient expertise or self-confidence. The communes constitute a huge reservoir of expertise brought in via formal training or picked up subsequently. And if expertise was not there from the start, then confidence was: 'It was crazy to leap into the country without knowing how to farm it, but we did succeed'. So perhaps, instead, lack of time or inclination have contributed most to the lack of energy technology.

Personal poverty and lack of material or spiritual comfort can also be debilitating, and a drag on achieving group principles. Opinions divided very evenly on whether relative poverty was or was not a problem. 'I don't hanker for material things: we've got all we need' and 'I'm never tempted to go out and spend lots of money' were minority statements. But so were the other extremes:

> We suffer from being poor: I'd like more money.
>
> It's not *natural* to desire material things: some people don't. But I *do*, and it's doubly difficult for me as I'm conscious of the need not to be materialistic.
>
> It's very difficult living on a tiny pension, but my fortune and affluence are good compared with others. However, it's difficult not giving in to temptation.

Many others described such temptations as minimal, or as impulses which *ought* to be given in to sometimes:

> At times I don't want to eat vegetarian food, and I want a new pair of jeans for £25 – obviously I can't, but I'll give in sometimes to my urge to eat meat. We must be nice to ourselves, and it's very difficult to get out of the middle class mould.

'Middle class avarice' was how one communard described the desire for more money. Most, however, see money as a justifiable enabler: to look after a family, to take education courses, to travel to see friends or have holidays. The last is an especially heartfelt want for money.

It was difficult to assess just how poor people really were. Income sharing schemes, with or without pocket money, meant low disposable incomes, often around £40 to £50 per month; though to those involved, lacking the common worries about money management could be compensation in itself. Salary schemes like that at CAT (£3,000 to £4,000 a year for single people; double this for those with two children) also seem to give little fat to live off, despite the richness of having access to many shared things.

However, for middle-class communards private money (for example, from parents) could often be available. Appearances were no guide to this. 'Smart' people could have very little; 'scruffy' (but invariably clean!) people might have a legacy. The equanimity with which some younger ones accepted apparent poverty could be connected with future material expectations or parental safety nets, which might make communalism a sort of game. But older communards more often push for private and material consumption, largely to gain comfort:

> I'd prefer WCs rather than ecologically-sound compost loos, they're more comfortable.

> Over the years our consumer side has got richer – it's partly age and wanting more home comforts. You can't keep up ideological purity for long.

As we have discussed, spiritual rightness is supposed to compensate for material poverty. However, many communards said or implied that the former was deficient:

> The moral and religious side of the issue is the cutting edge of the ecology debate, and every so often I take a trip to Findhorn. But our communal awareness gets lost in the daily round. It's a happy life, but the cutting edge is missing.

This was echoed by others who bemoaned a lack of intelligent conversation, or of discussion of principles, or, more often, of deep friendships and open discussion of feelings. This vital question of personal relationships, important to greens for material and spiritual reasons, is discussed below.

Not practising what you don't preach

Despite notional and real gains on the road to ecologically-sound lifestyles, communards very commonly feel that they themselves and their colleagues fall short of living up to their principles, whether they preach them or not: and they usually do not preach. The sharing process itself can be difficult. Sharing things, particularly cars, can fail, and a blunt view from Laurieston was echoed more mildly around most other communes:

> I got fed up with being the only one to fix the car. I stopped: now no-one does it. Vehicle sharing has gone wrong . . . there's no ecological purpose here, it's just written on a piece of paper.

Elsewhere, communal bikes and tools are the most common victims of a 'no-one owns, so no-one cares' syndrome.

Sharing space is also a problem for some:

> An ecologically sound future doesn't necessitate living on top of one another, so I have withdrawn and detached myself.

This problem is almost invariably recognised and appreciated; a high premium is put on individuals having their private space and their inalienable right to withdraw to it. Similarly, sharing control of one's own children in communal childcare could cause agonising.

The basic problem of 'bourgeois' people trying to be communists was summarised thus:

> It's difficult to share sometimes, because I think I deserve more, because I put in more work. It's a difficulty with the communistic principle – each person has a different concept of what they or someone else *can* put in.

Hence there is the problem of whether everyone pulls their weight. While this is much discussed among commentators on communal living, we found few examples of it being a bone of contention, though it possibly often simmered below the surface. It appears at Findhorn, of all places, however:

> Findhorn is a great cop-out for some people. They waft around in airy-fairy spiritualism . . . saying 'I don't feel like work today: I need some space' – and they go and relate to the beach.

Another Findhornian saw strong conflict between a professed ethic of communality – reflected in attitudes of stewardship towards the land, such that people cannot make money out of it – and strong individualism, where people profit from selling their work to each other. 'That's OK if you make and sell teddy bears, but it's not OK to charge for spiritual healing: we are too conservative and middle class'.

Elsewhere there were long catalogues of failure to live up to principle. Too many cars are used. People want independence and will not share them. Too much petrol is consumed in too many journeys in 'clapped out cars which emit all sorts of fumes'. However, the car is so tempting: 'I just get the use of a car, but it would be attractive to have my own'. There is energy waste – in cooking (pressure cookers not used), in central heating ('we're getting too soft') or generally, when it's 'free' (the HEP scheme at Laurieston 'encourages people to use too much'). At some communes increased privateness has meant individual TVs and freezers, as in conventional life. Or there are heaters in every room: 'this isn't very ecological. We don't put on extra sweaters, and we should all be in one room in winter'.

Often it is a case of not being bothered, an absence of that meticulousness which the ecological lifestyle calls for. So paper is not recycled, or biodegradable cleansers not used. '*We'll* have to change our way of life if we're to set an example', said one communard, using coal on his heating/cooking range. But at another commune it was the children who got blamed, the 10 to 14 age group being particularly contemptuous about 'sound practice'. Perhaps this was why a further group thought that they had 'too many children . . . thus restricting the advantages of communal living'.

However, elsewhere an older communard professed difficulty in recognising any of 'what the younger generation here call conservation. We're all hypocrites' – profligate with electricity, using cars instead of a horse and cart, and having milk and butter yet believing in respect for animals.

This last issue bothered others: 'People at Canon Frome walk around with guns, shooting animals. There isn't the respect for nature which you'd think would follow from organic gardening'. Aspiring vegans and vegetarians at several other communes described how they reluctantly had to abandon their principles, either because the majority did not share them or because it was impractical to operate them in grassland/livestock farming regions. Fromer (1989), writing about a community he called 'The Lodge', showed why simple pragmatism has to hold sway over green principle in the matter of veganism:

> When considering possible new members for the community, we are very clear on our reasons for rejecting vegans. It's nothing to do with

prejudice of course; some of our best friends . . . But vegans would make life far too difficult for cooks. Cooks at The Lodge don't need life to become any harder . . . Depending on who's in and who's out and whether there are guests and whether it's Sunday or Wednesday (in which case the 'smalls' eat with the adults), you're usually cooking for anything between eight and eighteen people . . . So we try to keep things simple and give the cooks the freest possible hand . . . In other words, in the best traditions of communal living we compromise for the sake of the common good.

Exploitation of people, as well as animals, occasionally led to concern. At Crabapple, for instance, 'We say we're non-exploitative, but those who work in our wholefood shop have long hours and low wages'. At Lifespan the worry is over self-exploitation for the achievement of no greatly revolutionary aim – long hours worked in the successful printing business, but sometimes printing sexist or otherwise ethically unsound material.

More generally, what can become a sheer grind of self-reliant living leads to insularity and failure to practise the principle of outreach which many believe in, either through action in pressure-group politics or more local community involvement: 'As a group we don't do enough to live up to our principles. We're not going anywhere, and we are cut off from our local community'. This important issue will be discussed in Chapter 6.

Guilt

Some communards expressed guilt over their failings:

> I'm guilty about using disposable nappies for my child . . . and we don't eat as simply as I'd like.

> I smoke, and miss having a vehicle: I feel guilty about this.

> I'm full of inner conflicts – what other people think you should be and what you think. Because I came in with a lot of high ideals, but in fact there aren't that many differences between what happens here and outside.

Some see guilt as positive:

> Our high consciousness level [about what is environmentally and socially sound] leads to high guilt levels, especially in the area of work. Everyone is self-regulating in their work hours [this goes for all communes] because they are driven by guilt.

But most see guilt as negative. Here they make a major, and wise, departure from conventional values: 'For people who don't feel good about themselves, failure to live up to principles can lead to one criticism after another, which is bad'.

So, many communards have abandoned guilt. One justification for deviation may be pragmatism:

> We flew on an airplane to Rhodes, and use the car for shopping and children, and our commune is terribly sexist and it hasn't put solar panels on the roof, but you have to be realistic about where people are at.
>
> I sometimes drop standards but I've let go my guilt – I'm a pragmatist, and I don't believe in fundamentalism.
>
> I feel dreadful about what we do to nature, but I *am* partly a competitive and manipulative person. I get a kick out of it.

Another justification is that having the right context is more important than individual striving:

> I'm not worried about personal behaviour inconsistent with beliefs – you don't have to be so conscious for yourself that every single act is environmentally sound: the institution [CAT] is set up so that you can't *help* being environmentally sound.

Or there is fatalism: 'Yes I have a car and I know I shouldn't: it causes a bit of a problem. But since the car was manifested it means it must be a good thing'. Or a more familiar justification, that *others* do it:

> You think: 'I had better not burn this piece of polythene and pollute the atmosphere' – then you remember that the Americans have just bombed oilfields in the Middle East. So you think: 'Why bother?'

And, most familiar of all: 'We don't talk about where we get food from. We don't have the energy'.

LIVING TOGETHER

So far we have emphasised 'first order' ecocentric practices. But in Chapter 1 we pointed out how second-order, *living together* practices are also pivotal to ecocentrism in action. Here, however, can be some of the greatest gaps between principle and practice:

> Others don't take their personal lifestyles seriously. I arranged a series of evenings here on personal development and got a poor response. Yet our AGM agreed that all hinged on personal development. The social side is our greatest deficiency. We do little in finding better ways of relating to each other.

and

> They've got the *idea* of being New Age. They talk about it but then get off on only one thing. They don't realise that New Age principles apply across the board. They're not New Age people really.

We now consider some problems of living together and how successful or otherwise communards are in second order practices. Those which they particularly emphasised were work and income sharing, democratic and non-hierarchical structures and processes, assertion of the individual and tolerance of others, and personal relationships and conflict avoidance.

Work and income sharing

Work in communes divides into three categories. There are 'non-specialised' domestic jobs like cooking and cleaning, 'specialised' jobs in the commune such as animal husbandry, and 'specialised' paid work outside. Most communes have successfully evolved a way of dealing with the first by rota, sometimes voluntarily signed: an informal and flexible system. However in two of the smaller groups the more anarchistic approach of leaving it to individuals to see what needs doing and respond conscientiously for themselves has operated. In one case, where members have been together for some time, it works:

> It's not hierarchical here; there are no rules or rotas. If someone sees that bread needs making they make it. No-one lays down the law for anyone else, we just live here. Some days the cooking doesn't get done, then we don't have a meal.

In another, newer group it did not work, and there were vast discrepancies in the amount of work different people did. However on the whole we found little evidence of 'an endless watching and checking to make sure that one is not being exploited by the very people with whom one is trying to combine – an endless, sad discovery that others cannot or will not give enough' (Abrams and

McCulloch 1976, p200); but then this was not a sociological survey. Although the problem of the 'free rider' clearly does exist, in most instances the best seems to come from people because the best is assumed, in a climate generally predicated on trust and optimism, though tempered by realism. Some non-oppressive devices are adopted to ensure that work gets done with the least entrenched hierarchy and a maximum of democracy. Periods of from half a day to a fortnight when everyone works together on specific tasks or on maintenance are a favourite institution, and the bigger communes like CAT or Findhorn have evolved specialised departments responsible for particular areas, such as catering or a bookshop. Elsewhere individuals may have specialised roles, but always the responsibility to the larger group is ostensibly understood.

CAT also has an ingenious 'ogre' system. A different person each week is appointed as the 'ogre', whose specific job it is to go round checking up on how well or otherwise jobs are being done. They also have to admonish slackers. In this way any unpopularity is temporary and is shared around.

As we have said, the problem often seems to be that too much work is done for too little reward. Canon Fromers and Lifespanners complained about their coops taking over their lives. At the same time people very often felt that they did not have much fun together. Sometimes this is because they look to friends and activities outside the commune for their leisure, and are constantly going away at weekends. Or it is because personal relationships are quite distant:

> You'd think people would lower barriers in a communal situation. In fact people put them up to keep a bit of a distance because they are living so closely. This interferes with the ability to have fun together.

Work outside the commune for income which is usually private can be a bone of contention. It gets increasingly necessary as social security benefit rules are tightened and as people's material desires increase. Those who are not working outside can feel resentment at those who are, or vice versa, as at Canon Frome where inside workers 'build up kudos and status. They are *seen* to work, and can turn round and ask why others aren't doing the same. We don't want this: we want labour to be shared'.

Total income pooling is now rare, but whether total or not it seems to work surprisingly well in most cases, as at PIC:

> It was difficult at first. People were unhappy at losing control over money and there were lots of unhappy scenes. But it's successful now

and it has changed attitudes. Everyone feels equally important and a job does not carry special status. However there are arguments between those who spend every week (on drink and tobacco) and those who want big things every so often. To share income you must trust people.

Participatory democracy

Every commune tries to achieve this by making individuals accountable to the whole group but also by trying to reach major policy decisions through consensus. In this process everyone must be able, and enabled, to say what they think and to avoid the 'tyranny of the majority' by in effect having a veto over every decision. The system can work by dint of good chairing of meetings, universally cultivating awareness of the feelings of others, and giving way from one's position for the sake of the progress of the group even if one disagrees with a decision.

Nearly half the communes feel that they have learned the art of consensus well, thanks to much hard work. 'After ten years, I've learned what consensus really is'. They say they are prepared to take a long time (weeks) over decisions, and do not go ahead if there are really strong objections from even one person. Here the time factor is usually important; in conventional society decisions are usually made (often unnecessarily, but to the benefit of the ruling hierarchy) against a limited time schedule. Goodwill is also a key factor:

> In consensus we have an unspoken veto. But if you're aware that five others want something, you go along with it.

> Consensus works extraordinarily well. Although I disagree politically with the others, I don't feel marginalised.

However, elsewhere another individual was experiencing just the reverse. As a relative newcomer he had found that despite the veneer of consensus, decisions were really reached by an inner group – a common situation where an experienced old guard is entrenched. Meetings had become structureless and extremely informal:

> Children, animals, cigarettes, lying on the floor, knitting, reading newspapers. The meetings were known as the 'X and Y show'. They spent all the time telling us what was going to happen. So, I worked to make meetings more formal. My anarchism tells me there should be underlying structure. People who do not want structure are youthful, zany anarchists.

But this was to little avail and he was successfully marginalised by the hierarchy and stigmatised as 'loony left', a faithful reflection of a process so common in wider society.

This problem, of not really being able to make an impression in a structure ostensibly designed to facilitate everyone's participation, does recur in many communes. Women particularly complain about it:

> X wants to join, and I don't want him to. I'll be in difficulties when the time comes to decide. I could exercise my veto, but all hell would break loose.

In the communes where consensus is most successful a lesson has been learned about psychology. When people disagree in meetings, dig their heels in and develop factions, it is commonly not because of the issue in question. It is because of personality clashes, 'because the people concerned do not like each other'. While conflict resolution mechanisms may be applicable in this situation, frequently the resolution comes by dint of one party to the dispute leaving the commune.

The question of hierarchies is linked to that of democracy. In all the communes except the small group at Glaneirw, hierarchies were admitted to exist. Smallness does not necessarily preclude hierarchy, since even at ZAP one person often dominated by dint of drive and ideas, longevity in the commune and doing so much of the work.

Most communards see expertise hierarchies as good and/or inevitable. However at Canon Frome, although 'knowledge is power', it was claimed that expertise hierarchies were not permanent; 'tendencies for them to develop are quickly squashed and experts are quickly reduced to the status of facilitators' [helping others to learn a job]. 'Farming here is therefore inefficient, but we aren't here for efficiency, but for hobby and pleasure'. But Canon Frome has had many difficulties arising from other hierarchies, based on people's length of time at the commune, their degree of articulacy, and 'leadership' instincts. A Lifespanner put the basic problem:

> Any group that's together for a while adopts a behavioural pattern. We all have roles within the group dynamic. People who have been here a long time are powerful and dominant, and the new ones fit in or leave.

This last is not inevitably true, for at Canon Frome, it is the 'oldies' – the former leaders – who had left or were going.

To have structure, which all communes increasingly want, is not necessarily to have power hierarchy, and devices such as job swapping can avoid the latter. In general, however, hierarchies have not been avoided. Skills or longevity hierarchies *need* not, in theory, be power hierarchies; but once again, what applies in theory does not hold in practice in many of the communes.

Individuality and tolerance

A key aspect of high quality of life in a green society should stem from ample opportunity for the individual to express him/herself and *be* an individual. This includes having his/her views tolerated and heard. This principle is important in the communes too: 'The importance of communes may be said to be the understanding they embody; that personal autonomy is concomitant with personal reciprocity' (Abrams and McCulloch, p96). But this understanding can break down over the issues of privacy and individual possessions. While privacy may be sacred in theory, it is easily violated:

> I can feel lost as an individual – all friends are shared. It's a loss of privacy. I'm leaving next year and looking forward to a place of my own.
>
> The feeling that there's always someone *there*, outside your door or downstairs, is too much. It's OK when you're up but not when you're down.

But others, especially women, find this liberating. There are always (women) companions around. Children are brought up in a sociable and safe environment, and childcare is shared – though less than used to be the case. This enables women, particularly, to learn skills they would otherwise not have learned and so gain in self-confidence. Many women spoke of such a gain. Emancipation, though, is not an easy process: 'People join communities sometimes because they don't feel good about themselves and can't cope. The challenge can be a disaster unless you are willing to change yourself'.

The change often involves learning how to be tolerant of others. However, racial and political tolerance are hardly deep issues in the communes, where white Anglo-Saxons are almost the sole inhabitants, while political discussions and strong ideological bonding are rarer than they used to be (see Chapter 4). Non-sexism is a different matter. In some communes like Canon Frome, despite non-sexist intentions, men and women occupied traditional roles. This was dismissed as a 'quirk of fate, not inherent in communes', and this seemed to be borne out at Lifespan where, however, there was a majority of women. Lifespan had a high awareness of sexual equality, and a tolerant atmosphere.

> Why do we find women easier? Sexist reasons. Women are *nice*, and polite. Men are arrogant and know-all – they pass on their knowledge in a patronising way and can be a burden, looking exclusively to women for emotional support. We often turn down men, but few women – unless they are single parents, because they need a lot of support.

Lifespan is an exception here. Most communes have more men than women. Although this does not necessarily stifle women's self-assertion, in practice it often does and men, together with a sprinkling of exceptionally assertive women, dominate. There then is created a subclass of women who do feel repressed. Such repression is often bound up with a repression of feelings in unfulfilling relationships.

Personal relationships and conflict resolution

It is in this area that the gap between green communal theory and practice is perhaps greatest. By living in communes, it is clear, people do not eliminate relationship problems. They merely swap one set of family problems (nuclear) for another (extended). Most communards prefer the latter. However, though their relationships were described generally as 'good', they were also sometimes thought of as 'shallow' and not as deep or close or satisfying as desirable.

Only in the two places where New Age thinking is most evident, Findhorn and Glaneirw, did people describe great openness and honesty in interpersonal dealings, although both communes had had major problems in the past. While Findhorn has many techniques for conflict resolution, 'the main thing is the aura of love and openness which exists'. Some Findhornians also believe, true to their doctrine of denying conflict, that:

> You can't have conflict unless there's an attraction of some kind between the parties. What you do is sit down and work out the attractive elements. This is a very successful approach.

Glaneirw's similar approach also succeeds:

> We're open and honest, and I can tolerate a lot of things as long as I can *talk* to people. We can disagree, but not in a brick-walled way. We can define areas for discussion and not for discussion, work on the former and not interfere with the latter.

Elsewhere there is often a less rosy picture with relationship issues ignored. For instance:

> We basically don't talk to each other. You can not speak to some people for four months, because of the style of being very cool and laid back.

> We don't spend much time on relations. We could be more open, but shouldn't be completely so.

> We've no set way of dealing with conflict here, except accommodating to the group who would be hardest to live with if they were denied. This is a disgrace.

> I pressed for the therapy day, and got little out of it. I want to confront differences between people all the time, but others don't want to.

The non-confrontational approach is widespread, although informal means of bringing two quarrelling people together to talk about their differences in the presence of a third often exist, because 'in conflicts it's often important to see where the other person's coming from'. But ad hoc approaches, or non-involvement, deeply upset some. The worst example of such angst was:

> At 'feelings meetings' I voiced my distress at being unclose to people, but others didn't respond. Feelings meetings ended last winter. When I tried to say how *I* felt in them, others went to sleep. I don't feel heard: there is no dialogue. If people are upset they just go away. They don't shout at each other, but they don't hug each other either. There's no physical contact.

This last cry was echoed in three other communes. 'There should be more physical contact here. There's plenty of warmth and love here, but *first* you have to show you can exist without it and be emotionally self-sufficient'. Such bourgeois hangups are found elsewhere:

> There should be more physical contact, but if someone comes up and hugs me I feel bad about it. I'd like to do it: it was good in the women's group but I find it harder to be hugged by men, because of my past experiences and socialisation. It would be nice if it was easier.

Hodgkinson (1990), however, described how the reverse applies at Findhorn, where

> hugging has become so much a way of life that it is known as the 'Findhorn handshake' . . . I've always been extremely wary of 'huggy' communities, feeling that they probably foster an entirely false closeness between people. But now, having given it a try, I can see why they encourage this kind of physical contact. I discovered that hugging can quickly dissolve the deep mistrust we tend to have of other people. It can give a cohesiveness to a disparate collection of individuals and also encourage a kind of group dynamic which enables you to work together . . . Hugging other members of my group allowed me to become more sympathetic and tolerant, to draw closer to them emotionally and physically. Through hugging, we were able to share in each other's triumphs, sadnesses and emotional upheavals . . . There are no power games played between those who are able to hug spontaneously.

However in about half the communes relationships were either going badly awry or had recently done so. Entering a commune frequently tests a couple relationship to its ultimate limits and beyond. One had four couple relationships a year previously, but now only one was left intact. Decoupling and recoupling is common elsewhere. Unlike conventional society, friendship has usually very definitely to come before a sexual relationship. But this changefulness does not mean that boredom akin to that of conventional marriage is absent:

> We don't stimulate each other any more, because we see too much of each other. It's like being married. We see each other in mundane situations. We need to be in touch with outsiders. A major contributory factor in poor relations is the lack of ability to see outside the community. If you aren't careful the cows and sheep become the edge of your world.

Communal break-ups sometimes occur because of this, or because a few too-dominant individuals do not anyway get on with each other. Then factions tend to form around them. Elsewhere, diversity may be seen as the weakness, with everyone pulling in different directions, and resentment building.

Conflict resolution by mass exodus of the disaffected group had happened in three of our communes over the previous two years, and in one, Canon Frome, conflict we have already discussed had not yet fully ended. There had been a 'gruesome' few years, at least for some, in which the oldies were pressured out; 'their security, comfort, home, tribe, were under threat'. But after a general collapse relationships generally recovered – principally because, said one Canon Fromer, people have got on with their work rather than dwelling on relationships. True, a therapist was brought in to deal with this institutionalised quarrel between the strong-minded remains of a paternalistic and powerful core group and new people wanting rapid change and power devolution. And the day of listening and awareness did bring out some interesting feelings. But the session had not been repeated. 'We felt close but the feeling didn't last. No-one was really challenged and put through the mill'.

The work-versus-therapy controversy

In Canon Frome, we found a split into two schools of thought on forging strong relationships and conflict resolution and avoidance, a divide clearly evident in at least six other communes also. On the one hand is the relations-through-work, or 'get-on-and-do-it-pull-yourself-together' faction. On the other is the therapy, or 'two-hour-chats-over-coffee-to-sort-things-out' school. Clearly, the communards' use of such epithets indicates that each side has some contempt for the other.

The work school maintains that relationships build and hold incidentally through doing tasks collectively. Frequently its members are the longer-lasting communards:

> I've been here for seven years . . . I want to get into *work*. Good feelings should naturally flow from working together . . . When you try and sort things out by changing others to fit a mould it all goes out of the window . . . We're more cohesive when working together. Living day to day is what makes it OK, not our ideals. I'm cynical about talking: there's a big discrepancy between people's theory and their practice.

Newer members may describe this attitude as

> boring and ignorant. It makes me angry when they say 'you think too much'. You can't tell people who've had a profoundly painful experience to pull themselves together.

The most common therapies which aim to bring barriers down and feelings to the fore are rebirthing, primal therapy, co-counselling, encounter groups, 'sharings' and attunements at the beginnings of meetings, and 'feelings meetings'. The therapy advocates point out how such methods challenge belief structures about one's personality. They are hard work and time consuming. They may build an understanding of others and their vulnerabilities, and then 'It's more difficult to hate someone if you understand what motivates them. But you need three months' training to help people to listen to each other without interruption'.

At Findhorn and Monkton Wyld the therapy approach probably held sway. At most other communes it did not. There have been divisions into two camps, or attempts at building a comprehensive therapy programme have been met with sizeable indifference (for example, 'emotional maintenance' meetings at Redfield were boycotted by sections of the commune), dismissal ('we have the do-er/talker split at Monkton Wyld too, but the important moments are when people get together to do things – the rest *is* just talk'), or cynicism ('she wanted some rebirthing to unlock her, but she couldn't afford the £20 a throw to do it'). At PIC however both approaches seem valued. Sometimes relationships held up through collective work, but on other occasions stressful undercurrents and personality clashes were reduced by co-counselling. But working together, under a shared world view, were thought to be the important elements in making relationships work.

There is a political dimension to this division between work and therapy approaches. It was clearly manifested at Redfield, where the 1970s core group founders were Marxist and believed in trying to change wider society by collective (*gemeinschaft*) approaches to community. However the newcomers' approach to social change was the liberal-individualist 'personal-is-political', which therefore emphasised the importance of 'personal development', and involved open expression and sharing of feelings and emotions. (They have a more *gesellschaft* view of community.) A Redfield old-guard socialist put her objections to the therapy school:

> It helps the individual, but not the community, and it scares off the good people. *My* therapy is being out there and doing the work that needs doing. *Their* therapy puts self before community. They are so tuned into their individuality that it's difficult for them to put the group first. It's a continual conflict between those who think that someone's feelings are more important and those who want to push the group along.

CONCLUSION

The influx of the 'therapy' school into most communes in the eighties together with the rise of New Ageism is just part of a broader move away from socialist notions of community towards liberal individualism. This in turn is part of a trend in wider society, against which communes are supposed to be part of a *counter*culture. That trend involves individualism, market economics and a shift of interest from 'public' to 'private' realms. We examine it further in Chapter 6 because it relates importantly to the issue of whether communes will help to transform wider society.

We can conclude from this chapter that communards have a world view that is indeed radically and overwhelmingly green. This view translates rather patchily into individual and group practice, but it is probably true that communes can provide an institutional context which encourages ecologically sound practices. However the social behaviour which accords with green principles is more difficult to attain, even in a commune. Partly this must be due to the influences and socialisation which communards bring in from wider society. We now turn to the question of relationships with that society, and how it might be changed to an ecologically sound one in future.

CHAPTER 6

Changing society: or being changed?

This book asks two major questions. Chapter 5 has answered the first: how green are the communes? We now consider the second question: how important are, and will be, communes in leading the way to an ecologically sound society [9.11]?

We ask, first, how communards themselves see this question: whether they believe that social change is happening and what are the best ways of facilitating it. This, their theory of social change, is important. For whether one adopts structuralist or non-structuralist, and materialist or idealist perspectives, and whether one emphasises individual or collective and consensus or conflict approaches, are factors that may materially influence just how effective one is in working for change. This book does not presume (as some communards do) that all of these approaches are equally valid, as will be made clear.

We finish this chapter by addressing practice. Are these communes in fact making any impact on wider society, and what evidence is there either way? Is influence achieved by just *being* there, as an example, or is there conscious 'outreach', locally or nationally, and is it sufficient?

Finally, to invert the question, we consider the problem posed briefly in the last chapter about the relationship between this element of the counterculture and mainstream society. Rather than the former influencing the latter, is the process more dialectical, whereby the counterculture itself modifies and adapts to reflect patterns of change in that society which it opposes? This chapter presents material germane to these issues: judgement is made in the next, concluding, chapter.

THE THEORY

Turning points, hundredth monkeys, Aquarian conspiracies and the 'more-and-more' syndrome

'We're at a turning point: more and more people realise there's a crisis'. This answer to the question, 'Is society changing generally towards an ecologically more sound one?' reflects the millenarianism of much of the green movement. Clearly expressed by Capra (1982), millenarianism was shared by some communards we interviewed, especially New Agers. Rather like the crudest Marxists, whom they trenchantly oppose, they saw themselves as part of an irresistible historical trend – a 'trend in history towards things getting better', as a Redfieldian put it. Many are convinced that change is already happening: 'The whole thing is on the move' . . . 'a process of changing expectation is occurring, more in towns than the countryside' (this last from Canon Frome, set, like many communes, amidst rural Toryism).

Whether they are overt New Agers or not, many greens display the 'more-and-more' syndrome that is part of such millenarianism, and about a quarter of our interviewees used either this key phrase or the allied ones of 'growing awareness' or 'heightened consciousness' to convey their preceptions.

> More and more people are growing food organically – and the government's listening.

> More and more are becoming vegetarian. Mainstream society's changing slowly.

> Consciousness is on the turn, away from the mechanistic world view.

> There's much greater awareness than ten years ago of alternative medicine and food ideas. People power is visible – Sainsburys is removing additives from its food.

One problem about this last, middle-class oriented, view is that little evidence is produced beyond the anecdotal to support it. 'The question of where society's going is subjective – you can produce evidence either way', admitted a Monkton Wyld communard, 'and my subjective view is that society's entering an Aquarian age'. 'Many people are doing things which will suddenly have a big impact', said a Redfieldian: 'I've no evidence; just a feeling – I know a lot of people like that'. Herein lies the rub of possible self delusion, for in relying on empirical evidence from one's immediate and wider circles for any perceived trend, one can so easily forget just how limited that circle is, and the communards' circle could be more limited than most. This Redfieldian did choose the example of how interpersonal awareness skills were being applied, along with 'consensual' decision making, in industrial management – an example lifted from Findhorn's 1988 conference, 'From Organisation to Organism', and this Findhornian New Age perspective had spread to individuals in many communes – along with its attendant elitist, anti-socialist/anarchist view of the importance of top-down rather than bottom-up change. It attaches primacy to environmental and spiritual awareness among 'people who'll get into positions of power in the next ten years'. From there it will take 'fifteen years for ideas like wholefood to spread from the muesli belt class to the working class'. The communard responsible for this last remark had been heartened by the readiness with which people on the street had taken leaflets about Chernobyl and the US bombing of Libya in 1986.

The top-down approach envisages that, firstly, a small and scattered minority will become imbued with the new consciousness (they will 'breathe together', or 'conspire', the Aquarian wind of change – hence *The Aquarian Conspiracy* (Ferguson 1982)) though the individual actors may not be aware of their co-conspirators. Then, when the number of quiet revolutionaries reaches a critical mass (about fifteen per cent of the population, including the powerful and influential) *all* of society will be transformed. The manner of transformation may involve some mass intuition, or extra-sensory telecommunication – part of a 'planetary intelligence' – rather than a mass consciousness arrived at rationally as in socialist revolutionary theory. That such a process does take place is constantly alluded to by New Agers, in their 'hundredth monkey' story of how innovation was allegedly spread in quantum fashion amongst geographically dispersed monkey communities (see below).

A less sanguine view

But such views were not overwhelmingly present. A down-to-earthness pervades the quiet optimism of most communards, which can, paradoxically, verge on cynicism. Wild, exaggerated assessments of what is happening in society, and the communes' role in it, were few outside the circle of the New Agers. 'Awareness', said one Canon Fromer, 'and enlightenment' may be spreading, but probably only to the educated. People are getting more aware, but only people I know of. I'm lucky to mix with people who respect nature, but I don't know that most people do.

Another Canon Fromer thought that change was taking place only in 'less challenging things, like giving up smoking', not in people's deep mental state, while a third said:

> We sit round knitting Arran jumpers from wool from our own sheep, but so what? The rest of the world's going up in flames. We're just doing things to satisfy ourselves. And while more and more people are aware, there's another big group pulling in the opposite direction.

This suggested a degree of political realism occasionally found elsewhere, as at Redfield:

> There's no real social movement for us to change our ways to alleviate the plight of the poor.

or Lifespan:

> Lots of people are more aware, but being prepared to *do without* is another matter.

or Lower Shaw:

> The response to crisis is cosmetic and piecemeal, as witness the Montreal protocol against CFCs.

Approaches to changing society

Chapter 3 discussed two sets of interrelated positions on social change. Bearing these in mind, interviewees were asked an initially open question on how they felt that change towards an ecologically sound society was most likely to occur [8.1]. They were then prompted, if necessary, to expand on this. Their views on the relative importance of individual or collective approaches were particularly sought [8.2-.3] because of the bearing of this issue on the perceived (and actual) role of communes in social change. For while the very existence of communes ostensibly suggests that their members favour a collective approach, this may not really be the case – if, that is, the communes are little more than a collection of individualists who are weakly bonded (in other words, lacking common purposes and action strategies related to social change). The attitude to the importance of changing the ideas and values of the individual was also probed by asking about the role of education in social change. For, to see education as the major force in social change probably means rejecting the structuralist/materialist position (where educational institutions mainly function to peddle the ideas that reinforce the collective consensus – and therefore the existing economic/social organisation) in favour of a non-structuralist/idealist perspective (where education is freer from the socio-economic structure, and can be used as a tool for changing perceptions and values). However education, in this context, need not be taken merely as the formal system, but as the whole range of arrangements and influences which lead people to form world views. Hence, education through people seeing and copying the *example* of those living alternative lifestyles comes into the scope of this question.

It was argued in Chapter 3 that there was a logical connection between taking collective, materialist and structuralist positions on social change, or, alternatively, taking individualist, idealist and non-structuralist approaches. In other words, if you believe in any one of either 'set' of three, then it would be logical also to believe in the other two in the 'set'. However, the responses from our interviewees sometimes challenged this supposition. In particular, they questioned the dualisms on which such a scheme is based, arguing, for example, that individual actions, when summed, represent collective action; or that when people's ideas and values change then they will consequently change their material circumstances; or, similarly, that by changing the way individuals see things you will at the same time change social-economic structures. These refutations suggest – even hinge on – a liberal conception of society and community as little more than the sum of its individual component parts.

This underlying political nature of the debate did occasionally surface in interviews, and aspects of it are pursued in the section on political approaches. The political issue was put in its essentials by two CAT members. One was a disillusioned anarchist, now much influenced by Findhornian idealism, and the other was an ex-trade unionist. The former emphasised how 'people' now think about political change in terms of *themselves* and how they feel. After a revolution, will it feel different? He replied:

> When I was younger, people talked about political change in order to get social justice. No longer. Now it's about alienation and feeling alive – now we're talking about the [environmental] problems of the *rich*, not the poor.

The former trade unionist, however, felt that because of this, environmentalists and communards are

> out of touch with the nature of the political forces they're up against. The solutions of people living here are too simplistic. They don't face up to reality, and lack class consciousness. Talking to 30,000 black kids in inner city Birmingham about compost loos is not addressing the issue. My coming here is a form of resting without doing much harm. CAT is marginal to social change and we shouldn't overrate its importance.

Individualist approaches

As Table 17 suggests, individualist approaches to social change were overwhelmingly favoured. The forty per cent who stressed the role of the individual did so with varying degrees of reference to the wider society. At one end of the spectrum, most attention was fixed on the *inner self* as the focus of change:

> Wider change is possible *only* through people changing themselves as individuals. You can tell people about ecology till kingdom come but they won't do anything till they feel good about it. What stops people taking action are blockages inside themselves – childhood and pre-birth traumas for example. I've seen fantastic changes in people through re-evaluation and co-counselling. They've gone on to change the world.

This statement refers to the importance of non-structural factors; behavioural patterns established at childhood or, as another put it, 'social and family conditioning'. Hence the significance of therapies which help to relive early experiences in helping to change oneself:

> The more I can change myself, the more it will reflect out. People empower themselves through acknowledging what they are. Rebirthing gives back to people a sense of themselves, enabling them to take back their [political] power.

Here, then, is the essence of alienation for so many communards – a sense of having been removed from or robbed of contact with their true selves and their power over their own lives (perhaps by conventional family life, and conditioning). So,

Table 17: **Summary of views on social change**

1. INDIVIDUAL has primary role (setting examples, raising consciousness, promoting spiritualism – 'the personal is political')	40% of all responses
2. COLLECTIVIST approaches most important (via political action, national and local strikes, demos, coops and communes)	13% of all responses
3. EVENTS will be most important (leading to individual and collective actions and different social organisation)	15% of all responses
4. EDUCATION (about 'facts', for cooperation, for better ideas)	9% of all responses
5. CONSUMER PRESSURE (leading to greater environmental consciousness)	4% of all responses
6. TOTAL MIX (impossible to single out any factor)	11% of all responses
7. CHANGE WILL NOT HAPPEN	6% of all responses

> The real politics is inside myself. The only power I'm interested in is a magical power: the power of myself. My hope is in myself.

It is a hope of true revolution: 'A social change coming *from people*, not relying on government to do it'. Hence people must take more responsibility for their own lives. For instance, women can take back their power rather than blaming men for the state of the world. This of course assumes that individuals can take back power, rather than its being deeply embedded in social-economic structures. If the latter were true then collective action might be the only way to wrest power from structures and organisations where it lay, but the 'extreme' individualists expressly rejected this route:

> Collective action isn't taking responsibility for our blame, which lies in a lack of respect for others. If we haven't disarmed ourselves we cannot disarm the world. I know it's a middle class thing to say, but *anyone* can change – there's a voice inside us that can't be stopped by anything.

Indeed, this sentiment *could* be an example of middle class preoccupations. The conviction about one's own guilt reflects, perhaps, one's relatively comfortable position in life. The guilt is transposed into taking blame onto oneself for the wider ills of society. In a way this is a modern version, too, of the medieval ideas of the self as a microcosm of the wider world, reflected also in Roszak's influential phrase 'person/planet': some communards put it almost exactly in this way:

> Change *must* be from within oneself. To change *the planet* one must change *individuals* first.
>
> You are part of the world and it's part of you. This is a really important part of the green message which we [ZAP] believe in. There's no division between changing yourself and changing the world.

The trouble with such sentiments is that they might contain the presumption that there is no significant material break in the social continuum. This leads to impractical and even elitist assumptions; for instance that 'people in inner cities can also wake up and change their lives. They should grow their own food, so that they know what's involved'. Statements like this suggest that the realities of social and political stratification are being forgotten.

These people see the locus of political power rooted in the self. But while some kept this focus very much on the individual other individualists were a little further along the spectrum towards collectivism. To them, the much-used aphorism 'the personal is political' meant acknowledging that the individual is part of a society, but that to realise this social role, self-realisation must come first. They therefore brought some notions of collectivity into their analyses of social change through individual action:

> *Collective* political action is the only way. That does not conflict with the importance of changing individuals, because collective political action stems from a group of individuals.
>
> People must feel better about themselves before they can do anything about the environment. They must feel their individual power: collective action then follows.
>
> I used to be a collectivist: now I'm more into individualism. Those who say wider political change starts with the personal might be right.

This last represents a 'defection' which is not uncommon. Some communards are 'ex-collectivists' disillusioned with revolutionary or party politics, who now prefer to focus on individual, personal change.

For some this link between the personal/individual and the political/collective lies in the notion of change by *example*:

> Individual change, to make a model available to society, is all you can do.
>
> If one can individually adjust lifestyle, one can show others what can be done.

To believe in this power of example can lead in one of two directions. On the one hand it may imply an idealist position – the notion that people can be diverted from their set ways, and the ideologies that support them, by the power of example, logical reasoning and persuasion. On the other it can be to propose that when sufficient changes in material circumstances have taken place people will be looking for new ways to live, and then, at such a time, it is important that living, working examples of ecologically sound lifestyles should be available. We will explore the latter position shortly, but first we will note some features of the extremely individualist perspective of New Age spiritualism. This, in Findhorn, supports the sovereignty of the individual while also attaching importance to the idea of the collective, enshrined both in its own community and in concepts like the 'planetary village'. However it also explicitly rejects the idea of the collective as the *motor* of social change.

Bringing in the New Age

New Age thinking hinges on the idea that spiritual forces underlie all life; therefore social change must be at the spiritual rather than material level. Already the 'spiritual is getting into politics', we were told. The changes in Eastern Europe were attributed by all the Findhornians we interviewed not to material, economic circumstances (namely that the USSR could no longer afford the cold war). Rather, together with spiritual movements and communities in the US, they stemmed from an Aquarian energy from beyond Earth which was expanding people's consciousness – their 'global awareness' or consciousness of the 'noospere' (a term coined by Teilhard de Chardin). 'There's a deep moving spirit which shapes events' said one Findhornian, explicitly accepting Hegel's idealism and rejecting Marx's materialism; 'It comes from people's collective consciousness. By working with it you can have an enormous influence for change'. As CAT's Findhorn 'representative' put it: 'consciousness not economics is the driving force of history'.

Findhorn is one 'hole' or 'light centre' whereby Aquarian energy – the moving spirit – enters Earth. There are other such geographical 'cosmic conduits', while each individual who gets the New Age spirit also becomes an energy channel. If individuals get their channels together, the resultant hole gets bigger. It does so by a power of two, so one individual allows one energy unit through, but two allow four units through. Here, incidentally, is an acknowledgement that the collective effort is more than the sum of its individual components.

The process which admits this energy of change to Earth – 'allows things to occur' – is meditation. In it, people direct thoughts and feelings towards an object, 'altering the frequency of vibrations around it' (energy is vibrations). Meditation can change material events. It can lower the crime rate in an area (see Chapter 4), bring 'light and love to Nicaragua', remove apartheid or the arms race: 'It's a directing of thought and wishing for things'.

At first the meditational process is a concentration on oneself:

> . . . then on things going on around you. You get to know you're connected with them. The deeper you meditate the more you recognise your bonds with everything, in flashes of insight. They get more intense, building up to peak experiences.

These resemble religious ecstasy – for accounts, see Caddy 1988.

So, once more, changing the wider world starts by focusing on and changing oneself. Detractors of the New Age wonder if it really goes further than this. Such scepticism might be justified by one Lauriestonian, who had devoted his life at one stage to following a yogi. 'My hopes [for social change] are pinned on meditation, in spiritual life, and my yogi's teaching', he told us. 'It's such a positive thing in my own life. But I don't think I *can* change the world. Individuals are up against a machine and can't cope'.

And while in one breath they talked of worldwide change, in other parts of the interviews Findhornians told us:

> It's a *personal* empowerment. People take responsibility for themselves; not for anyone else.

> Because Findhorn's a light centre, people grow and cleanse *themselves* of what's not 'harmonic', i.e. flowing with nature.

> What can *I* change? Nothing outside of me, but I can change me. I can't control anything outside myself; even my child has its own karma. If you try to change the world you're disempowered and frustration starts. I get a new value system and start to send out love. Then others get changed by my energy and my power to communicate.

Herein lies the feature of New Ageism which collectivists, structuralists and political activists might particularly object to. For the formula seems to be a spiritual equivalent of Adam Smith's 'invisible hand', whereby liberals justify their individual economic selfishness on the grounds that it somehow 'coheres' into a force for collective good. 'Better not to take conscious action to improve the lot of the less fortunate', it seems to say. 'Improving your own sense of wellbeing is the best you can do for them'.

This kind of sentiment came through in responses to our questions on what one does about unemployment:

> We did advertisement programmes to help the unemployed to change their value systems – *this made us feel real good* about what we were doing [emphasis added].

> Don't worry about unemployment. This and other problems will go away when enough people tune into their spiritual benignness. They must not view poverty as a drudge but as a gift. Some of the best things in life are learned when you are poor.

We have already noted a similar response to the problem of Third World exploitation.

Hence the individual does not attempt to change other people, or social-economic political structures, by material action in conscious concert with others: 'We can't do it as a collective. Only as individuals who recognise what good stuff they're made of'. Yet it is maintained that others *do* change – partly through contact with New Agers and following their example (here, the communicative power of new technology, such as satellites, is invoked). People change also through the intuitional spread of New Age consciousness. When enough people – the 'critical mass' of fifteen per cent referred to earlier – have gained such consciousness, suddenly there will be wholesale change and most people will gain it. This is how monkey populations, it is claimed, learn new habits such as washing their food. First one monkey stumbles across an idea, and communicates it directly to others. Then, after a symbolic 'hundredth monkey' has learned it, entire populations of monkeys geographically separated simultaneously start to do it. By the same token, it is no coincidence that new scientific discoveries are often made at the same time in different places on the globe.

It all relates to the monistic 'morphogenic theory', whereby thoughts are things and energy is matter, which we described in Chapter 4. Carrying this idea one stage further, we can say that something 'new' is not really new – it exists in the cosmos all the time. Discovery of 'new' things or ways of living and perception is in reality just 'tapping in' (through insight) to thought/energy fields that are already there. The New Age is a process of increasing numbers of people tapping in, or gathering insight; suddenly they will open up such a big hole, or channel, that Aquarian energy will pour in to affect everyone on the globe (see Lyall Watson's *Lifetide*, 1980). This critical mass theory means, for some Findhornians, that:

> It's OK that we're the privileged middle class. You needn't try to change everyone. We're a vanguard – a group who are waking up: dreaming dreams that others can't comprehend. But we're not that special – just different from others.

The elitism of this bothers others. As Bloom (1987) put it, New Agers can 'seem irrelevant' in the midst of a 'poignant planetary scenario' involving starving children, resource maldistribution, war and 'the greenery of the planet being stripped away':

> With our circle dancing, meditation and personal processes, we appear like any other alienated social group seeking solace in the emotional prop of an illusory but comforting belief system. We can be accused of being the middle class sixties generation selling a cartoon reality.

But currently Findhorn directs much effort towards a critical mass of politicians and business executives: 'Acting on them – the key people – you can get business to do different things'. Business can 'change its relationship to the planet', as the oft-quoted Body Shop is thought to show. And, 'Yes – you can even change burger-chains to new values. Even nuclear weapons manufacturers will put social consciousness into what they're doing'.

Lots of Japanese and US businesses are already, we were told, adopting New Age cooperative, consensual techniques in 'win-win' management: those lower down the firm are made to feel part of the whole, which is no longer split into workers and management, winners and losers. They have realised that personal empowerment of everyone in the organisation leads to higher creativity and higher profits, and 'there's nothing wrong with profits, with people's creativity being rewarded by money'. One Findhornian told us that evidence of businessmen gaining New Age consciousness came in the form of an organisation with the startling title 'Millionaires for World Peace'. Clearly, theories of structural violence have little place in New Age thinking.

Collectivists

As we have said, at one level all communards are collectivists. But within the ostensibly collective framework overwhelming importance is attached to changing the individual self as a method of simultaneously transforming society. While we have acknowledged those communards who see no incompatibility between the two approaches, we found that a smaller group (see Table 17) did specifically reject individualism and self-change, while also advocating collective approaches. This minority was mainly drawn from the longer-stay communards, who had been part of the first, more ideologically motivated (to the left) wave in the mid-seventies and were also part of the relationships-through-work school.

We have already touched on some of the objections which this group has towards individualism. They include its perceived selfishness;

> I'm not convinced by the person-is-political argument; it's just a way of making *yourself* comfortable.

> Changing the world through individual 'consciousness' raising is a *reactionary* solution. You only worry about the problems of the world as you relate to them.

its 'apoliticism';

> The we're-all-responsible-for-ourselves attitude is a way of escaping from political action, whereas we do need to confront things.

its 'arrogance in thinking people will be converted by *your* example – in fact individuals can change themselves, but not others'; and its ineffectiveness;

> Revolutionaries are into the notion of external enemies, while Taoism tells us to look into ourselves. The latter isn't enough. The radical movements of the sixties melted away into therapy and inward-looking.

It was pointed out that in working collectively for political change individuals in any case change themselves. Of the possible collective approaches, political campaigning from the top – 'by such people as Bruce Kent or Petra Kelly' or 'via socialism and the Labour Party' – were favoured by only two or three people. Localised and decentralist 'participative socialism' and pressure groups and political campaigning were hardly any more popular. *Doing* things, via communes and coops, was seen as a better way of 'taking control' in the anarchist sense, as part of a voluntary, devolved, federated and non-exploitative green society. 'You have to *take* control – you can't set up a political system which then *grants* you that control'.

Others in this group linked their collectivity clearly to structural and material perspectives, by emphasising the need to change economic power relationships, since these are also political power relationships. Here, demonstrations and strikes were regarded as important tools, for it would be a matter of removing capitalism. But while collective 'revolutionary' action might be important, neither it nor quieter, example-setting communes and coops would succeed without accompanying material changes. For instance, people will have to reach a certain level of affluence before they can think and act in ecologically sound and socially just ways. Alternatively 'things will have to get worse and worse: this is what will initiate social change'.

Events

About one in six interviewees, whether collectivists or individualists, stressed this importance of material changes as a vital trigger to changes in social and economic-political organisation or individual and mass values and attitudes, or both.

> Disaster and crisis will take society in the way I'd like it to go. You must change yourself as well as getting political change. My solution is to experiment with ways of living as an example to people – but they have to be disillusioned before they will follow the ideas.

> Lack of social deprivation equals lack of revolution. Social change will come through famine and the breakdown of the world banking system. The only way new ideas will spread is through major upheaval. The present system has so much inertia and things aren't bad enough to move people out of it.

Some spelled out a series of cause and effect 'reactions'. For instance, increased pollution would lead to changed consciousness in individuals, who would then come together to effect change. Or a similar sequence would be triggered by a specific disaster, leading to flowering of the 'Aquarian Conspiracy, with education and TV chipping away at people's consciousness, and producing social change without revolution'. Or there will be a 'sudden environmental event producing a final flip to a different society – most social change happens by accident: that propounded by institutions has never turned out as intended'.

For New Agers this all fits into their millenarian perspective. However, a different historical model was offered by an anarchist/materialist communard:

> I believe in historical cycles. The bubble burst on the fifties, then sixties attitudes came. The cycle's almost repeating itself. When the

yuppy bubble bursts and they want something more, we will be there to offer something else. The cycle isn't totally repetitive – more helical. Communes have died away in the eighties but there's more ecological awareness now.

Inertia

Such historical determinism borders on fatalism, and just a few communards displayed this. Fatalism's anarchist form took the line that:

> There won't be a collapse; too much energy is put into sustaining the system. The only answer is not to participate – get into alternative communities, the black economy and squatters. The society I'd like to see isn't attainable. I'm an idealist – a romantic.

The New Age form might be astrological:

> Social change is a bit of a chimera, because the astrological charts show that people have certain potentialities which no amount of influence by others can destroy.

Or it might see the Aquarian Conspiracy as predetermined:

> That's the way it is. There's nothing anyone can do about it. But there might not be any problems. Nothing might happen. They might put all the rubbish into a rocket and shoot it into space. Yes, I'm fatalistic. Whatever happens, happens.

Fatalist tendencies are perhaps more common than our categorisation suggests, as is sheer puzzlement. Sometimes, after a long discussion on social change mechanisms, people would say (in their anxiety to get to dinner?): 'I don't know the answer: I just worry'.

Optimistic idealism

If the above seems a trifle pessimistic, the views of those who saw education or consumerism as motors of social change gave the reverse impression. Some saw rationality, with 'correct' ideas and values, as a major force; 'We'll get there via education' because it will tell people 'the facts'. Thus equipped with greater 'environmental awareness' young people will 'change the mode of production and industry' towards cooperative working and sharing. As we have seen (Chapter 4) many communards criticised education for *not* teaching the values of cooperation and sharing. Just a few believed that fundamental value changes come through education:

> You can't just change the economic system through revolution, though I used to believe this. You must change people's *ideas* first, by changing the structure of education towards cooperation. Then they'll change their minds.
>
> Education for basic values – health, Third World, all living things – will lead to individuals changing. They will form local groups which will become political movements.
>
> You can't make people do what they don't want. It's done by educating people to know they can control their own lives.

The educational orientation of communes is less strong now than their founders might have wished. But it is still there in nearly half the communes from our small sample (see Table 4). Hence the above sentiments are not those of such a minority. The world view of this highly-educated group of people (see Table 8) must inevitably have implicit faith in the power of education, and this was reflected in most of our conversations. Very few, however, were prepared to say that education constitutes a main motor of social change.

Surprisingly, for a group which itself has moved a few steps towards the consumer society (see below), even fewer people saw consumer power as of any great significance. Just two or three thought that 'consumer pressure and the influence of the market is a major force for social change'. They had the current popularity of green consumerism in mind, and were optimistic enough to believe that this force will eventually produce an ecologically sound society – a society which paradoxically will not be a consumer society at all.

Capitalism and class conflict

To probe further their support for structural or non-structural perspectives on social change, communards were asked whether they supported the idea that environmental and social problems stemmed specifically from the capitalist form of economic organisation, and if they believed in 'class analysis' – i.e. that society is divided significantly into economic classes, and that conflict between them is a key to social change [8.5].

Less than one in three did support these contentions in any strong way. Those that did drew attention to the need to grapple with economic relations that, in their view, presently give capitalist entrepreneurs no choice but to produce in environmentally harmful ways. 'You don't make money out of environmentally benign goods', thought one. 'Where profit is the most important motive the environment will suffer' said another. A third emphasised the 'necessary' short-term perspective of the system.

It followed for some that revolutionary change is needed:

> Given that people at the top level have a vested interest in the status quo, the only thing to do is get rid of those at the top. Non-violent direct action is not very effective, so we may have to use force. A slow, gradual move to communal ways may not be enough. I have a sense of urgency.

The difficulty of removing the resource-owning class, however, was underlined. 'It's difficult communicating ideas to the working classes', said one revolutionary, while another bemoaned false consciousness whereby the exploited are bought off with material goods, and working class people vote Tory rather than in their own interests. Because Western capitalism 'can keep its workers happy, it will not founder on class struggle'. For this reason one communard had visited Nicaragua to support the revolution there: 'I've put my energy into changing Third World society, because if this happens the elite in this country would founder. If the Third World is freed, this will have a profound effect on Britain'. Another had withdrawn from the struggle, while a third wanted voluntary, not imposed, commun(al)ism. This would, hopefully, achieve common ownership of land, a solution which all the communards had opted for in practice in their own lives, although surprisingly few saw it as a key factor in achieving their preferred future on a wide scale.

Others accepted capitalism, with its class divisions, as significant, but did not see possibilities for other than limited action to change it. For one, the underlying truth of class analysis held, but, perceptively, she saw limitations in applying it because 'people don't see themselves as part of a distinct class, and if people don't have class consciousness they're alienated from what should bind them together'. For others the class system in Britain was 'incredibly strong'; although it might be forced to change, or burn itself out because of environmental contradictions, there was little that class conflict could achieve to help the change.

> Capitalism has many self-perpetuating vested interests, who aren't going to allow threats to the status quo.

> Violent revolution might be a solution in South Africa, but the English system seems to bend to what people want.

> Only a limited fight – with limited success – for workers' causes within capitalism is possible. We must be pragmatic.

A third group held that capitalism as it stands is to blame for many environmental and social ills, but they hoped that 'capitalism will be flexible enough to provide for more sophisticated market desires, such as anti-pollution measures and vegetarianism'. Such self-confessed 'revisionists' accepted that 'we can't get away from the big boys who command the heights of our economy'. They also saw signs of 'some big industry looking to the longer term'. These people included the Findhornians, discussed above, working to encourage 'holistic' attitudes in business.

They would probably agree with the Crabapple member resigned to the fact that:

> Capitalism's obviously fun for some people, so they're going to go on wanting to do it. Hence there must be room for capitalism in an ecological society, though I don't think there ought to be. But it has to be a controlled and responsible capitalism, though I don't know if there is such a thing. I'm impotent in any class struggle, because *I'm* from the dominant class. But Britain is class ridden and the green movement must meet the working classes half way.

For the rest, the majority, capitalism or communism were irrelevant. One in four used a favourite green phrase: 'they're as bad as each other'. Economic class was also held as immaterial. The class division between men and women was more significant; 'If women had more power, you'd have less capitalism'.

Class distinctions, in this view, are not necessarily denied. They do exist, and it may be important to eliminate them. But 'having a classless society will not, of itself, produce an ecologically sound society', and 'class struggle does not achieve relevant social change; you won't get a stable society through revolution'. Predictably, environmental ills were blamed on 'industrialism' per se, rather than on capitalist industrialism, by some who were active in green politics, while anarchists blamed the nation state. Most of this group blamed people's ideas, values and state of environmental and social consciousness.

What caused consciousness to be as it is was not always explained, though a popular line was to blame 'not capitalism or communism' but 'human nature', 'greed', not being 'good enough', or 'fear'. Thus, very often the argument was thrown back from structural to behavioural, psychological explanations, or even to explanations in terms of 'original sin' or 'hubris' (insolent pride, or presumption, that leads to downfall):

> People aren't good enough to go along with Marxism.
>
> It's human nature, not capitalism, which is the environmental bogey.
>
> Private enterprise is about individual expression. We don't want to oppose this, but greed. This is where anarchism comes in.
>
> I don't believe in class struggle or conflict. Seeing things in these terms means that one doesn't blame oneself, but one must take responsibility for oneself.
>
> We could live quite soundly under communism or capitalism. It's not this but greed which is the issue.

Finally, there is the total rejection of conflict – with economic structures, between classes, or within oneself – which is seen in the New Age view.

> We must *avoid conflict*. If people are angry, they send out angry energy. The New Age movement puts out love energy to counter this. Anger just promotes defensiveness and more anger. You have to make people change *their* energy and stop exploiting nature, and you do this by showing them how much *you* love nature. That's what's wrong with the anti-nuke movement: it's anger and hate. There's no difference between an angry government official and an angry anti-nuke person. We're *one* – brothers and sisters on planet Earth. Greens must stop being anti – must stop trying to stop the old. We New Agers are building the new.
>
> If we *think* capitalism hinders us, it will. We only give away our power to the extent that we think we have.

One communard who worked in Milton Keynes Cooperative Development Agency had successfully applied this philosophy. He shared offices with 'anti-coop' people and made it his job 'to contact their chief executive and talk to him. He's now flipped to the other extreme and is enthusiastic about coops. The reason people are as they are is because of their early life experiences. It's deficient ideas that are to blame'.

Again, these are non-structural, idealistic perspectives on change. So idealistic are they that they maintain: 'You can *think* yourself out of a class if you want'. They refuse to

> address the capitalism-communism thing. Socialism forces people to do things; I'm into running the planet by the power of the spirit. No-one is forced to join in. The terms 'capitalism' and 'communism' are outmoded. We now need the model that when the individual is nourished the group is nourished.

Here is the essence of the New Age conception of 'group' and 'community'. It is a mirror-image of the socialist idea that when the group is nourished, so too is the individual. Findhornians accepted that 'capitalism must change, but Russia has failed too though it's full of feminine energy. A marriage of the two is needed, a *third way*'.

This phrase – a 'third way' between capitalism and communism – is beloved of greens, as Bramwell (1989) has noted. Used here, it signified a search for something between socialism and capitalism, where the former suggests state bureaucracy and the latter the 'free' market. It is, at best, an ambiguous concept. At one time it was used by decentralist socialists after World War I and again in the sixties new left movement to support their contention that 'people should shape their own destinies' (Barbrook 1990), but it was also a slogan of fascism, and led to the very opposite of such self-realisation (Bramwell 1989).

Conventional politics [8.6-10]

Following much of the above, it is predictable that two-thirds of our interviewees were either cynical or doubtful about conventional political routes to social change or rejected them totally (see Table 18). For them such politics represented essentially collective approaches which simultaneously relegated the importance of individuals. 'The personal is political' was held to have no role in conventional politics, whose adherents clearly do not usually live up to their grand principles. Scorn was particularly directed at national party politics, whereas people had more time for pressure group activities. Many were, or had been, in Greenpeace, Friends of the Earth or the Campaign for Nuclear Disarmament. Given the anarchistic leanings of about a fifth of the sample, and the green or socialist views of many more (Table 12) it was a little surprising that support for change through local community-based politics was slight.

About one in three did have some time for conventional parties, mainly Green and Labour. And although a sizeable consensus was built around anti-Conservatism, especially anti-Thatcherism, nonetheless it was quite common to hear support for the Thatcherite Victorian virtues of 'standing on one's own two feet', 'taking responsibility for one's own life' and making the state's institutions apparently accountable to local communities (there was a perhaps mistaken impression that the Thatcher versions of these shibboleths

Table 18: **Attitudes to conventional politics**

Rejecting conventional politics *absolutely*	43%
Cynical/doubtful about politics	22%
Green Party member or supporter	18%
Labour member or supporter	13%
Liberal member/supporter	15%
Conservative member/supporter	15%

somehow embraced anarchism's cherished beliefs – but then perhaps they partly do).

The anti-politics/ideology school divides roughly into two categories, anarchistic and New Age. Anarchists stress their rejection of the concept of political power and its corrupting effect:

> Because politics involves power, automatically it's not an acceptable route to change.

> I've no time for conventional politics. Anyone who wants to be a top-notch politician must be very egotistical or narrow minded.

> Most national politicians are megalomaniacs. Pressure groups and community politics are, too, subject to the problem that you can't tell people what to do.

> Political power means centralised power – this is corruptible. Everyone's open to corruption but when you concentrate people's interests at one point it's easier to corrupt.

> Politics of any sort is just a form of control. Pressure groups just mimic those who oppress them.

The New Age view closely relates to its rejection of conflict, and its historical determinism:

> Findhorn's apolitical and this is good. We shouldn't expend our energy on what's going to change anyway, but should build the new.

> I wouldn't try to make the system work by agitation. The government can create only a certain number of jobs. I lead the meditations on government and the political process. I get our group to send out waves to the planet about things which need change. I don't want to get into sanctions against South Africa. Sending energy, the inner word, is more valuable. I wouldn't picket or take sides.

By no means everyone in this rejection-of-politics school has such a clear position. There is quite a large third group who simply say,

'I'm not interested in politics and know nothing about it', or words to this effect.

Among the more political minority, there is probably more sorrow than anger about the labour movement, together with a feeling that its politics are somehow outmoded – or, as greens often put it, are about 'the old' politics of left and right, not the 'new politics of life'. Labour was seen as 'stuck in its ways', 'bankrupt' and failing to take up 'new' – black and women's – issues. 'Trades unions are still built on racism and sexism', said a male ex-trades unionist, while a female who had never belonged to the movement (but 'would join to kick Maggie out') thought it 'encouraging that union leaders are talking about bringing women into the movement'. She went on to regret that the so-called 'loony left councils won't make it, because the Conservative-backed tabloids are too widely read'. Others similarly baulked at the weight of an establishment which had, for them, nullified the unions:

> Trades unions are unlikely to be a force for change. They've done much to dignify their members in the past, but now they've been sucked into the system.
>
> The unions have been defeated by Maggie, so I've lost confidence.

Others were slightly more optimistic but still tentative:

> Environmentalists should work on the unions. They're a good idea even though undemocratic. But it is difficult to change the movement via infiltration. You're banging your head against a brick wall.
>
> I work for Labour because they would provide a better framework for cooperatives. But you won't get social change from one Party.
>
> Labour *might* be a way forward, but its history doesn't give me much hope. A lot of impetus for the seventies alternative movement came from disillusionment with the political parties, and wanting to go out and at least *try* to build islands of socialism in a sea of capitalism. We've done it, but we're more a pebble than an island.

And so it probably remains in the nineties. Despite the ideological fragmentation and diffuseness discussed earlier, there is still a groundswell of socialist fundamentalism in the communes. 'But the Labour Party doesn't represent "*our*" socialism', is the common complaint.

While the Green Party resonates with the concerns of so many communards, socialist communards think it lacks 'policies on fundamental issues like common ownership of land'. They are alienated from Labour, as many socialists have been down the years, but cannot stomach the Greens. One ex-Labourite summarised the dilemma:

> I feel incredibly muddled and politically ineffectual. The Green Party is so far from effecting major political change. It isn't red enough and the Labour Party isn't green enough.

Greens, however, were at times hardly less muddled:

> I'm in the Green Party, but I'm not political. The Green Party won't get in. I vote Liberal. Labour is as bad as the Conservatives. They're both about confrontation and making enemies. I don't agree with Mrs Thatcher, but she's sincere.

Though there was also some confidence that the future did *not* lie with Labour:

> Die Grünen are trying to synthesise red and green and it's not working. The reds have had their chance and they've fucked it. They've created giant monopolies as employers. To me, red means state socialism. Small and local level is not a socialist tradition.

But then confidence in the Green Party was also less than total:

> I'm not sure about their social policy.
>
> It's too party-oriented, instead of having close links with pressure groups.
>
> They constitute a useful voice, but as soon as they get political success I won't have any faith in them.
>
> They have some right wallies standing for them.

How important are communes? [8.11]

If conventional politics are out, and collective solutions are secondary to individual self-change, where do communes fit in? This question, 'How important are communes in leading the way to a socially more just and ecologically more harmonious society?' was central to this study (see Introduction), and it was put directly.

The 'green' academics, theorists and visionaries cited in Chapter 2 might be surprised by the answer. It was that while they, who do *not* live in communes, are 'likely to suggest that something like a federation of communes is the only viable political-institutional form for the sustainable society to take' (Dobson 1990 p123-4), those who *do* live in communes are most unlikely to suggest this! Over six out of ten of our interviewees thought that communes are not important in leading us to a green society, and do not constitute a significant part of the blueprint for survival. Less than three in ten thought that they might be significant, and under one in ten was prepared to be enthusiastic and unconditional in supporting the idea.

'Yes, they are central to change', said one of this minority. 'The Aquarian society will be made up of communes like these', said another, 'especially if they abolish money. If people can't get money or power they will not be corrupt – they'll help each other and live together'. Here, of course, is the anarchist and pure socialist view. A more 'mainstream' green view was that 'our commune [Redfield] is quite compatible with green values and gives people a chance to live them out'. While a Lauriestonian acknowledged 'slippage' from green practices, she, too, believed that

> despite this I'd hold this alternative community up to the green movement as an example. We're showing that it's possible to live outside the system. It would be possible to run the whole country like this, but the present system would have to *collapse* – not just change – and be replaced by a society of communes.

Characteristically, half of this small group of eight unqualified optimists were Findhornians. 'We're just trying to build a new civilisation', claimed one modestly. 'We're not just a replay of nineteenth-century communes, we're part of a new spirit and people are here because they feel they are making a difference', claimed another. The others thought it would be possible 'to have the country made up of small units – it could be done, with commitment'.

Of those generally in favour, some did not see communes as complete blueprints. Rather, communal living fosters elements of a green society, such as honest and open human relationships – and the 'green movement does not pay enough attention to social relations' – or 'being in tune with nature'. Hence communes will be a help, but they also have lots of problems, so constitute only indirect ways forward. In particular they do help to change individuals who might later go out to forge the green society.

Some enthusiasts saw very practical drawbacks however. 'Communes are a leading edge of the green movement', said one, 'and an example to others. But it would be impossible for all society to live like this. There aren't enough seventeen-acre houses to go round'. Another thought that they could be a leading edge, but are prevented from so being because the communards do not get the time to broadcast their existence and lifestyle to a wider world. A third explained that Britain does not have enough communes for them to lead the green movement. Out of 47 in the Communes Network, only fifteen write regularly for the *Newsletter*. Furthermore, though communes might be

> the best way to a green society, it *is* true that the bulk of the work which goes on in them is what conventional people do only at weekends or in evenings – gardening and cleaning. These things take over in communes, which is difficult for those of us who see more to life. You spend most of your lifetime keeping going, or having meetings to decide to how to keep going. The place can attract people who aren't motivated to do much else, then it gets motiveless and goes round in circles.

For rather more people such drawbacks outweighed the advantages, making communes of limited or no influence in the green venture – certainly not as effective as other forms of community. Most Quarry members, for instance, saw CAT as simply a demonstration, to give urbanites in particular some ideas and stimulation. And it is a way for people

> already into social change to renew their batteries. But it's not a way to change society. I'd like the green movement to promote communes, but it's more important for it to get political power.

'We're hardly the start of a revolution', said one Canon Fromer: 'We don't anywhere near reach our potential to change things', said another. 'We're not a serious alternative that everyone can do, just a small demonstration of what might be possible. Urban cooperatives would have more influence'.

Others enthused about street level communities 'but not lots of communes with people living in the same household'. The most likely future communal form, which environmental problems and the disintegration of the family would strongly encourage people to adopt, was seen as something of the order of a street or neighbourhood, comprising individual dwellings but with resource sharing and communal spaces (for instance the Rainbow Housing Cooperative in Milton Keynes). Communes might thus be one feature, but not an absolutely necessary one, of a green society. The stumbling block to going any further than street communities, many agreed, is the problem of the interaction of people. Put euphemistically, 'A lot of people can't handle the richness of the relationships in communes'. Put more bluntly: 'I don't think many people would want to live this way. They'd want more domestic control than we have, and not to be *so* close together'.

One of the People In Common group suggested that the ideal size for communal interaction depends on activity, but it is not more than eight for cooking and eating, or twelve for unstructured meetings. And even with such small numbers private space is also essential. Another communard proposed that communal villages might be more visible than communes. With these, and common land ownership, the countryside could be more people-intensive: however no ways were seen of fully achieving the green dream of doing away with cities altogether.

Among the most negative responses, this was one theme – reflecting the sheer lack of room in Britain to create a commune-based society *à la Kropotkin*: 'We're the elite here, we have nearly an acre per head, which is not possible for most people. We're very fortunate'. And 'There isn't room to live as we do. We're privileged'. Another was that the lifestyle would not appeal on a mass scale to the British, 'who like urban life and anonymity'. 'Not many could live as we do, relinquishing control over our personal life. It's an experiment, but not the answer for the whole world'. And, the lifestyle is 'so frantic – it's hardly ideal'. Or 'lots of people find it difficult to cope with all the power you're given'.

The British also would not like sharing income, one Findhornian pointed out:

> People get pocket money and so are separated from the products of their labour. But if people should be responsible for their own lives this means they should have their own money. Here they don't get enough money back from their work. It's too collective.

'If it was a better way then more people in Britain would do it', said a Lifespanner: 'In fact few do it, because sharing only really works when you're on rock bottom. The answers which communes give just aren't appropriate'. This cultural dimension came up repeatedly. Other cultures could be based on communes, we were told; Bangladeshis who came to Britain had a communal culture, and were trying to maintain it in a country where communes are but 'a drop in an otherwise unfriendly ocean'.

I used to think the answer was to live like this and people would join in. It's striking that in the eight years since I've been on the scene unemployment has risen, and this *hasn't* led to more people living communally: in fact the reverse.

The class barriers of British society were deemed relevant. For one thing, it is economically impossible for most people in Britain to buy enough land. But also:

> Unlike the middle class people who founded Laurieston, the working classes do not have a sense of being able to break out.

> There's a lot in the idea that communes are means whereby white Anglo-Saxon protestants solve their personal problems. You won't get communes on a large scale in Britain. The more difficult things get here, the less likely that people will want to go into communes. Class differences are a major problem. Communes in other countries – Israel and Scandinavia – are not predominantly middle class, as here. [In fact they are predominantly middle class nowadays – see BBC 1989.]

One Monkton Wyld member's class consciousness extended to suggesting that 'we're an example, but not a particularly sparkling one, and if we *did* become extreme enough to threaten the ruling elite then . . . well, the history of these places ends with the troops coming in'.

Others, too, saw communes as insufficiently 'threatening', in the sense of lacking dynamism and a high public profile. 'We're not strident'; 'People don't hear about us – British communes' publicity is pathetic'. And, 'The communes don't evolve because we keep going back to involve new people'.

There is a sense that at the root of this problem lies an isolation from the rest of the British people.

> To change society you need to be closely involved with people, but we're detached.

> Isolated communities won't have influence. It's important to change the system from within. We must get in touch with people and integrate, at least partly, with conventional society.

> I don't see us having a commune-ist society. In communes we have control over our *own* lives, but what's the point if we don't control society? Communes don't confront the power structure of society. Living like this is a political action, showing there's an alternative. But we can get out of touch with the problems that are out there. Now and then you need to go back and live in grotty conditions.

> The trouble about being in a community is that you can't get much involved outside. We grow our organic food but it doesn't change things. And when you've been here so long, you lose your way and can't see the wood for the trees. You assume that things outrageous and revolutionary are the norm. They are not the norm for outside. We're out of touch with real life.

This is a frequent charge, which outsiders usually level at communes that dare to suggest they might be part of a social change movement. It was echoed by a member of Redfield:

> To change society you must live in it. We just create our own society here.

Now we will explore how much this is true or whether there is in practice an attempt at effective outreach to the 'world outside'.

THE PRACTICE

Active outreach [7.1-11]

Nearly all our communes' founders imagined that their projects would in some way impact on wider society as well as benefitting those who were part of the group. This would be achieved particularly through educational projects (see Chapter 4). Today, just seven actively pursue outreach with any vigour; ironically, of the two most active, CAT and Findhorn, the latter did not start with outreach in mind. CAT's success in becoming a display centre for alternative technology 'to educate ordinary folk' has, on the face of it, been resounding. 55,000 visitors a year go to the site and see examples of soft energy generation, organic gardening and farming, recovery of energy and materials from 'waste', and recycling. They may visit the thriving wholefood restaurant and bookshop – or ask questions about community and cooperation, though people rarely do this latter. There are education services – *Green Teacher* magazine is run by people connected with the Quarry, and a new complex of timeshare chalets is used by schools doing some of their standard 12-15 year olds' curriculum studies on the site. There is also a virtually continuous schedule of educational courses – mainly practical – for schools, colleges and the public. Dulas Engineering develops 'electronics for environmentally sound purposes', especially for the Third World (e.g. portable windpowered battery systems for Mongolian nomadic herders). And there is a shop and cafe in nearby Machynlleth and an offshoot of Dulas Engineering in Aberystwyth.

Notwithstanding all this, a feeling that it was unviable for the 'enterprise' – for such it is – to stand still led to a decision in 1989 to pursue a massive growth project: in order, as coordinator Roger Kelly put it, to 'offer our visitors in the nineties a "total experience" that involves all their senses and emotions'. As well as upgrading the exhibits and expanding the cafe, there will be a centrepiece waterpowered cliff railway. The whole project is blessed by Prince Charles and the Welsh Tourist Board and supported by a £1m issue on the Stock Exchange and the attainment of 'public limited company' status (Blackwell 1990). While most CAT members have some misgivings about this 'Disneyfication' project, many are also acutely aware of being 'out of touch' with their public. 'People are interested, but they realise it's another tribe's domain'. The complex displays which describe the exhibits have to be radically changed in the new scheme, for they epitomise this barrier with the public:

> They are like books on walls. There are lots of intellectuals here who make the classic mistake of assuming that everyone else is at the same level.

> It's sad that CATians spend so much time living up to their principles that they don't have time for people outside – even the CAT children don't have a clue what it's all about, they're embarrassed about bringing their mates to the Quarry.

Hence the perceived need to put visitors in a more receptive mood and promote a 'soft' image, though one CATian wanted to sell 'harder political conclusions on collectivity'. Promoting this side of the Quarry's work is difficult. 'The truth is that simple things like eating together probably contribute more to energy saving than all the machines we use. But people like seeing new machines and gadgets. You can't put the community on displays', said Roger Kelly.

CAT also has the same problem as most other communes concerning relationships with local people. Overcoming a 'hippy in the hills' prejudice is exacerbated by the commune's position as an 'English' enclave in rural Wales. Some Quarry people think that relations with the locals are good – there is participation in local music making and the schools – and others think they are bad. 'It does not cross locals' minds to come and get our advice on matters like barn conversions and energy conservation', said one, while others thought there should be open days to promote organic farming and windmill use by local people. But local outreach is effective by comparison with other communes, partly because local people are employed at the Quarry and because they generally approve of the influx of tourists attracted by CAT.

Of the other 'outreach' communes considered here, Findhorn, Monkton Wyld, Lower Shaw and Laurieston produce a plethora of residential courses in deep ecology, therapy and healing, creative arts and related themes. To a large extent they are, unlike CAT, preaching to the converted, as many of their members admit.

Findhorn's outreach efforts are prodigious. The outreach department's brief is to 'share the Findhorn principles with wider society'. It promotes specialist publications (books and calendars) and a range of New Age paraphernalia. The audio-visual department promotes writing for TV and film to publicise the message, and 'New Age music' products. For visitors, there are youth programmes, tours, family weeks or caravan holidays. And on 'experience weeks', 'living in the community' months and being a 'departmental guest' you could pay, in 1988, £165 or £350 or £125 respectively, for the privilege of spending at least half your time working for your board and keep. 'Work is an integral part of life here, through which many spiritual lessons are learnt', says the brochure, perhaps warding off objections. 'For this reason the working sessions are an integral part of the programme'. Other central parts of the educational outreach are the two international conferences per year, and the residential workshops and courses. There were twenty-three of these in spring/summer 1988, costing £175 to £350, on topics like 'Nuclear Energy: New Clear Energy', 'Creating Your Own Reality', 'Devas, Fairies and Angels', 'Being a Couple' and 'Listening to Love', as well as on dance, song, art and theatre.

The object is to demonstrate 'what it is like to work every day with love and light'; however, 'we're open to anyone, but a lot can't afford to come to us'. Mindful of this, some interviewees were unhappy about exclusivity and felt a need to reach out to '*Mail* and *Sun* readers' by speaking to them without jargon, and generally 'interfacing' with society – not to mention influencing mass building firms like Barratt and Wimpey: 'Get them here cooperating with nature and building ecologically sound homes'.

Monkton Wyld's courses are similarly spiritually focused on deep ecology, rebirthing, 'Education Otherwise' (helping people to teach their children at home), co-counselling, Tai Chi, circle dance and 'The Art of Loving', for example. Their twenty-two courses on offer between February and September 1988 cost between £30 and £180 each. As with Findhorn, there was the concern about exclusivity, and not bringing in enough city people or the underprivileged. Also, relationships with locals are tricky, partly because of the 'tearaway' reputation of the original school and partly because the courses do not appeal: 'Our one-day workshop on aromatherapy for locals was not successful. Reichian therapy is threatening to the man in the street'. But efforts are made; a winter solstice ceilidh and a jumble sale had brought people in.

Laurieston and Lower Shaw told similar stories. The former's 'People Centre' ran twenty four courses in 1988 (costing from £50 to £180) on Gay Men, Selfheal Training, Polarity Energetics, Reichian Bodywork, The Wildman Within and Deep Ecology. By no means was there total belief in this outreach attempt, which partly involves merely making premises available to outside groups, and when our interviews were occasionally punctuated by the far-off sound of visitors' 'primal screaming' this provoked wry mirth. Some communards here, and elsewhere, felt that

> more than outreach, it's important to preserve our way of life. I'd *like* others to do it but I don't want to proselytise it, or spend more time defending my way of life. I don't want lots of new people looking at us. I get fed up of explaining and repeating myself.

This does however contrast with those, particularly in the low- or no-outreach group, who mainly felt endangered by isolation, and wanted outreach. In addition, Lower Shaw people, who again facilitated but did not organise their courses, felt encroached on by suburban Swindon. 'We've lost country, fields and privacy. A pagan men's group with ritual, drums and way out things is not now so possible'. But there is a desire to relate locally, which the yoga, massage and shiatsu, craft, meditation and circle dance weekends (nine in spring 1988 at £30 to £40 each) do not do.

Lifespan's outreach used to hinge mainly on hosting visitors – 150 per year – and working in Sheffield's feminist, anti-nuclear and anti-racist groups. But now there is a 'lack of time' – a constant theme here because of the energy needed for the printing business. This at least enables other radical groups to publicise their message, but now conventional economic pressures mean that some work is taken on which is considered unethical.

Something similar partly applies to ZAP. In 1990, nearly three years after the first interviews there, we learned more about its shift of focus. The desire to change society towards 'green economics' remains, but the educational programme is much diminished. Selling food is now the means whereby it is hoped to divert money away from the mainstream market economy and into the informal, 'alternative' sector. The outlets are a wholefood cafe in Birmingham (low-cost vegan and vegetarian, for people without much money), and a travelling catering business, selling at festivals (such as Glastonbury) and other gatherings, like motor-bike rallies. Most of the food is 'ethical', much coming from ZAP's own allotments. But there is less fastidiousness here than there used to be (see Chapter 5); chocolate bars are now a sideline, and some food comes from tin cans. Much attention is focused on making money. The core group exploit themselves, aiming to pay themselves a basic wage and then to use profits to support other cooperatives in the 'Radical Routes' network. At Manchester there is veganic gardening, at Northampton a collectively run school, in Hull a house restoration concern for the unemployed and homeless. And the original purpose of buying more houses to add to the network also remains.

Outreach among the other communes is sporadic and sometimes half-hearted. 'When people visit and know us, bits of what we're doing rub off on them' was a typical but lame reaction to this question [7.11]. Or there was commonly reference to interaction with the community through sending children to the local school, where the commune children can be regarded suspiciously by their school mates. But most people in this group conceded that they do less than the original founding group intended, or that anyway the community is there principally to benefit the people in it and not outsiders. Crabapple's wholefood shop in Shrewsbury centre is slightly different, being seen as a 'publicity centre for green values'. Both Crabapple and Redfield have run poorly-attended open days. On the whole the groups are too busy with the need to survive daily and earn enough money to keep going. Individuals do still get involved with local pressure groups, but this has fallen off, and ideas about actively supporting urban political movements have floundered through the problem of transport to and from a rural location.

A sense of isolation and guilt at all this may persist:

> Communities like this should be in cities and be more politically oriented.

> Our purpose is to set an example to those outside in the move to a voluntary, decentralised Britain, but we're so busy keeping ourselves going we don't have the time.
>
> We need more *social* contact with outside.
>
> Facilities like ours should be used by the local community.
>
> We should be less insular, and have people with jobs who are changing the world staying here.
>
> Here, I'm almost back in the rut which I was in in conventional society.

And there is the persistent reference to concern, in these rural centres, about the relationship with the locals. Some people are not overtly worried:

> The hippy image haunts us. We *do* use drugs and people outside don't respect this.

Others are worried:

> We have a negative image with some people round here. It's partly our fault: we've earned a hippy reputation. A lot of the original people dressed badly – Earth mother stuff, ragged clothes. There has been no attempt to face up to the social context here, which is conservative.

Over the decades the balance of opinion about the desirability of meshing in with conventional society has probably swung away from the perspective of the first statement towards that of the second – part of a larger process in the tension between changing society and being changed by it.

Nudging the already-converted

Evidence is slight that the outreach communes are actually changing many people's views or lifestyles beyond their doors. The two major communes, Findhorn and CAT, provided interesting contrasts in their attitude towards this issue [9.1-2]. The former's members were often initially quite certain and strident in asserting that they were affecting people: it is a position which followed logically from their millenarianism. But even Findhornians became circumspect when probed about their effect on the grand pattern of social change. Thus: 'Humanity is on the verge of a major evolutionary step' is followed by 'but we do appeal to a very small, select group', and 'A big shift in consciousness is happening on the planet' becomes, on further reflection, 'Maybe I'm changing and nothing else is'. Of course, many visitors and students on the courses do pass through the site annually. This provokes some optimism that 'normal everyday people, from housewives to kids to businesspeople from the US and Europe' are being affected, and that 'it's spreading – the people who come here say they're working on friends and relatives'. But others are aware of a large 'preaching to the converted' element, and that 'the people who come here are limited to white, well-educated middle classes'. Perhaps most typical of this commune was the response: 'The evidence is in the way *I* have changed – but I also see people changing and growing around me . . . I hope for the hundredth monkey thing'.

Quarry members were far less sanguine and more down-to-earth about their experiences with a less select public. And CAT was the only commune to have attempted some market research. Their view of this was laced with typical Quarry downbeat humour. 'We have cards that visitors fill in voluntarily. This produces a totally biased sample of interested, articulate people who like filling in cards'. Eight out of ten responses had said 'interesting' and were positive, but the Quarry people's concern was more about those who had not filled in cards. 'On the whole I'm sure people don't like, respect or admire our work . . . I've overheard things and seen the way people look. We have done surveys, but people are too polite'. 'We don't impinge in the slightest on people who control our lives, except perhaps Prince Charles', said one, but another pointed out, correctly, that establishment firms and decision makers are now more receptive to alternative technology than when the Quarry started. The renewables debate is on the agenda and CAT has certainly played a role in it, partly through constant exposure on the media, as witness the increasing market for CAT's products.

The view that 'this is just a Mecca for the converted' is probably too harsh and less justified here than for any other of our communes. Certainly, our own ten-year experience of taking classes of undergraduates on short courses to the Quarry suggests that its members have a great talent for reaching out to 'ordinary', un-green and suspicious people. This is achieved through a mixture of frankness, seeing issues from the perspective of the conventional wisdom but quietly insisting on the need for change, admission of obvious human frailty and respect for others. The great majority of the students approached CAT over this period as bigoted lions, only to leave a few days later like lambs – if not converted, at least more open-minded and curious.

It is perhaps only in the latter state of mind that people should visit most other communes. The well-known phenomenon of 'visitor alienation', coupled sometimes with an outward appearance of scruffy and unkempt premises, could otherwise turn off the uninitiated for ever. Once sympathetic visitors do come, the analysis we heard at Monkton Wyld seems to hold for all the communes:

> We get a lot of feedback from people who go through personal change after coming here. We're having an effect. We haven't changed wider society much but have made *visitors* think about their lives. And people respond to our example by asking to live here, or coming as volunteers. We influence them on lots of small points, like income sharing, which they see can work.

But, the important rider to all this is that it concerns 'people *already* looking in our direction. We give them a nudge'. Anything more than this seems unrealistic, pious hopefulness and a minority view. For example:

> The very *existence* of our community must have made some marginal difference.
>
> I'm setting an example to the people who know me.
>
> If we felt it wasn't having any good effect we wouldn't be doing it.

BEING CHANGED: 'THATCHERISATION' OF THE COMMUNES

As this study progressed, an aspect of the dialectic of social change became clearer. In the interplay of opposites which move society through change – the interaction of the 'thesis' and 'antithesis' – the wisdom and lifestyles of conventional society are at odds with those of the counterculture. But because this is a dialectical relationship between the two, they are constantly affecting and are, indeed, part of each other. Hence, in this issue of social change we cannot merely examine how much communes might change wider society: we must also consider the reverse, a 'counter-revolutionary' process where communes may change in sympathy with trends in conventional society. By analogy, we have seen how the resurgence of 'free' market liberalism in the 1980s set the agenda for its opponents in the political mainstream, as witness the ludicrous and embarrassing ideological contortions of Kinnockite Labourism to capture the 'middle ground'. So too has the agenda of the counterculture changed in the eighties, mirroring the shift in the 'centre of gravity' of political debate. A trend that we can conveniently call 'Thatcherisation' has set in.

We noted four main related elements of this trend, reflecting directions in mainstream society. They are privatisation, rampant individualism, materialism and profit seeking via managerial efficiency. Of course, such trends can partly be accounted for by the attainment of 'late youth/middle age' by a substantial group of communards, for as most of us get older, radicals or not, we are more drawn towards creature comforts. But a substantial part of the trend seems to relate to the ideological direction of wider society.

Privatisation and individualism

Many communards have tended to withdraw from the 'public' to the 'private' realm. This partly means a retreat from the high political-ideological profile of the founding wave and its evangelising intent to change society. It also means a loss of collective activities, focusing more on the importance of the individual and relegating elements of community and sharing.

The most marked example of the latter has been at Laurieston, which stopped being a commune and cooperative in 1987 and became solely a cooperative. At that time eleven people lived as the commune within the wider housing coop, sharing income, and six others lived in the spacious grounds of the large house or its outbuildings, non-communally. But six commune members 'wanted their own car, and not to income share or eat communally all the time or have rotas', we were told. The process of breakup and change of direction was achieved without the mass exodus which many communes periodically experience, even though some communards (who had already determined on leaving) did fight to retain the commune. 'It was smooth, not catastrophic, through a carefully organised series of meetings. This was gratifying. Laurieston's a very mature place with smart, intelligent people. There are no fools here'. It was the culmination of a gradual process of disenchantment with 'excessive communality', the advantages of which became taken for granted while the disadvantages became magnified. A Lauriestonian described both by reference to a previous time spent living in Crabapple from 1980 to 1984. On the plus side:

> There were good exciting things about it. You could work through frustrations and the chaos, filth and crap. There was a feeling of pig shit and contentment. You had to be involved in the basics like cooking. There was caring and nurturing and people got together to share problems. Sharing was a matter of course.

Then bad feelings crept in. They were

> to do with personal irritation between folk and petty irritations – the 'top of the toothpaste syndrome' – and lack of privacy. I couldn't move without telling another dozen people why. And I felt resentful about having to share income with people who did not work as much as me.

Similarly, after the communal phase at Laurieston, people

> felt constrained and wanted to be individuals. Most people didn't like each other very much. The worker did not like the lazy person; the single person did not like the family.

And there had been a gradual slippage where people found it 'more convenient' to work outside for cash rather than in the community. People no longer wanted to follow socialist principles and eliminate income disparities. The new liberalism was encapsulated by one Lauriestonian who had joined when she was sure it was not going to be a commune, on the grounds that she did not want to share income with those who lacked the same 'money sense' as her; and another who said, 'We're cooperative, not communal. We're free as individuals – free to drive our own car'.

On our first visit in the experimental year, 1988, communality was still clearly apparent, with fifty per cent of meals being taken together (though there was also a 'sense of relief' that 'we can have our own breakfast and tube of toothpaste'). On another visit, in 1990, we had the impression of less communality, with independent living units well established in the house, each with separate kitchen and eating arrangements. Only those who ran the People Centre still took communal meals to any degree.

At Canon Frome, too, people spoke of a retreat from sharing; the community had become a collection of separate living units, with a common meal only once a week. At Redfield and CAT many meals are still taken together, as are grand policy decisions. But some

Redfieldians bemoaned a loss of collective responsibility and purpose. 'I thought communal responsibility would be indigenous when I joined, but it isn't: It's all down to the individual in the end'; 'People originally wanted communally to promote ideas, but now, for most, it's just a home'.

A similar turning inwards 'from changing the world to therapy and personal relations' was colourfully described at Monkton Wyld:

> Everyone is really into themselves. They have no bloody time for anyone else . . . [the second-generation communards are] a self-orienting, free-choosing, ecologically-minded, freedom-living, anti-establishment bunch of layabouts.

Materialism and creature comforts

There is growing desire for the creature comforts associated with the high-consumption lifestyles which radical greens often decry. This extends to a deepening concern with appearances, so that 'pig shit' and 'contentment' no longer go together. Though still a minority of the communes were tidy and 'attractive' in a way which would appeal to middle class suburban values, some communards across the board hankered for such attractiveness: 'Look at the state of this place: it's a disgrace', was heard more than once.

In Laurieston, again, the move to Thatcherite values seemed well advanced:

> There's a general tendency to more materialism and cash income. We've done being freaky: we want to be normal now.

> I'm not critical about conventional society. In many ways I'm still living in conventional society.

While, at Findhorn:

> We're more establishment. We desire more material things and accept that it's OK to make life more comfortable. It helps others to have a living if you buy things.

And at Canon Frome:

> We don't want squalor, sharing a dirty bath or kitchen. We don't want poverty, or to live with free-riding ex-hippies, exploiting people they live with. *They* want material things too, but pay lip service to alternative ideas.

However, others see hypocrisy as extending beyond 'hippies' to middle class communards. At Laurieston we heard:

> They say they'd like to care for the environment but can't afford to – in order to defend their driving to Sainsburys and buying avocados from Israel.

At Lifespan:

> Things that are supposed to be important about living here take a subsidiary role because we spend a lot of time increasing our standard of living and developing the material foundation of the place . . . This is obviously what people want. The temptation of money is very strong. Living here is very different from what I imagined it would be.

While at Crabapple:

> The founders were very anti-materialist – they were more radical than us. As with most communes, we have moved closer to the society we live in. Communes are less radical but more comfortable places now, and more appealing to people outside.

Similarly, at Monkton Wyld, 'ideas of simplicity have changed. It was spartan and cheap to visit in earlier days. Now it's comfortable and there's no self-sacrifice to principles'.

Someone who had joined Lifespan from a lesbian separatist commune noted that 'by comparison, we do nothing here to improve on the patriarchal capitalist culture of conventional society – we're hooked in to consumerist values. Women here are strong but are competing to be more masculine'.

Profit-making and managerial efficiency

We have already noted how ZAP, in 1988, anarchistically rejected conventional market economics. Now, in 1990, it has moved towards acceptance of a perceived need to make profits in order to promote an economic thinking which relegates profit-making in favour of environmental and social goals. So far so 'good', though ZAP could be treading a well worn path on which the next step, for many other communes, has come when the 'need' to make money to achieve financial 'viability' has largely taken over from the ideological purpose.

Hence, at Lower Shaw:

> We now do financially less risky things than we used to. What we have in common is just that we can manage to live here . . . There's no common ideology now. It's got more hazy. Now we are primarily a business . . . we're very confused . . . we don't know what the purpose of what we're doing is.

While at Lifespan:

> The print business success has really confused a lot of people. It's come at a time when we've started behaving in a way which is very acceptable to the state. We're doing exactly what Thatcher's Britain wants us to do, which is running a successful small business, working long hours for low wages and not taking any state subsidy. We're no longer idealistic . . . realism has set in.

For some, rejection of state subsidy is largely pragmatic: it is now more difficult than a decade ago to get it. For others, the rejection is more ideological. For instance at Laurieston:

> There's a part of everyone here which wants things to be more commercial. People from a middle class wealthy background, especially, like to earn cash and think it's wrong to get state money. 'Individual liberty', 'entrepreneurial spirit' and Thatcherism have come to Laurieston. Growing herbs for sale, in a way which erodes communality, is the latest idea.

While at Findhorn the 'free' market liberal version of 'taking responsibility for your own life' is celebrated:

> We're much more part of mainstream society than we used to be: it's not that we've changed so much, the rest of the world is catching up.

Many Findhornians have left the commune to become independent from its income sharing element (everyone gets pocket money – £75 a month in 1988 plus £35 per child – though some have private incomes). They live in the local areas as part of the small business complex attached to the Foundation. 'This is good', said one on-siter, 'Capitalism grows here'. The associated capitalist feature of growth and agglomeration to large monopolies would, however, be avoided 'because Findhorn capitalism is practised with spirituality, whereas Thatcherism does it without compassion or spirituality'. However, Thatcherite language has certainly crept in. 'I want to get out to people beyond here, to market the product', said the producer of New Age music albums: 'You've got to put entertainment in the message'.

At CAT, however, some members still talk uneasily of their basic purpose having been 'compromised because of the need to make a profit', especially by the Disneyfication scheme and share issue referred to above:

> The contradiction for CAT [as for most other communes discussed here] is that its survival depends on economic success in conventional terms. So, day to day, ideology is of no benefit. Agreed, this *is* ecocapitalism, and there's not now a lot of difference between CAT and the Body Shop . . . It's a capitalistic community in a tourist area. With that business opportunity it's doing very nicely.

For longer serving Quarry people like Peter Harper this retreat from CAT's anarchistic roots has been essential to avoid the failure associated with so many other seventies radical ventures (Landry et al 1985). He describes how 'things which haven't stood the test of time' have been abandoned, including

> self sufficiency . . . radical arcadianism . . . deindustrialisation . . . beards and sandals . . . don't-need-experts-it's-all-mystification-anyone-can-do-anything . . . don't-bother-about-organisational-structures-things-will-work-themselves-out-spontaneously . . . capitalists invariably have top hats and cigars and their sole purpose is to exploit workers.

In their place have been adopted 'ideas or practices we wouldn't have been seen dead with ten years ago'. They include some very Thatcherite elements:

> profits . . . interest . . . markets and marketing . . . the importance of good management . . . the bourgeois virtues of thrift, punctuality, order, cleanliness, due process and efficiency (Harper 1990).

While these elements of his list might be part of some green visions, they could also be interpreted as a retreat from green radicalism – particularly that anarchistic form which insists that process is necessarily as important as end result. This would hold to the value of consensus decisions as against 'representative democracy', even if 'efficiency' is the price to pay. At CAT the former still ostensibly holds for major decisions, but Harper places the latter on his 'acceptable' list. It certainly seems that in many communes power has devolved from the consensual mass meeting to specialist 'departments', 'topic groups' or whatever. This may have been necessary for good management, but it may also have led down a slippery slope towards Thatcherite notions of power being acceptable – as is obviously so in the response of one Lauriestonian, which might have been scripted by the Iron Lady herself:

> You shouldn't worry if someone has more power than you. Power is responsibility, it's work, it's energy. You *need* certain folks to take responsibility. We all have our little places.

CHAPTER 7
A vanguard for Ecotopia?

We have found that the communes we visited do have overwhelmingly green values and attitudes which they do try to put into practice. Therefore communes *could* be a significant, even major, part of a green society – of Ecotopia. But they probably will *not* be so, nor are they likely to constitute a leading edge in any move towards radical social change.

Chapter 4 showed that when these communes were set up, mostly in the seventies, many of their founders shared the concerns of the time about imminent environmental crisis and limits to growth. Such concerns were part of the first wave of post-war popular environmentalism – an outgrowth of peace, hippy and other sixties countercultural movements, of which the second wave came in the mid eighties.

The founders generally saw their communes as part of a trend of needed social change towards a greener society, a trend that also implied more social justice and better social relations. As such, they echoed the nineteenth and early twentieth century back-to-the-land movements, with their emphases on organic farming and gardening, self-sufficiency, holistic lifestyles and mysticism, mixed in with utopian socialist or anarchist ideas. Though anti-urban, the seventies communards were not escapist romantics, as witness the strength of their intent to set up educational centres: they wanted to proselytise with their ideas and their example.

Since then, with successive waves of newcomers and a fall in the numbers recruited, evangelising zeal and ideological intensity dissipated, while the importance of individual fulfilment through escaping the alienation of mainstream society – especially the nuclear family – increased. In the late eighties there was a further drift towards loss of collectivity and sharing, the rise of private over public domains, and a perceived need to earn a financial surplus, some of which would be spent on increasing creature comforts. Despite, or as part of, these changes, the communards have some very green ideas, and have been strongly influenced by green writers and media coverage. They strongly support radical ecocentric positions on human-nature interdependence and ethical treatment of nature. Other popular green ideas – of environmental crisis and of limits to growth, tinged with Gaia, mysticism and anti-urbanism – are also widely held.

And there is an impressive list of ecologically sound practices which most communards have some commitment to (see Table 16). They try to be environmentally aware in what they do, while their institutional context of sharing and low material lifestyles also militates in favour of ecologically sound practices.

THE POTENTIAL FOR CHANGING WIDER SOCIETY

However, by their own admission they often fall short in living up to this awareness. As ever there are particular difficulties with what we call 'second order' environmentally sound practices to do with harmonious, loving, peaceful and cooperative social relations. All this constitutes one form of impediment to being effective agents for social change. It means that the 'example' which communards might want to give to wider society (of course, some of them do not particularly want to provide an example but others do) is diminished in its exemplariness. Therefore their credibility as part of an Ecotopian blueprint is also lessened.

Secondly, we find that contact with a wider audience through effective outreach is generally lacking. This is the same problem which Rigby identified in the seventies. As he said, it stems partly from a failure to channel enough energies into making connections with other radical social change movements (such connections seem to have diminished), and partly through being so thin on the ground that there is not enough person power left over from the pressures of daily living to spare for concerted outreach. As a Glaneirw communard succinctly put it:

> Glaneirw, Canon Frome, Crabapple – we're all suffering from lack of people. This problem of insufficient support must be solved before communes can play their rightful part in leading the way to a new society.

A further criterion of effectiveness as agents for social change concerns ideological clarity. Here again, the communes fall short.

Most no longer have a clearly defined ideology of which they constitute a lived example, nor do they worry much about ideological cohesion. There are advantages for internal relationships in not doing so, but it is correspondingly less clear to the outside world what they are trying to achieve.

Related to this is a fourth criterion of effectiveness: how much will people sacrifice individual desires for a collective goal? By and large, the 'possessive individualism' and shunning of collectivity which, according to Abrams and McCulloch, sixties communities displayed, reasserted itself in the late eighties. This is part of a potentially major weakness which the communards seem to share with much of the wider green movements. This lies in their theoretical and practical approach to social change. As Chapter 6 shows, it is idealist rather than materialist, so it emphasises changing people's ideas and values and relegates the importance of changing, for the majority in society, the material reality on which those values are founded. It also favours non-structuralist, behavioural/psychological explanations of what is wrong, which revolve around assumptions of hubris and original sin, rather than interpreting conventional anti-social anti-ecological values and behaviour more in terms of their supporting social and economic structures. And it regards the individual rather than the collective as the fundamental unit of social change. Some objections to this idealist-individualist-consensual approach have been outlined in Chapter 3.

Overweaning individualism seems paradoxical for people who live in communes. But it is understandable when one recalls the middle class liberal backgrounds and upbringing of so many communards, and that, inevitably, people will bring with them to the collective life the attitudinal baggage of their previous conventional existence. The privateness of that existence with its counter-revolutionary implications are captured in Sennett's (1978 pp4-6) eloquent prose:

> Each person's self has become his principal burden; to know oneself has become an end, instead of a means through which one knows the world . . . The obsession with person at the expense of persons is like a filter which discolours our rational understanding of society; it obscures the continuing importance of class in advanced industrial society; it leads us to believe community is an act of mutual self disclosure . . . Masses of people are concerned with their single life histories and particular emotions as never before; this concern has proved to be a trap rather than a liberation . . . Western societies are moving from something like an other-directed condition to an inner-

directed condition – except that in the midst of self-absorptions no-one can say what is inside. [This is a] romantic search for self-realisation.

Sennett (pp10-11) describes the state of narcissism which 'enters systematically and perversely' into conventional Western human relations. It is an obsession, in dealings with others, with the question: 'What does this person, that environment, mean to *me*', and it is part of a search for *self* identity. Hence relations of communality with strangers for social ends are not really possible. Group activity and identity, every time, is 'perverted by the psychological question': that is, people cannot relate unless they get to know each other as persons, or individuals. This process involves acts of reciprocal self-revelation, mutual 'open-ness' through disclosure of intimate details about the self, and the like. Without them, relationships cannot proceed. Impersonal relationships seem to offer nothing of value. Sennett points out that this is a process analogous with 'market exchange' where one is calculating one's own benefit all the time, a process based on the same assumptions as material exchange in capitalist society. Seabrook (1990 p12) also thinks this, and he draws attention to the very vocabulary of this perversion of human relations under market liberal philosophy. It resounds with notions of market exchange: we talk of the 'returns' we get from relationships, and whether they pay 'dividends' or are 'profitless'; of our 'stock' with others and our 'assets' of looks or brains; and indeed whether we are in the 'market' for an affair. This is perhaps not *gemeinschaft* communality, but *gesellschaft*: seeking a mutually beneficial contract with others, and like all contracts there is usually an expiry date, and we look over our shoulders to see if we should have got, or could get, a better deal elsewhere. It is not that enriching synthesis of the self with others which true communism is about. To the extent that there is a sense of collectivity – a *gemeinschaft* – it is what Sennett calls 'destructive *gemeinschaft*': based on collective *being* rather than collective action in pursuit of true economic class interest.

The narcissism of such relationships, says Sennett, is also underlain by insecure notions of self justification and ratification: concern with the question 'Am I good enough/adequate in the eyes of others?' And this, he further points out, is the 'most corrosive element of the Protestant ethic', far removed from any 'alternative', more liberating set of values.

We came away from many (but not all) interviews with the impression that many personal relationships in communes were indeed conducted very much within these bourgeois parameters. This was especially true where New Ageism was prominent. Here there may well be what Sennett calls a 'discoloured' sense of community based over much on 'mutual self disclosure' and a world view posited on the self as starting point, i.e. on the liberal values of the conventional culture. This was the essence of objections which the doing-things-together school raised against the relationships-by-exploring-feelings school: the first desired relationships based on collective action, the second emphasised collective being and the abandonment of social-economic 'text' (Sennett p238).

THE CLASS PROBLEM

This study also supports Abrams and McCulloch's findings about the class background of the communards, and confirms that they feel alienated from capital but lack affinity with labour and its tradition of collective political action. Again, there is a strong parallel with the wider green movement.

Scott (1990 pp145-7) describes the paradoxical nature of this for greens who are, he says, largely third-generation displaced working class. They are from relatively privileged but not over-wealthy backgrounds, and highly educated; but lacking power and excluded from political negotiation. In neo-corporate states like Britain (and even more strongly on the European mainland), Scott says, power still lies largely with groups such as industrialists or trades unionists. Decision making is still technocratic, based on what has been a stable agenda for a long time (in which economic growth is the main item). Real disagreement has been swallowed up in the apparent consensus between narrowly circumscribed groups from capital and labour.

Excluded groups therefore tend to mobilise at grass-roots level. Having a high proportion of tertiary sector white collar professionals, they make up pressure groups on behalf of a range of causes: civil rights, women's liberation, peace and ecology – what sociologists call 'new social movements'. And they feed into the new 'classless' political parties like the Liberal Democrats and Greens, and into the lifestyle movement of which communes are an ultimate expression.

Perceptively, Scott suggests that their predilection for green causes is strongly rooted in ecology's anti-industrialism, which is therefore anti the main actors in capitalist industrial society and pro the new middle classes. In Ecotopia, by contrast, these people – academics, teachers, carers and community activists and planners – would effectively be the most politically influential people. If Scott's materialist analysis is right, then, it is no coincidence that so many writers and commentators on green issues finish their works by stressing the need for more research, education and caring, and that these activities should have more status and financial recognition. Take, for instance, the call which Trudgill (1990), a soils and environmental researcher and academic, makes for more research and teaching as the lynchpin of a strategy to solve environmental problems.

Scott's conclusion is that, paradoxically, new social movements like the greens will be agents for social reform, but not *transformation*. For although they seem to challenge society's whole basis, they do not really do so. Instead, they articulate the grievances of excluded groups in an attempt to end their exclusion and gain acceptance. This being so (and it *is* a moot point), integration into mainstream society and the ultimate disappearance of the movement would become the criterion, not of failure, but of success.

Where communes might fit into such an analysis is further discussed below. But we have indeed found that their effectiveness as agents of social transformation rather than reform is questionable. For reasons well documented elsewhere (Weston 1986, Ashton 1985, Ryle 1988, Dobson 1990), their politics of wanting to by-pass rather than confront the powerful economic vested interests that are ingrained in socio-political structures are not likely to destroy those interests.

More than this, however, we have already seen that a process of assimilation, if not total integration, is in fact happening.

ASSIMILATION INTO CONVENTIONAL SOCIETY

Perhaps the greatest potential barrier to communes acting as agents for radical rather than reformist social change towards an Ecotopian society is the process whereby they become absorbed into conventional society, that culture to which they have previously run counter.

We have discussed how it is inevitable and appropriate that any counterculture will be coloured by the mores of its opposite – 'conventional' or 'mainstream' society – in a dialectical interaction which produces social change. The problem arises, however, when that process goes a stage further, and the counterculture is actually nullified – coopted or gobbled up – by its opposite. Bookchin (1980 pp12-13) put it thus:

> The market has absorbed not only every aspect of production, consumption, community life and family ties into the buyer-seller nexus; it has permeated the opposition to capitalism with bourgeois cunning, compromise and careerism. It has done this by restating the very meaning of opposition to conform with the system's own parameters of critique and discourse.

Radical ecocentrism does constitute 'opposition to capitalism', and many elements of the capitalist philosophy of market liberalism are now being taken on board by at least some communes. The logical corollary of this is that such communes no longer constitute opposition to capitalism. They have abandoned their original intended role as part of the counterculture to capitalism.

There seem to be three stages by which such a position is reached:

1. Intent to *bypass the system* by setting up an alternative social and economic organisation as self-sufficient and independent as possible from mainstream society. This anarchist approach intends that mainstream society will ultimately be brought down and changed through more and more people joining in the bypassing processes. For this to happen it is held essential that revolutionary thought and deed will not be compromised by any attempt to make a financial surplus to sustain daily life. Any discomforts, practical failures or incompetences which stem from this lack of 'realism' are deemed a fair price to pay for preserving an ideal.

2. Intent to *use the system* as a means to subversive ends. This can mean a range of things, from drawing social security benefits to working on purely income-generating projects while also working towards the ultimate goal of overthrowing the paternalistic state and the materialistic society which it supports. At this stage there is still a clear vision of ends, although it is convincingly and rationally argued that compromises are necessary and justified in the cause of an ultimate revolution which may take a long time before it comes about.

3. Less consciously, perhaps, becoming *part of the system* through acting increasingly in response to its demands, so that eventually the values of the system are taken on. As Chapter 6 suggests, a growing

realisation of a 'need' to generate financial surplus to achieve things, together with a more down-to-earth tiring of constant material deprivation – these have played their part in 'Thatcherising' the communes.

Some have completed this *Animal Farm*-like sequence and have accepted the liberal values of rampant individualism, profit chasing, abandonment of sharing and collectivity, and privatisation.

One communard described communes as now 'divided between the more radical left/green types and those which have become privatised'. Another confirmed that this process basically involves a left-right political distinction:

> The socialists want a caring community and say *we* should take responsibility if something goes wrong with the individual: conservatives sympathise, but say they have their own problems. They have pulled out from collectivity, own cars and houses and go on holidays.

Of the communes studied here, Glaneirw and PIC seem to be somewhere between stages 1 and 2, Redfield and Crabapple are at stage 2. Lifespan, CAT, LSF, Monkton Wyld and Findhorn are further along, between stages 2 and 3, and Canon Frome and Laurieston have virtually arrived at stage 3. The last moved perceptibly 'rightwards' in the less than two years between our original visit and a revisit in 1990, while in the same period ZAP also moved, from stage 1 towards stage 2.

The implication is that those at stage 3 are no longer actors in the movement to establish a *radical* ecological society, while the group of five communes behind them could soon cease to be. This does not imply that they will not continue to play a part in social *reform*. Findhorn, Monkton Wyld and LSF, for instance, may successfully occupy a niche in the green consumer/New Age movements, usefully helping to 'clean up' capitalist society, especially spiritually. CAT may perform a similar role, though at the more practical and technological end. As such, its acceptance into the bosom of the establishment may be all the quicker (see Dobson 1990 pp147-9). Perhaps it has already arrived: PLC status and the £1m share offer in 1990 were augmented by the ultimate in assimilation: a July Sunday morning slot on comfortable, middle class Radio 4's 'Week's Good Cause' appeal. (It did however net £8,000, which no sane revolutionary would sneeze at!)

Assimilation of opposition is, par excellence, a process used by the British establishment to avoid the excesses of popular revolutionary zeal occasionally experienced elsewhere in the world. But it is by no means an exclusively British phenomenon.

Take, for example, the kibbutzim in Israel. They started in 1909, and developed as attempts at new forms of human settlement; socialist collectives based on the ideas of social justice, self-determination and self-motivation, with no bosses, no wages and common ownership of the means of production. Many of their intended features were similar to those highly regarded by seventies ecological communes: participatory democracy, lack of hierarchy, people before profits (e.g. willingness to employ aged people even though this reduces 'efficiency'), the extended family/tribe and small-scale organisation (humility before nature or respect for women were not conspicuous, however). Their claim was to have created a society without class, poverty, crime, unemployment, homelessness or snobbery, and in the 1980s this prospect attracted 128,000 people to live on 280 kibbutzim. Now, however, much of this has changed and the kibbutzim have increasingly taken on the features of the society in which they are set (BBC 1989). The original desire, to change that context, has gone, and people join largely to enhance their own quality of life, as an escape from a competitive and soul-less urban life. Longstanding communards assert that among this new generation the original cause has become an embarrassment, and real socialism and community are disappearing. Most kibbutzim have become materialistic, and increasingly part of the surrounding economy (hiring outside workers for cash, for example).

Many kibbutzniks complain about working too hard for insufficient money, but they may have their own private sources and bank accounts. Indeed, some groups are trying to save their kibbutzim from bankruptcy or lack of new members through individual incentives. No longer are people 'confined' by a pocket money system, they can earn wages for doing at least part of their formerly unpaid work. The implications are heretical, involving rejection of a collective discipline in favour of the needs and wishes of individuals. Indeed, one kibbutz now earns money from a fashion and costume design business and holds fashion shows for its own members – catering for individual wants to an extent that was previously shunned and regarded as ideologically unsound. The parallels between all this and the individualism, privatism and conventionality now appearing in our sample of communes (Chapter 6) are obvious.

COMMUNES AND THE NEW SOCIAL MOVEMENTS DEBATE

All of this is of considerable interest to social change theorists. As Chapter 2 demonstrated, academic writers on green issues have queued up in the past to hail communes as harbingers of eco-Nirvana. And, sometimes embarrassingly, many still do it. Thus Young's (1990) *Post-Environmentalism* came out just when CAT's share issue was getting maximum media exposure: however that book described alternative communities, particularly CAT (plc), as testimony 'to the survival and re-growth of an inherently subversive ideology in the minds of the Chernobyl generation' (p175). The author wrote: 'A large number of experimental and educational organisations in Western society do excellent business undermining the ethos of capitalism. The Centre for Alternative Technology... is one of the best known'.

Young could be described as 'post-modernist'. This term means many different things in different contexts. Here it implies an end to the search for grand theories of history, and of how social change happens – an end, therefore, to the 'goals and theories of the Enlightenment'. No longer are laws of social motion and change believed in. Rather, the post-modern, post-industrial society will be created by a plurality of groups and forces, each operating within their own contexts and not part of any grand movement or design, conscious or unconscious. These groups are seen as not necessarily driven by rational considerations (such as the utilitarian attempt to maximise material wellbeing). Indeed the 'fight of women and gays for a legitimate social and sexual identity outside the parameters of male heterosexual vision and the search for alternatives in our relationship with nature' are regarded by post-modernists as a 'critical deconstruction of Enlightenment rationalism' (A Huyssen, cited in Frankel 1987 p184).

Of course, one grand theory of history is that of Marxism, where the conflict between economic classes in society is regarded as the motor of social change, and the working classes (more strictly the proletariat – those who have only their labour to sell) will play the major role in instigating the revolutionary transition from capitalism to socialism and communism. Many social commentators, while they have reacted against the conventional functionalist/pluralist model of society which underlies the parliamentary system, have also expressed doubts about this Marxist model of social change, though they largely accept Marx's analysis of capitalism. In particular, there is dissatisfaction with the notion of the working classes as social change agents (see, for instance, Gorz 1982). Some have therefore rejected class analysis in Marxist terms, without necessarily or totally rejecting Marxism's structuralist approach or its 'modernist' search for laws and principles of social change: they include the so-called 'neo-Marxist' or 'Frankfurt' school, whose theoreticians include Marcuse, Habermas and Touraine. (Others such as Smith (1984) perhaps rightly refute the notion that these are in any sense Marxists, since they reject Marxism's central tenets of class analysis and conflict.)

To this school, new social movements are (or are to become) the prime agents of social change, replacing the working class in this role. Scott (pp16-23) gives a detailed definition of new social movements. They are 'primarily social or cultural in nature and only secondarily, if at all, political'. This means that they are less concerned with political power than with values and life-styles, and they see the struggle as less for control over economic processes than over the 'cultural' realm and particularly the production and dissemination of information and images through the media. They are

> little concerned to challenge the state directly. Their aim is instead to defend civil society against encroachment from the increasingly technocratic state (Touraine), or from 'inner colonisation' by the state's technocratic substructure (Habermas).

So their technique is to try to bypass the state, by 'creating other relation networks which radically oppose the "mass" and its atomisation', and to 'bring about change through changing values and developing alternative life styles' and through 'the discursive reformulation of individual and collective wills'. Indeed, the distancing of these movements from politics is seen as a very condition of their success. Instead, they emphasise 'such psycho-social practices as consciousness raising, group therapy, etc: the attempt to create a free social and geographical space for experiments in life style'. Personal autonomy, 'the personal is political', 'insistence on the independence of their concerns from those of the male or white working class' and non-hierarchical, network, grass-roots organisation are further important principles. This 'loose organisation and a focus on a limited spectrum of issues does not require a high degree of ideological agreement, or agreement on ultimate ends' (p31).

This description quite clearly tallies in detail with the approach and beliefs of the great majority of those whom we interviewed.

Thus the communards, like the larger green movement, constitute a 'new social movement' in the descriptive sense at least. However, when one examines the communards in relation to the potentially *revolutionary roles* ascribed by various theorists to new social movements, the correspondence is less striking.

Marcuse, for instance, believed that new social movements in the sixties, students and other 'privileged groups', were among those most oppressed by capitalism's creation of false needs and suppression of real needs. Therefore they were most likely to form the vanguard of a new, post-capitalist, unalienated society. Our interviews, however, showed that most communards, except the Findhornians, are very unhappy with the idea of their being part of any vanguard for social change.

Touraine's criterion for successful social movements, those which engender social change, is that they should identify with and fight in the interests of a clearly defined social group, should engage with a defined enemy, and should have an alternative, not 'regressive', model of modernity to the technocratic one widely offered. Not being regressive suggests that the struggle is to create a new society, not to be integrated and legitimated into the existing one. Scott considers that whereas Poland's Solidarity movement fulfilled all these criteria, and was thus successful in Touraine's terms, the antinuclear/ecology movement was not: it failed to meet the first two criteria. By exactly the same token, our researches suggest that the communes do not constitute a 'successful' social movement.

For Habermas, new social movements indicate that there is a 'legitimation crisis' in late capitalism. Habermas' evolutionary view of history sees it, in a modernist way, as a process of increasingly developing rationality. As a result, libertarian and secular morality (which is rational) has gained ground universally at the expense of deference to authoritarianism (which is irrational). Herein lies late capitalism's contradiction, for it requires the state to control the economy's mechanisms, and it needs people to kow-tow to the state, in other words to accept authority from above. Yet rational argument suggests the need to be self reliant, and not to accept any authority unchallengingly. New social movements therefore naturally rebel, and also express disillusionment with the paraphernalia of capitalism: its familial-vocational privatism, its consumerism and its achievement ideology. They embrace what are, for Habermas, the 'new politics' of quality of life, equal rights and participation and individual self-realisation. While there is much in this model that initially resonates with our view of the communards, further reflection shows serious disjunctures. In particular, the widespread 'Findhornian tendency', with its reconstruction of myth and religious experience and its stress on 'traditional' communal/extended family values bucks the rationalist evolutionary trend and strongly embraces romantic anti-rationality. It may reject state authority, but it cheerfully accepts that of gods like Shiva or Gaia.

Hence, the theoretical revolutionary potential of new social movements in these various neo- or post-Marxist models is not one that we have strongly identified in *practising* communards. Still less would it be possible to see communards as part of a revolutionary proletariat, in any more orthodox Marxist scheme: the majority of answers to the questions in Section 8 of our interview schedule rule this right out.

One social change (or adjustment) model which might more aptly fit the communes as they now are (rather than as their founders intended) is that of functionalism/pluralism. In this model society is a responsive democratic system made up of a plurality of interest groups that co-exist in dynamic equilibrium. When one group is particularly dissatisfied, it sets up stresses in the system by articulating dissatisfaction and possibly behaving in a subversive way. The whole system then accommodates in response; some of what is demanded is granted, and reform therefore takes place. The previously alienated group is now more accepting and accepted. As suggested above, at least some of the communes, such as CAT, Canon Frome, Laurieston, Monkton Wyld and Findhorn, could be seen as actors in such a reformist scenario. They would accord with Scott's view of new social movements as groups of alienated middle class people struggling for integration into conventional society. At the same time, some of the counterculture values that communards embrace are gaining more popular currency in the mainstream society – alternative technology, 'sound' consumerism and so forth.

We can also agree with Scott's representation (p32) of the new social movements as ideologically and politically heterogeneous, if the communes are anything to go by. This, for Scott, 'produces problems in, and limitations to, the development of new social movements into the kind of coherent oppositional force which analysts and some movements hope to expect'. This is exactly the same verdict which we have expressed above on the communes in particular.

MOBILISATION THEORY AND CONSCIOUSNESS-RAISING

Scott does appear to believe that the effectiveness of new social movements is increased by dint of a collective consciousness which they foster, whereby individuals do not simply act so as to optimise their own advantage: 'free riding' individualism is not nurtured. Rather, an 'alternative collective will . . . takes shape, which provides a basis of solidarity and self-identification with the movement'. The individual is bound to the movement through 'cultural practices common within social movement spheres, ranging from the dissemination of alternative information to consciousness-raising and forms of psychotherapy' that lead to self-understanding. Furthermore 'loose social movement spheres provide friendship networks. They guarantee the individual contact with others who are likely to share their interests and values' (pp124-5).

All this, Scott thinks, helps to mobilise people in the movements to become more effective social change agents. 'By providing individuals with alternative lifestyles and identities, social movements break down barriers to collective action, challenge "civil privatism", and substitute values of solidarity for instrumental rationality'.

Our work suggests that communes cannot be perceived in this way. Cultural practices such as consciousness-raising and psychotherapy have been sources of dissent and division rather than group solidarity, except in Findhorn perhaps. Instrumental rationality and civil privatism have been on the increase, with a corresponding perception that collective action has been on the decrease.

This, as we have stressed, is because communards are no more capable than anyone else of 'making their own history', to use the Marxian phrase, in a vacuum. Their actions and thoughts reflect the values of the culture they have left, but are still surrounded by. In Marx's famous dictum, 'Human beings certainly make their own history, but they do so not under conditions of their own choosing, rather under conditions given and transmitted from the past'.

Too many commentators have simply forgotten this dictum, when they have eulogised the communes movement as 'builders of the new dawn'. Frankel (1987 p178), however, has not forgotten it, and he chastises the 'mindless pluralism' of post-modern writers like Bahro and Toffler and many anarchists, environmentalists, Maoists and utopian socialists. They foresee a 'post-industrial' society in which the old ideological problems, divisions and conflicts no longer apply. It is a society made up of diverse, decentralised, demassified groups which no longer cohere by virtue of socio-economic class but simply express idealistic unity in vague obfuscations like 'planetary consciousness'. Says Frankel:

> Socialist society is conceived as a tranquil, simple harmonious answer to the complex, conflict-ridden, bureaucratised, monolithic and alienated present. The 'basic commune' is basic in its very essence – back to nature, back to basic needs, back to face-to-face relations, back to small communal experiences and peace . . . what is missing from these utopian longings is an awareness that life may not be able to become so uncomplicated, so free from cultural contradictions.

To Frankel, these post-modernist dreams of the end of conflict and ideology in such forms as communes are unrealistic. He says that it is one thing to reject the 'negative legacies of the Enlightenment', but:

> It is quite another thing to believe that, once women, gays and environmentalists have defined their values and priorities [which is what communes are about, in a practical way], all questions of rationality, equality, democracy in the public, as well as interpersonal private spheres, disappear. There seems to be a tendency to believe that, just because social movements articulate legitimate values and concerns which are not identical with those of the traditional labour movement, then somehow all these women, gays, greens etc., are not living in the same society, not encountering similar problems . . .

We acknowledge the accuracy of this: not to do so is unfair to the communards themselves.

THE PRACTICE: STRATEGIES FOR INCREASING EFFECTIVENESS

Of course it is easy for comfortably-off academic 'radicals' to be idealistic; or equally for them to be cynical when the theoretical social change potential of communes is not borne out in practice. And those who are sweating it out at the 'doing it' end are entitled to be correspondingly irked, and to ask: 'What else do you expect? What do you think we *can* do?'

'Very little' is the probable answer. Nearly everyone in the communes we visited already works extremely hard and thinks sincerely but practically about radical environmentalism and righting the wrongs of mainstream society. But in the end they put a priority on their own lives, as normal people do. As Chapter 4 clearly shows, social change came a very definite second in the priorities of most people when they joined their commune. The improvement of their own lives came first. It needs to be stressed that in these terms the communes are, by and large, extremely successful. For most people who have experienced commune life, the experience has been enriching in some way. Even though they may not have wanted to put up with the disadvantages of commune life any longer, they have often carried with them, on rejoining conventional life, the good effects of their experiences. Hence, in this sense there is no need here to suggest how communes could be more 'successful'. However, as we have also shown, the social change function is also of potential interest to a sizeable group of communards. For them it is valid to ask: What *can* be done to make communes more effective agents in the green movement's drive to establish Ecotopian society? Two broad approaches are worth mentioning.

The first is a form of the old 'networking' theme, which radical movements of the sixties onwards always seem to have come up with as a panacea for all problems. But, as Landry *et al* (1985) suggest, and this is critical, it should first and foremost be an *economic* network – as near as possible to an 'alternative political economy', capable of sustaining itself (a) by interaction with the 'sea of capitalism' in which it is set, (b) by economic interchange between the network's members and (c) by such interchange with other elements of an alternative economy, for instance as part of local green currency systems (see Ekins 1986 – we have been told of one such well developed system that already exists in the hinterland of one of the communes studied here). This network should attempt to maximise the communes' potential for economic productivity and generate enough surplus to pay people adequately, so that communards do not have to be boundlessly energetic, enthusiastic and willing to exploit themselves all the time to be effective. Generating surpluses by interacting with those afloat in the capitalist sea runs the risk, as we have seen, of ideological slippage, revisionism and eventual assimilation. Hence the need always, 'as in political warfare', to be careful to assess

> the strategies and tactics of these relationships [with capitalism] in terms of how far they allow us to retain economic advantage while extracting the maximum possible political advantage (Landry *et al* p98).

Potential projects must be evaluated, then, not just for their money-making potential, but also for their 'political advantage'; that is, their revolutionary as opposed to reactionary potential. If undertaken, they will then represent a stride forward for the movement itself, and not just towards a reformed and more effective capitalist system in which the counterculture has unwittingly and unpaid, as Landry *et al* puts it, done much of the research and development for capitalist firms to come along later and capitalise on (as has been the case in alternative technology, organic husbandry and consensual management). But when political advantage to the movement is unlikely to come, the enterprise must be deemed less justified than when it does and probably not proceeded with. To assess this, a return to the 'old days' of regular discussions about overall purpose and strategy has to be contemplated. The absence of these in many communes today, while understandable, is a weakness as far as the political effectiveness of the communes is concerned, and it is not good enough to take aims and ideologies simply as read. This in turn has implications for recruitment strategy.

Of the communes we visited, ZAP's work seems most to correspond with the approach we have outlined. For ZAP does not work in isolation, but attempts to build economic solidarity with other political partners in the Radical Routes network – the basis of an alternative political economy. Of course, all the other communes (except Findhorn, which is part of its own international network) belong to 'Communes Network'. But reference has already been made to the moribund nature of this grouping. As the Communes Movement, its membership jumped from 24 to 340 people between 1968 and 1971 (Wood 1989 p15). The Movement intended to be a tightly-knit federal society of communities, and it started a fund to buy property. But, says Wood:

> as a campaigning organisation the Communes Movement petered out by 1975. It was beset with organisational, administrative and financial problems, most of which it brought on itself... In addition, no cohesing ideological basis emerged upon which a campaign could be based. What the groups had in common was a commitment to communal living, not a common agreement about what the 'Alternative Society' would be like.

In truth, the communes do not seem to have been very good at collective solidarity, as witness a further failure of an attempt to do what Radical Routes is now trying. In 1981 there was a seven-member network (including four of the communes in this study) called Fairground Cooperative Ltd. According to the prospectus its purpose was, along Mondragon lines, to create:

> a secondary housing cooperative providing a range of services to its member coops, including advice on legal and financial problems, support for major maintenance or construction projects, and a pressure group to represent the interests of communes;
> an alternative financial institution in which people can safely invest their savings where they will be used to buy cooperative-owned property;
> a federation of independent communes.

This project appears to have sunk without trace, foundering on that lack of solidarity and sound management which sinks so much radicalism.

More, then, would be needed to propel any alternative political economy towards a breakthrough to a radical ecological society. A second, parallel, approach is needed. This involves working on the *context* in which the communes operate to help to transform it into a more supportive political and economic environment. In such an environment, the need to generate a surplus would not always be paramount. This capitalistic *sine qua non* of radical 'anti-capitalist' activity was in fact overcome to an extent in the days of the Greater London Council. That body subsidised, politically supported, and gave a voice and some political power to many countercultural groups. It allowed them some autonomy, so that they could 'extract themselves from the prerogatives and priorities of the dominant capitalist system' (Landry *et al* p99).

Today, from Glasgow to Liverpool, from Bradford to Wales, elements of this supportive environment are still there. But

> ... many of the [countercultural] groups and projects have not thought in strategic terms about the economic and political power at their disposal, and so far have missed the opportunities of mobilising that power in concert. They have at their disposal a number of strategic assets – these include the consumer-based cooperative supermarket chain, the 'Co-op', the purchasing power of certain Labour-controlled councils, the investment funds of trades unions, etc. (Landry *et al* p98).

Just how readily available these assets might be to a communes and cooperatives network is open to question. But one aim of political activity should be to make them more available, as they ought to be.

Another should be to strengthen the hand of those who mind the assets and their ability to increase them. This amounts to working on the economic and political structures of society through collective political action. Nothing less will suffice. As Wall (1990 p63) tellingly puts it:

> Green politics is about collective action. Personal change, heroic as it may appear to its exponents, is not enough. Individuals should support and empower each other . . . Rather than expecting ever greater sacrifices from the unwilling and undeserving, greens should aim to change structures so that living non-exploitatively becomes easier.

This means, for Wall, working in various grass-roots movements, largely predicated on liberal green politics. However, it must also be necessary to bite the bullet and to build up the affinity with labour and its tradition of collective political action which so many greens and communards are wary of. For this tradition is likely, even today, to provide some of that more sympathetic context for communes. This applies to local, municipal socialism rather than the national Labour Party, of course, though as a few communards realise, in order to strengthen the former it is still probably necessary to support the latter.

As well as working outside the political mainstream, therefore, it would be desirable for communards to grit their teeth and overcome their antipathy towards working within the conventional political arena, by engaging in a dialogue with the actors in party politics, pressure groups and, perhaps most of all, trades unions and community groups.

But they have as little time to spend on all this as on other forms of intensive outreach. Hence they greatly need reciprocal support from both labour and green movements if they are to be an effective political force. These movements should publicise and subsidise what the communes stand for and do. There should also be continuous personal contact and liaison between the movements. And labour and green movements should be more encouraging in public pronouncements and policies towards communes and coops. At least the same orders of financial subsidy which are available to people who set up homes and businesses in the mainstream economy should be available to communards. This seems a tall order. Communes did not figure at all in Labour's 'greenish' election manifesto in 1987 (though coops did). And, more surprising, Kemp and Wall's (1990) 'Green Manifesto' does not mention communes either.

More collective, materialist and structural perspectives on social change are needed. Unfortunately, as we have said, the wider green movement, like the communards, tends to shun such perspectives. The extent to which the New Age idealism of Findhorn permeates *all* corners of the green movement is substantial, which is one reason why this book devotes a fair space to describing such ideas. While elements of the 'New Age tendency' are to be admired, on the whole the critics who describe it as a counter-revolutionary tendency are probably correct. Rather than promoting a genuinely new age, it has more to do with sustaining the mores of the existing age.

LETTING COMMUNALISM SLIP

The notion that the ecological future will be secured by proselytising with New Age ideas is a weak one. Nor is it likely that many of the public will want to follow the practical example set by the people considered in this book, and live in communes. This much is clear from the responses of the communards themselves. While it has its rewards, commune life is too difficult for most of us. While it *is* a 'green' lifestyle, it is not necessarily the most appropriate green lifestyle for most people. Communes could usefully figure more prominently in the green movement for social change, but they will not constitute a leading edge of that movement. Nor will they be major elements of an Ecotopia. Most communards think not.

But despite the firmness with which our research has driven us to these findings, such a conclusion seems partly counter-intuitive. For, as Chapters 1 and 2 show, *some form* of collectivity and communality, if not *this* form, is a central part of the green vision. However, conventional society is presently so removed from *gemeinschaft* that it is hard to disagree with those communards who believe that only material events like Chernobyl or the build-up of greenhouse gases will give a significant impetus to people to radically change their ways and, simultaneously, their ideas. These events will not be very pleasant, especially for those of us who have been spared 'environmental crises' up to now (and since the Industrial Revolution, if not before, only minorities, at first in the West and now in the Third World, have not suffered from degraded environments).

To avoid or mitigate the harmfulness of such events, prior political action towards a more communal society seems urgent, as Johnston's (1989) recent analysis of the dynamics of contemporary economics amply demonstrates. Such action would represent, as Porritt acknowledges in the quotation that introduces this book, a move leftwards, for by invoking democratic communalism Ecotopia harks back to a popular theme in socialist utopianism.

The communes movement could be part of such a move, but our survey has suggested that at present the drift is in the opposite direction, towards becoming part of the society they were originally set up to oppose. This is a problem for those inside and outside the communes who see them as potentially a leading edge of the radical green movement. The dilemma was aptly summed up by a Lauriestonian, with whom we leave the last word:

> To move to the left is difficult – you have to push everyone else. To move to the right is easy – all you have to do is opt out of the collective struggle. And in the end you think: 'Fuck it, it's easier to opt out'.

The significance of critical utopian socialism and communism bears an inverse relation to historical development. In proportion as the modern class struggle develops and takes definite shape, this fantastic standing apart from the contest, these fantastic attacks on it lose all practical value and theoretical justification. Therefore, although the originators of these systems were, in many respects, revolutionary, their disciples have, in every case, formed mere reactionary sects . . . They still dream of experimental realisation of their social utopias . . . and to realise all these castles in the air they are compelled to appeal to the feelings and purses of the bourgeois. By degrees they sink into the category of the reactionary conservative socialists . . .

Karl Marx and Friedrich Engels, Manifesto of the Communist Party, **part III.**

APPENDIX 1

Communes and radical environmentalism: interview schedule

Many of these questions were not asked directly, but the answer to them often came out of the conversations.

Section 1. History and type of commune

1.1. Could you tell me what you know about the founding of this community and its history? What was the group like who founded it – what did they believe in?

1.2 Was it founded mainly for reasons to do with the individual (to provide a sanctuary for alienated/dissatisfied people) or with the general state of society (to promote social change)?

1.3 Was it founded specifically as a route to establishing an ecologically more sound society?

1.4 Therefore how would you describe the commune – was it meant to be an 'extended family' or a 'purposive' commune?

1.5 Did it have the characteristics of a (quasi-)mystical commune?

1.6 How important was ideology – was there a specific ideology intended to unite the members and form a common bond? (Was it an environmental ideology?)

1.7 What is the situation now – have any of these things changed?

1.8 How?

1.9 Why?

1.10 Has any ideological intention and/or unity been fragmented, dispelled, diffused or totally lost?

1.11 If so, why?

1.12 How often do you talk about your aims, purpose and principles?

Section 2. Individual motivation

2.1 Tell me about how and when you joined this community.

2.2 From what background, and education did you come? (Age? Place? Parents' occupation?)

2.3 What were your reasons?

2.4 Were your reasons mostly to do with yourself as an individual?

2.5 What was it about your life which dissatisfied you?

2.6 Were your reasons mostly to do with a concern about society?

2.7 How would you describe your most deeply held convictions about society? I.e. what sort of things do you feel most strongly about?

2.8 Are you an anarchist? If so, what kind? How would you define anarchism?

2.9 Are you a socialist? If so, what kind? How would you define socialism?

2.10 How much did any concerns about the society-environment relationship motivate you to join?

2.11 If so, what made you initially concerned – how did it come about?

2.12 What books and people have most influenced your views about the society-environment relationship?

2.13 What is meant by 'the environment' in your mind?

2.14 Should environmental concern be mostly to do with 'nature' or with the socially produced environment?

Section 3. Critique of conventional society

3.1 What are some of the main things which you regard as wrong with or improvable about conventional society?

3.2 What do your fellow members of the commune think are the particularly wrong things?

3.3 Specifically, what is wrong with modern economics?

3.4 Specifically, what is wrong with modern society?

3.5 Specifically, what is wrong with the nature of work?

3.6 Specifically, what is wrong with modern education?

3.7 Specifically, what is wrong with modern technology?

3.8 Specifically, what is wrong with the way we treat nature?

3.9 What is wrong with the attitudes to nature?

3.10 Why are these things wrong?

3.11 Won't human ingenuity and technology be able to find ways out of any environmental predicament which we may now be in?

Section 4. Ecocentric beliefs

4.0 Tell me about your beliefs concerning:
    a) the relationship between human society and nature
    b) the implications, if any, which these have for human behaviour and for the nature of a future society (what it should be like).

4.1 Tell me, first, about those beliefs which you hold most strongly.

4.2 To what extent are they shared by members of the commune?

4.3 Are there any which strongly shape the life and work of the community – to the extent that they might be part of its written or 'unwritten' constitution?

APPENDIX 1

(Checklist of ecocentric beliefs in Appendix 2)

Section 5. Ecologically sound practices
5.0 What practices in the community follow directly from the beliefs you have described above?
5.1 To what extent are those which are observed, wholly or in part, observed specifically as a result of the community's beliefs about what is necessary for an ecologically sound lifestyle?
5.2 Are any of the practices you describe part of the *group* code of practice: or are they just observed by you, or other specific individuals or groups within the community?
(List of ecocentric practices in Appendix 2)

Section 6. Intentions and outcomes
6.1 What practical difficulties are there for the community as a whole in following any of the above practices which relate particularly to an ecologically sound lifestyle?
6.2 What difficulties are there for you?
6.3 Do other individuals share your problems in living up to the principles?
6.4 Why are there clashes between intentions and outcomes, if there are?

Section 7. Relations with conventional society
7.1 How much do the difficulties arise because of constraints imposed by the wider conventional society?
7.2 To what extent do difficulties arise because of the attitudes and habits brought in by the members of the community from conventional society?
7.3 Are there economic problems in keeping the community going?
7.4 Would you like to be more independent from conventional society, or do you think it essential for the community to be a part of that society, as much as is possible?
7.5 In what ways do you not relate to the wider society, but think that you should?
7.6 Would you say that the community is here mainly to benefit the people in it, or those outside it?
7.7 Should this community's outreach consist mainly of preaching and teaching (ecologically sound) values and practices to the outside world?

7.8 Should outreach be attained principally through conversion by example?
7.9 Should outreach principally consist of joining in with local community action (e.g. to improve the environment and social problems) and/or instigating it?
7.10 Will you improve the environment in which local people live by action directed specifically towards environmental improvement, or through seeking to solve or ameliorate social problems?
7.11 Can you give examples of action you have taken with and for the local community?

Section 8. Attitudes to economic and social change
8.1 Could you describe how social/environmental change in the direction you most wish to see is most likely to come about?
8.2 Is individual consciousness raising and reform of yourself the first or most important route to social and environmental change?
8.3 Is collective political action more or less important? Or is it doomed to failure? If so, why?
8.4 Is education a main motor of social change?
8.5 What is your attitude towards capitalism and the ownership and owners of capital, as agents of change towards a social/environmentally better future? Do you believe in a *class* analysis of society?
8.6 What is your attitude towards organised labour as an agent of change etc.
8.7 What is your attitude towards conventional political parties as agents of change etc.
8.8 What is your attitude towards The Green Party as an agent of change etc.
8.9 What is your attitude towards community/municipal politics as agents of change etc.
8.10 What is your attitude towards pressure group activity as an agent of change etc.
8.11 How important are communes in leading the way to a socially more just and ecologically more harmonious society?
8.12 Which is more important – social justice or ecological harmony? To what extent are they separate?

Section 9. Degree of success
9.1 How much have you changed or influenced people and the society in which you operate?

9.2 How? What is the evidence?
9.3 Is society changing generally towards an ecologically more sound one, where nature is valued more for itself?
9.4 What is the evidence for such a change?

APPENDIX 2

Ecocentric principles

First order

Directly concerning nature
1. Bioethic – respect for/worship of nature. Need for spiritual communion with. Moral obligation towards.
2. Holism – interdependence with nature. Humans a part of natural systems, not divorced from or above them. A harmonious relationship of stewardship required.
3. Nature may be seen as female (Mother Earth, Gaia).
4. Anti-urbanism/pro the pastoral.
5. Nature is strongest in diversity and variety (plenitude)*.
6. Ecosystems should be stable*.
7. Interdependence. We are part of a global ecosystem – what we do affects the environment globally, and we bear responsibility for much environmental degradation elsewhere.
8. There are ecological laws of carrying capacity, which are being exceeded. There are limits to growth (population, economic).
9. There is an environmental crisis (pollution, resources, population).

Second order

Direct implications for society and lifestyles
1. Social behaviour and personal morality should observe ecological laws (like those marked * above) and/or nature is a model for human society.
2. Fundamental changes are required in attitudes and values, and social organisation.
3. This will entail fundamental changes in human relationships.
4. We should be non-violent towards nature and ourselves.
5. There should be a better balance between yin and yang, feminine and masculine:

Femine	*Masculine*
contractive	demanding
responsive	aggressive
cooperative	competitive
intuitive	rational
synthesising	analytic

6. Economic accounting should recognise and feature environmental factors – it should be holistic.
7. Outer ecology should be respected and valued: inner ecology should be the same (health; wellbeing of humans).
8. Nature is non-hierarchical (?) – we are not at the top of a natural hierarchy, but are a link in the chain of being. Society should not be hierarchical either.
9. To have minimal impact on ecosystems, society should be small-scale.
10. We need low-impact, non-polluting technology (human products should be biodegradable), and soft, renewable energy – and an economics which favours this.
11. Western society must de-emphasise materialism and consumerism to stretch the planet's resources less.
12. There should be population control.
13. Self-reliant, self-sustaining communities/countries are less ecologically demanding and more stable, and they make for greater human cultural variety.
14. The economic dependency of the South on the North must cease; the former should have independent development.
15. Better resource distribution and more social justice are necessary to solve environmental problems.
16. Anti-industrialism, anti-mechanical society, anti-giantism, anti-high technology.

More indirect implications, and quality of life
17. Personal lifestyles are important; the personal is political.
18. There is a need for self fulfilment and self-actualisation.
19. We must take personal responsibility for outer and inner ecology.
20. The subjective, emotional and spiritual are underrated and should be elevated.
21. Feminism and feminist principles are advocated.
22. Inner-directed philosophies and practices, mysticism, philosophies emphasising the unity of humans and nature, should be embraced.
23. Well-being and personal satisfaction should be important economic parameters. All human activity should be incorporated into economics (informal economy).
24. Human needs should be satisfied by the economic/social system, rather than wants being satisfied through the market. Many wants are artificial i.e. generated by the market.

APPENDIX 2

25. Meaningful work (as distinct from employment) is a human need.
26. Work should not be degrading, boring or alienating; it should combine hand and brain, involve craft, not emphasise the division of labour and not be governed by the cash nexus.
27. Society should be a genuine participatory democracy.
28. There is a need for collectivism – in the sense of community and extended family, by which people take collective responsibility for their lives (environment, health and welfare, production).
29. The state is an enemy.
30. Private or state ownership of resources (land), and private enterprise or state socialism are incompatible with an ecologically sound society; unless they are small scale.
31. Education is a motor of social change, but its reform is needed to emphasise ecological imperative.

Sources: O'Riordan, Capra, Pepper, Porritt, Ekins.

Ecocentric practices

First order

1. Sharing resources for greater efficiency (communal eating, organising as a cooperative)
2. Recycling resources – e.g. waste (using recycled paper and products – reusing materials).
3. Vegetarian/vegan – consciousness about food and health; inner ecology. Consumer ecocentrism includes buying 'sound' products, for health and non-exploitation, esp. of less industrialised countries.
4. Home-produced foods and crafts – moving to a self-sustaining economy.
5. Using soft, renewable energy sources.
6. Using less energy in lighting/heating.
7. De-emphasise cars; emphasise mass-transit, cycles, walking.
8. Non-polluting practices e.g. biodegradable cleansers.
9. De-emphasise consumer goods. Living on little money.
10. Food coops/city-country exchanges.
11. Using and developing alternative technology.
12. Using alternative medicine.
13. Organic gardening/farming.

Second order: Quality of life

1. Less division of labour.
2. Combining hand and brain.
3. Work sharing, work tokens, rotas.
4. Expertise does not carry connotations of authority.
5. Democratic participative structures and processes; e.g. consensus decision-making. Emphasis on cooperation. Non-hierarchical.
6. Non-sexist, non-racist: diversity of beliefs tolerated.
7. Paying attention to quality of relationships. Time taken to focus specifically on relationships. Emphasising gentleness/loving/non-aggressive. Facilitating others to assert themselves.
8. Assertion of the individual. Consciousness-raising, speaking one's mind, expressing feelings and emotions.
9. Liberated attitude to sexual relationships and proclivities – permissiveness and tolerance.
10. Mechanisms to avoid conflict – group dynamics considered important/consensus decisions/co-counselling/therapy sessions.
11. Taking time for communal activities; eating, playing, campaigning, working.
12. Collective or individual mysticism (to emphasise spirituality and emotions, and/or to express unity with nature and Earth). Ceremonies/activities involving meditation/transcendentalism.

REFERENCES

Abrams P and McCulloch A (1976) *Communes, Sociology and Society*, Cambridge: Cambridge University Press.
Albury D and Schwartz J (1982) *Partial Progress*, London: Pluto Press.
Allaby M (1975) *The Survival Handbook: Self Sufficiency for Everyone*, London: Pan.
Ansell V, Coates C, Dawling P, How J, Morris W and Wood A (1989) *Diggers and Dreamers: The 1990/91 Guide to Communal Living*, Sheffield, Lifespan Community: Communes Network.
Ashton F (1985) *Green Dreams: Red Realities*, Milton Keynes: Network for Alternative Technology and Technological Assessment.
Bahro R (1986) *Building the Green Movement*, London: Heretic Books.
Barbrook R (1990) 'The third way', in *New Ground*, 25, 12–13.
BBC (British Broadcasting Corporation) (1989) *Heaven on Earth*, in 'Everyman Series', BBC1.
Blackwell T (1990) 'Shares and share alike', in *The Guardian*, 23 December, 27.
Bloom W (1987) 'New Age – any meaning?' in *One Earth*, 7(4), 6–7.
Bookchin M (1980) *Towards an Ecological Society*, Montreal: Black Rose Books.
Bookchin M (1982) *The Ecology of Freedom: the Emergence and Dissolution of Hierarchy*, Palo Alto, California: Cheshire Books.
Bookchin M (1987) 'Social ecology versus deep ecology: a challenge for the ecology movement', in *Green Perspectives*, 4 and 5.
Bramwell A (1989) *Ecology in the Twentieth Century: a History*, London: Yale University Press.
Caddy E (1988) *Flight into Freedom*, Shaftesbury, Dorset: Longmead Books.
Callenbach E (1978) *Ecotopia*, London: Pluto Press.
Callenbach E (1981) *Ecotopia Emerging*, Berkeley, California: Banyan Tree Books.
Capra F (1982) *The Turning Point*, London: Wildwood House.
Christensen K (1989) *Home Ecology: Making Your World a Better Place*, London: Arlington Books.
Cosgrove D (1990) 'Environmental thought and action: pre-modern and post-modern', in *Transactions, Institute of British Geographers*, 15(3), 344–58.
Cotgrove S (1982) *Catastrophe or Cornucopia? The Environment, Politics and the Future*, Chichester: Wiley.

Cotgrove S (1983) 'Environmentalism and utopia', in O'Riordan T and Turner K (eds) *An Annotated Reader in Environmental Planning and Management,* Oxford: Pergamon Press.

Devall B and Sessions G (1985) *Deep Ecology: Living as if Nature Mattered,* Utah: Gibbs M Smith.

Dobson A (1990) *Green Political Thought,* London: Unwin Hyman.

Ekins P (1986) (ed) *The Living Economy,* London: Routledge and Kegan Paul.

Elkington J and Burke T (1987) *The Green Capitalists,* London: Gollancz.

Elkington J and Hailes J (1988) *The Green Consumer Guide,* London: Gollancz.

Elsom D (1987) *Atmospheric Pollution,* Oxford: Basil Blackwell.

Ferguson M (1982) *The Aquarian Conspiracy,* London: Paladin Books.

Fox W (1984) 'Deep ecology: a new philosophy of our time?' in *The Ecologist,* 14, 194–200.

Francis D (1985) 'New Age or New Right? Findhorn: a feminist view', in *Green Line,* May, 4–6.

Frankel B (1987) *The Post-Industrial Utopians,* Cambridge: Polity Press.

Fromer R (1989) 'You are what you (don't) eat', in *The Guardian,* April 27.

Fromm E (1956) *The Sane Society,* London: Routledge and Kegan Paul.

Fry C (1975) 'Marxism and Ecology', in *The Ecologist,* 6(9), 328–332.

Goldsmith E and others (1972) 'Blueprint for survival' in *The Ecologist* 2(1), 1–43

Goldsmith E (1988) *The Great U-Turn,* Bideford: Green Books.

Gorz A (1980) *Ecology as Politics,* London: Pluto Press.

Gorz A (1982) *Farewell to the Working Classes: an Essay on Post Industrial Socialism,* London: Pluto Press.

Gorz A (1985) *Paths to Paradise: On the Liberation from Work,* London: Pluto Press.

Gould P (1988) *Early Green Politics: Back to Nature, Back to the Land and Socialism in Britain,* Brighton: Harvester Press.

Hall P (1983) 'From ideology to utopia: towards feasible solutions for 2000 AD', in O'Riordan T and Turner K (eds) *An Annotated Reader in Environmental Management and Planning,* Oxford: Pergamon Press.

Hardy D (1979) *Alternative Communities in Nineteenth-Century England,* London: Longman.

Harper P (1986) 'AT and the Quarry: looking forward and backward', in *Quarry News,* Autumn.

REFERENCES

Harper P (1990) 'Told you so', in *Clean Slate*, 2, 4–5.

Hay F (1989) *Setting an Example: Communal Living and Environmental Awareness*, unpublished BSc Hons dissertation, Sunderland Polytechnic.

Hays S P (1987) *Beauty, Health and Permanence: Environmental Politics in the US, 1955–1985*, Cambridge: Cambridge University Press.

Hawken P (1975) *The Magic of Findhorn*, London: Fontana Books.

Henderson H (1981) *The Politics of the Solar Age*, New York: Doubleday.

Hodgkinson L (1990) 'Gripping yarns', in *The Guardian*, July 10, 38.

Johnston R (1989) *Environmental Problems: Nature, Economy and State*, London: Belhaven.

Kamenka E (ed) (1982) *Community as a Social Ideal*, London: E Arnold.

Kanter R M (1972) *Commitment and Community: Communes and Utopias in Sociological Perspective*, Cambridge, Mass: Harvard University Press.

Kanter R M (ed) (1973) *Communes: Creating and Managing the Collective Life*, New York: Harper and Row.

Kemp P and Wall D (1990) *A Green Manifesto for the 1990s*, Harmondsworth: Penguin.

Kropotkin P (1899) *Fields, Factories and Workshops Tomorrow*, London: Freedom Press (1986 ed).

Landry C, Morley D, Southwood R and Wright P (1985) *What a Way To Run a Railroad: An Analysis of Radical Failure*, London: Comedia.

Lovejoy A (1974) *The Great Chain of Being*, Cambridge, Mass: Harvard University Press.

Lovelock J (1979) *Gaia*, New York: Oxford University Press.

Lumley-Smith (1978) 'The road to utopia', in *New Ecologist*, 1, 13–16.

McLaughlin C and Davidson G (1985) *Builders of the Dawn*, Massachussetts: Sirius.

Mercer J (1984) *Communes: a Social History and Guide*, Dorset: Prism Press.

Merchant C (1982) *The Death of Nature: Women, Ecology and the Scientific Revolution*, London: Harper and Row.

Milbrath L J (1984) *Environmentalists: Vanguard for a New Society*, Albany: State University of New York Press.

Mosse G L (1982) 'Nationalism, fascism and the radical right', in Kamenka E (ed) *Community as a Social Ideal*, London: E Arnold, 27–42.

Murtagh J and Robinson K (1984) *Living Simply: How and Why We Came to Believe in an Anti-Materialist Lifestyle*, Manchester: Whose

World?, c/o The Old Vestry, St Ambrose's Church, 395 Liverpool Street, Salford, M6 5RU.

Naess A (1988) 'The basics of deep ecology', in *Resurgence*, 126, 4–7.

Nash R (1974) *Wilderness and the American Mind*, New Haven, Connecticut: Yale University Press.

Nicholson-Lord D (1987) *The Greening of the Cities*, London: Routledge and Kegan Paul.

O'Riordan T (1981) *Environmentalism*, London: Pion, Second Edition.

O'Riordan T (1989) 'The challenge for environmentalism', in Peet R and Thrift N (eds), *New Models in Geography*, 77–102, London: Unwin Hyman.

Osmond J and Graham A (1984) *Alternatives: New Approaches to Health, Education, Energy, the Family and the Aquarian Age*, Wellingborough: Thorsons.

Papadakis E (1984) *The Green Movement in West Germany*, London: Croom Helm.

Pearce D, Markandya A and Barbier E (1989) *Blueprint for a Green Economy*, London: Earthscan.

Pepper D (1984) *The Roots of Modern Environmentalism*, London: Croom Helm.

Pepper D (1985) 'Determinism, idealism and the politics of environmentalism', in *International Journal of Environmental Studies*, 26, 11–19.

Pepper D (1988) 'The geography and landscapes of an anarchist Britain', in *The Raven*, 1(4), 339–350.

Pepper D and Hallam N (1989) 'The Findhorn tendency', in *New Ground*, 20, 18–20.

Phillips A (1990) 'The kids are alright', in *Weekend Guardian*, January 13–14, 2–4.

Porritt J (1984) *Seeing Green: the Politics of Ecology Explained*, Oxford: Basil Blackwell.

Rigby A (1974a) *Alternative Realities: A Study of Communes and their Members*, London: Routledge and Kegan Paul.

Rigby A (1974b) *Communes in Britain*, London: Routledge and Kegan Paul.

Rigby A (1990) 'Lessons from anarchist communes', in *Contemporary Issues in Geography and Education*, 3(3), 52–62.

Robertson J (1983) *The Sane Alternative: a Choice of Futures*, Ironbridge, Salop: James Robertson.

Roszak T (1979) *Person/Planet*, London: Gollancz.

Ryle M (1988) *Ecology and Socialism*, London: Radius Books.
Sale K (1980) *Human Scale*, London: Secker and Warburg.
Sarkar S (1983) 'Marxism and productive forces: a critique', review of Ulrich O (1979) *World Standard: In the Blind Alley of the Industrial System* (in German), Rotbuch Verlag: Berlin, in *Alternatives*, IX 145–76.
Schumacher E F (1973) *Small is Beautiful: Economics as if People Really Mattered*, London: Abacus Books.
Schumacher E F (1980) *Good Work*, London: Abacus Books.
Schwarz W and D (1987) *Breaking Through: Theory and Practice of Wholistic Living*, Bideford: Green Books.
Scott A (1990) *Ideology and the New Social Movements*, London: Unwin Hyman.
Seabrook J (1990) *The Myth of the Market*, Bideford: Green Books.
Sennett R (1978) *The Fall of Public Man*, New York: Random House.
Shenker B (1986) *Intentional Communes*, London: Routledge and Kegan Paul.
Simon J and Kahn H (1984) *The Resourceful Earth*, Oxford: Basil Blackwell.
Skinner B F (1948) *Walden II*, New York: Macmillan (1976 ed).
Smith N (1984) *Uneven Development*, Oxford: Basil Blackwell.
Toffler A (1981) *The Third Wave*, London: Pan Books.
Trevelyan G (1987) quoted in 'Sir George, bright-eyed leader of the movement', in *The Guardian*, 19 August.
Trudgill S (1990) *Barriers to a Better Environment: What Stops Us Solving Environmental Problems?*, London: Belhaven.
Van der Weyer R (1986) *Wickwyn: a Vision of the Future*, London: SPCK.
Vogel S (1988) 'Marx and alienation from nature', in *Social Theory and Practice*, 14(3) 367–88.
Wall D (1990) *Getting There: Steps to a Green Society*, London: Green Print.
Watson L (1980) *Lifetide: the Biology of Consciousness*, New York: Simon and Schuster.
Weston J (ed) (1986) *Red and Green: the New Politics of the Environment*, London: Pluto Press.
White L (1967) 'The historical roots of our ecologic crisis', in *Science*, 155, 1203–07.
Wood A (1989) 'History and overview', in Ansell et al *Diggers and Dreamers: The 1990/91 Guide to Communal Living*, Sheffield: Lifespan Community.
Young J (1990) *Post Environmentalism*, London: Belhaven.

INDEX

Abrams P and McCulloch A 3, 4, 31, 32, 33, 47, 54, 55, 56, 57, 59, 60, 61, 62, 64, 66, 86, 126, 146, 150, 201, 203
ages of communards 84-5
Albury D and Schwartz J 115
alienation/disaffection 28, 33, 37, 39, 40, 43, 53, 54, 55, 60, 62, 64, 69, 89, 95, 97, 112, 114, 115, 120, 126, 130, 161, 162, 168, 173, 199, 203, 211, 213
Allaby M 45
anarchism/anarchists 8, 10, 14, 16, 18, 20, 27, 29, 30, 31, 32, 38, 41, 42, 56, 57, 61, 64, 66, 67, 70, 74, 76, 80, 84, 89, 95, 97, 98, 103-5, 106, 110, 112, 113, 114, 115, 118, 126, 131, 146, 148, 161, 169, 170, 174, 175, 176, 180, 195, 197, 199, 205
animism 75, 99, 106, 109, 128
anti-urbanism 11, 25, 28, 29, 45, 126, 199, 200
Aquarian age/conspiracy 44, 75, 108, 129, 158-160, 165, 168, 170, 171, 180
asceticism 23, 25, 26, 30, 31, 32, 37
Ashton F 48, 56, 204
assimilation (into conventional society) 204-207, 211
astrology 95, 120, 128, 171

back-to-nature/back-to-the-land movement 25, 26, 28, 29, 30, 42, 65, 66, 69, 71, 89, 92, 136, 199, 213
Bahro R 25, 36, 37, 38, 41, 58, 64, 212
Barbrook R 176
Birchwood Hall 133
bio-dynamic 92, 136
bioethic/animal rights 10, 15, 16, 17, 26, 123-5, 135, 143
bioregions 42, 95, 107
Blackwell T 185
Bloom W 168
Blueprint for Survival 2, 36, 37, 39, 76, 130
Bookchin M 16, 17, 41, 42, 43, 58, 112, 205
Bramwell A 12, 30, 31, 32, 44, 65, 176

Caddy E 38, 99, 100, 166
Caddy P 80, 81
Callenbach E 2, 38
Canon Frome 3, 71, 72-3, 78, 81, 82, 83, 85, 86, 87, 94, 96, 122, 133, 135, 136, 139, 143, 147, 149, 150, 153, 154, 158, 160, 181, 193, 194, 200, 206, 211
capitalism/capital 10, 25, 30, 40, 41, 51, 52, 54, 57, 58, 62, 67, 76, 103, 112, 113, 114, 116, 118, 123, 131, 170, 172-6, 178, 195, 196, 197, 203, 205, 206, 208, 209, 210, 214, 215, 216
Capra F 7, 17, 44, 117, 120, 158
car sharing 132, 139, 142, 143, 193
Centre for Alternative Technology 3, 46, 69, 70, 72-3, 74, 77, 79, 80, 81, 83, 92, 94, 104, 121, 127, 132, 135, 136, 137, 139, 140, 141, 145, 147, 161, 162, 165, 181, 184, 185, 186, 189, 190, 193, 197, 206, 208, 211
Charter 88 53
childcare 71, 95, 142, 150
Christensen K 23
class identity of communards 41, 57, 59, 62, 86, 87-9, 94, 140, 143, 158, 163, 168, 183, 201, 203-4, 211
class (conflict) and social change 48, 52-4, 57, 62, 157, 172-6, 209
class consciousness 57, 58, 162, 173,

237

183
collective consciousness/politics 48, 49, 51-2, 58, 62, 157, 160, 161, 163, 164, 165, 166, 168-170, 176, 203, 207, 209, 212, 218, 219
collectivism/collective ownership 20, 22, 30, 42, 55, 61, 62, 63, 71, 79, 81, 104, 130, 142, 167, 182, 194, 199, 201, 203, 206
communards' critique of conventional society 7, 8-10, 32, 89, 112-115, 119-121
communards' lifestyles 20-24, 30, 33, 41, 56, 60-1, 70, 72, 132-139, 165, 200, 218
communards' values:
  on nature 10-12, 15, 89, 105, 123-9
  on society 12-14, 15, 89, 129-131
communes:
  before 1800 25-6
  definition 4
  nineteenth and early twentieth century 27-31
  1960s 31-5, 48, 54, 59, 62, 64, 69, 81, 93, 201
Communes Network 181, 215
conflict resolution 149, 151-4
consensus decisions 21, 31, 41, 48, 71, 85, 105, 107, 130, 148, 149, 159, 197
consensus of values/conventional wisdom 49, 52-4, 56, 57, 157, 161, 190
conservation: of energy 21, 23, 39, 45, 137, 140, 143, 186
conservatism 8, 17, 28, 36, 48, 62, 63, 65, 66, 67, 101, 110, 127, 131, 143, 189, 206
Conservative Party 20, 179
cooperatives 31, 40, 45, 46, 103, 114, 169, 170, 175, 181, 192, 216
Cosgrove D 17
Cotgrove S 7, 59, 65, 66, 88
counterculture 25, 30, 31, 54, 56, 58, 126, 156, 157, 191, 192, 199, 204, 205, 211, 215
Crabapple 3, 46, 71, 72-3, 74, 83, 87, 97, 135, 136, 144, 174, 188, 195, 200, 206

craft production 13, 26, 28, 29, 40, 42, 43, 71, 86, 106, 130, 132
critical mass theory and social change 159, 167, 168

Dartington movement 76, 115
decentralisation 36, 38, 40, 42, 43, 45, 64, 67, 97, 101, 104, 169, 189, 213
deep ecology 14-17, 29, 38, 65, 69, 105, 106, 107, 108, 112, 118, 127-9, 186, 187
democracy: direct/participative 21, 30, 31, 37, 43, 45, 55, 64, 146, 148-150, 207
Devall B and Sessions G 15, 16, 75
Devas 109, 128
Diggers 26, 28
Dobson A 10, 180, 204, 206
dualism 108, 109, 110, 117, 126, 127, 161
Dulas Engineering 184, 185

ecocentrism/ecologism 10, 121, 126, 130, 135, 145, 200, 205
economics:
  conventional 29, 113-14
  green 26, 33, 39, 74, 89, 114, 188, 214, 215
  and social change 50, 51, 54, 170, 172, 208
Ecotopia 2, 29, 38, 199, 200, 204, 214, 218, 219
educational centres 70, 71, 72, 73, 74, 76, 88, 132, 172, 184, 199
education and social change 32, 43, 49, 50, 59, 70, 89, 95, 117, 120, 130, 161, 171
Ekins P 7, 33, 114, 214
Elkington J and Burke T 114
Elkington J and Hailes J 23
Elsom D 36
environment: definition of 48, 52, 102
example: social change by 32, 47, 48, 49, 50, 56, 57, 59, 67, 69, 71, 87, 143, 165, 169, 170, 191, 200

Fairground Cooperative Ltd 2167

family:
   extended 14, 26, 38, 43, 71, 96, 130, 151, 207, 211
   nuclear 10, 22, 32, 33, 41, 43, 55, 70, 76, 89, 95, 96, 104, 113, 117, 151, 193, 199
fascism/nazism/National Front 30, 38, 65, 106, 107, 131
feminine values 8, 13, 45
feminism 3, 12, 13, 14, 30, 32, 38, 44, 51, 59, 89, 94, 97, 103, 105, 126, 130
Ferguson M 159
financial pressures 139-141
Findhorn 2, 3, 5, 15, 38, 69, 70, 72-3, 74, 75, 77, 80, 81, 82, 93, 96, 99, 100, 108, 109, 110, 112, 113, 114, 116, 120, 127, 128, 129, 133, 135, 136, 137, 138, 141, 142, 147, 151, 153, 155, 159, 161, 165, 166, 168, 174, 177, 180, 182, 184, 186, 187, 189, 194, 196, 206, 210, 211, 212, 215, 218
Findhorn Foundation 80, 81, 133, 196
Findhorn tendency 17, 110, 211
Fox W 15, 75
Francis D 75
Frankel B 64, 208, 212, 213
Frome Society 71, 78
Fromm E 2, 31, 40
Fry C 29
fundamentalism 77, 78, 81, 145, 178

Gaia/Gaianism/mother earth 11, 12, 16, 17, 44, 108, 121, 125-6, 200, 211
gemeinschaft 62, 63, 64, 65, 130, 155, 202, 218
gemeinwesen 64
gesellschaft 62, 63, 66, 155
giantism 9, 32, 89, 130
Glaneirw 3, 46, 71, 72-3, 83, 84, 95, 120, 128, 133, 136, 137, 149, 151, 200, 206
Goldsmith E 36, 65
Gorz A 40, 64, 209
Gould P 28, 29, 67
Great Chain of Being 44, 127

green consumerism 23, 58, 138, 172, 206
green critique of conventional/Western society 7, 8-10, 32, 89, 112-115, 119-121
green lifestyles and practices 20-24, 30, 33, 41, 56, 60-1, 70, 72, 132-139, 165, 200, 218
Green Party 2, 33, 52, 102, 106, 117, 131, 176, 178, 179, 203
green values:
   on nature 10-12, 15, 89, 105, 123-9
   on society 12-14, 15, 89, 129-131

Habermas J 209, 210
Haeckel E 44
Hall P 43, 44
Hallam N 58, 110
Hardy D 27, 29, 30
Harper P 77, 78, 79, 197
Hawken P 74, 109
Hay F 79, 133, 138
Hays S 88
Hegel G F 109, 165
Henderson H 44
hierarchy (rejection of) 13, 16, 26, 30, 58, 61, 64, 65, 71, 75, 76, 89, 103, 105, 112, 115, 146, 149, 150, 207, 209
Hodgkinson L 153
holism 11, 13, 14, 15, 26, 44, 46, 65, 75, 89, 106, 108, 109, 113, 121, 126, 127-9, 130, 174, 199
human nature 116, 117, 174, 175
hundredth monkey 158-160, 167

idealism 46, 48, 50-1, 54, 56, 57, 105, 109, 120, 126, 157, 161, 165, 171, 175, 201, 218
income sharing 5, 26, 33, 40, 141, 146-7, 182, 191, 192, 193, 196
individualism 9, 10, 13, 20, 22, 30, 32, 37, 45, 48, 49, 51-2, 54, 56, 57, 58, 61, 62, 66, 67, 78, 82, 107, 112, 113, 116, 117, 130, 138, 142, 146, 155, 156, 160, 161, 162, 163, 164, 167, 168, 169, 170, 172, 176, 180, 192-4, 199, 201, 206, 207, 209,

211, 217
industrialism 9, 11, 28, 46, 55, 120, 123, 130, 174, 203

Johnston R 14, 218

Kamenka E 63, 64
Kanter R 4, 25, 26, 30, 45, 63, 114
Kelly R 79, 185
Kemp P and Wall D 217
kibbutzim 31, 39, 60, 207
Kropotkin 29, 30, 40, 66, 182

labour movement (and trades unions) 52, 53, 64, 80, 178, 213, 217
Labour Party 53, 102, 106, 169, 176, 178, 179, 216, 217
Landry C et al 197, 214, 215, 216
Laurieston Hall 3, 46, 70, 71, 72-3, 79, 82, 83, 85, 86, 93, 112, 117, 122, 133, 135, 136, 137, 139, 142, 143, 166, 180, 183, 186, 187, 192, 193, 194, 195, 196, 198, 206, 211, 219.
liberalism 17, 20, 29, 45, 48, 49, 51, 52, 56, 57, 61, 62, 63, 67, 78, 95, 103, 113, 121, 155, 156, 166, 192, 193, 196, 202, 203, 205, 206, 217
Liberal Party 52, 93, 179
Lifespan 3, 46, 72-3, 83, 84, 122, 133, 136, 139, 144, 147, 149, 151, 160, 182, 187, 195, 196, 206
Lightmoor 45, 106, 199
limits to growth 70, 92, 200
local authorities 52, 56, 177, 216
local economy/community 137, 144, 176, 181, 185, 187, 189
Lovejoy A 44
Lovelock J 44
Lower Shaw Farm 3, 46, 70, 71, 72-3, 80, 82, 93, 133, 136, 160, 186, 187, 195, 206
Lumley-Smith R 55

MacLaughlin C and Davidson G 3, 81
managerial efficiency 195, 197
manifestation 108, 109, 128
Marcuse H 209, 210

market economy 41, 43, 103, 156, 176, 188, 196, 202, 205
Marxism/Marxists 10, 14, 17, 29, 33, 50, 52, 58, 64, 85, 103, 106, 109, 117, 118, 155, 158, 165, 175, 208, 209, 211, 212
masculine values 13, 126
materialism (consumerism) 3, 8, 10, 12, 14, 22, 24, 32, 37, 40, 52, 70, 87, 89, 116, 123, 130, 138, 140, 141, 171, 194-5, 205, 207, 210
materialism, historical 50, 58
materialist perspectives (on social change) 48, 50-1, 53, 54, 57, 64, 105, 110, 112, 157, 161, 165, 170, 201, 218
meditation and social change 109, 128, 166, 168, 177
Mercer J 26, 30
Merchant C 7
Milbrath 1
millenarianism 38-46, 158, 170, 189
mobilisation theory 212-3
monasticism 23, 38
Mondragon 31
monism 44, 108, 127-9, 167
Monkton Wyld 2, 69, 70, 72-3, 76, 77, 80, 82, 84, 85, 87, 95, 112, 115, 132, 133, 135, 136, 155, 158, 183, 186, 191, 194, 195, 206, 211
Morris W 28
Mosse G 65
motivation for joining communes 89-100
multinational companies/corporations 9, 16, 23, 113, 117
Murtagh J and Robinson K 23
mysticism 17, 27, 32, 33, 44, 65, 131, 136, 200

Naess A 15, 75
Nash R 31
neo-marxism (Frankfurt School) 209, 211
networks 209, 212, 214, 215, 216
New Age 3, 5, 16, 27, 38, 43-6, 47, 75, 77, 95, 108-110, 127-9, 146, 156, 158, 159, 165, 166, 167, 168, 170, 171, 175, 176, 177, 186, 196,

203, 206, 218
News from Nowhere 29
new social movements 203, 204, 208-12
Nicholson-Lord D 36, 45
nuclear power/nuclear state 76, 115, 122, 175
nuclear weapons/disarmament 33, 92, 121, 168

organic farming/gardening 3, 27, 30, 44, 46, 65, 71, 72, 74, 76, 92, 132, 133-6, 143, 186, 215
O'Riordan T 1, 7, 16
Osmond J and Graham A 46
outreach 144, 184-192, 200, 217
overpopulation 10, 11, 12, 15, 39, 92, 117, 123, 130
Owen R 27, 56

pacifism/nonviolence 3, 26, 30, 32, 33, 50, 57, 73, 92, 105, 173
paganism 33, 65, 106, 109, 187
Papadakis E 52
Paris Commune of 1871 64
Pearce D 22
People Centre, Laurieston 72, 78, 187, 193
People in Common 3, 46, 72-3, 76, 77, 80, 84, 94, 132, 139, 147, 155, 182, 206
Pepper D 2, 7, 16, 29, 31, 58, 110
personal is political 14, 51, 56, 87, 155, 163, 164, 169, 176, 209, 217
phases of commune development 84-6
Phillips A 70, 71
planetary village/culture/awareness 75, 108, 109, 127, 159, 213
pluralism 53, 208, 211
pollution 9, 10, 11, 21, 36, 37, 53, 70, 76, 105, 121, 132, 170
political ideologies:
    and communards 100-110, 130-131
    and community 62-7
    and the greens 17-20, 48
politics: parliamentary/party/ conventional 51, 57, 60, 164, 169, 176-9, 217
population: see overpopulation

Porritt J 7, 12, 17, 219
Postlip Hall 71
post-modernism 208, 212, 213
pragmatism 81, 82, 83, 86, 106, 107, 143, 145, 173, 196, 205
pressure groups 51, 57, 92, 94, 144, 169, 176, 177, 217
private and public domains 61-2, 142, 143, 150, 156, 192, 199, 201, 207, 210, 212, 213
privatisation 192-4, 206
profit making 195, 197, 206, 207
protestant (work) ethic 51, 202
psychology: behavioural, and of perception 49, 55, 74, 118, 174, 201, 202, 212

quality of life 13, 15, 22, 37, 130

Radical Routes Network 3, 188, 215
Rainbow Housing Cooperative 181
Raine P 79
rebirthing 76, 154, 155, 162, 186
recycling 12, 20, 42, 45, 76, 132, 133, 136, 143, 184
Redfield 3, 71, 72-3, 74, 78, 79, 82, 85, 86, 87, 92, 93, 96, 133, 135, 136, 155, 158, 159, 160, 180, 184, 188, 193, 206
reformism 204, 206, 211
Reich W/Reichian therapy 58, 76, 187
relationships: personal/communal 21, 30, 32, 33, 37, 42, 46, 54, 55, 60, 66, 76, 77, 82, 89, 129, 130, 141, 146, 147, 151-4, 155, 180, 194, 200, 201, 202
resource sharing 93, 130, 132, 138
responsibility for self 103, 163, 166, 169, 175
revisionism 79, 214
revolution 48, 51, 56, 58, 60, 61, 62, 82, 163, 164, 170, 172, 173, 174, 205, 208, 210, 211, 215
Rigby A 3, 4, 27, 31, 32, 33, 38, 47, 54, 55, 56, 57, 59, 61, 66, 200
Robertson J 40, 41
romantics/romanticism 27, 28, 29, 42, 63, 65, 92, 93, 102, 115, 121, 126,

136, 171, 211
Roszak T 26, 163
Ruskin J 28
Russell P 125
Ryle M 20, 64, 204

Sale K 31, 39, 45
Sarkar S 43
Schumacher E F 39, 120
Schwarz W and D 46
scientific world view 8, 108, 117, 120, 131
Scott A 203, 204, 209, 210, 211, 212
Seabrook J 47, 52, 202
self: fulfilment/assertion/discovery 14, 22, 26, 32, 41, 54-5, 61, 66, 69, 76, 85, 87, 89, 100, 109, 110, 113, 129, 150, 151, 155, 161, 162, 164, 166, 169, 170, 176, 194, 202, 203, 210 212
self-sufficiency/reliance 29, 36, 39, 41, 43, 45, 47, 69, 72, 73, 76, 82, 43, 89, 92, 107, 124, 133-6, 144, 199, 210
Sennett R 201, 202, 203
Seymour J 69, 133
Shenker B 4, 55, 60, 61, 82
Shindig 133, 139
Skinner B F 49, 74
Skolimowski H 74, 120
small-scale organisation 12, 42, 43, 65, 102, 103, 105, 130, 207
Smith N 209
social change 32, 33, 44, 45, 46, 47-68, 69, 76, 77, 84, 86, 109, 110, 116, 118, 157-197, 199, 208, 209
social ecology 16, 17, 106, 112
social justice 12, 13, 36, 64, 101, 102, 130, 161, 207
socialism 8, 14, 17, 20, 27, 28, 29, 30, 32, 33, 36, 38, 40, 42, 43, 47, 48, 53, 56, 57, 62, 63, 64, 65, 66, 67, 70, 78, 84, 85, 87, 89, 95, 101-4, 105, 113, 121, 122, 130, 131, 136, 155, 169, 175, 176, 178, 179, 180, 193, 199, 206, 207, 208, 212, 213, 217, 219
Socialist Party of Great Britain 43

socialist/red greens 16, 27, 48, 62, 64, 102
soft energy 12, 42, 74, 132, 137, 140, 184
spiritualism/spiritual revelation 26, 32, 36, 38, 44, 46, 58, 65, 73, 75, 76, 80, 92, 93, 99-100, 105, 108-110, 112, 116, 142, 159, 165, 175
stereotyping: of social roles 32, 61, 89, 105, 126
structuralism 48, 49, 53, 54, 116, 117, 157, 161, 163, 164, 166, 174, 201, 209, 218
sustainability 70, 123

technocentric 1, 16, 115, 121, 210
technology:
  high 9, 40, 115, 130
  alternative/intermediate/appropriate 16, 21, 26, 43, 46, 70, 77, 92, 115, 123, 132, 184, 190, 211 215
Thatcherism/isation 50, 103, 176, 191-8, 206
therapy 21, 58, 73, 82, 85, 94, 110, 154-6, 162, 169, 194, 209
third way 176
Third World/North-South relationships 9, 13, 21, 23, 41, 110, 114, 122, 123, 124, 138, 167, 173, 184, 218
Toffler A 40, 212
Tonnies F 63
Touraine A 209, 210
traditional/tribal societies 22, 38, 55, 65, 107, 122, 211
tree/hedge planting 132, 133
Trevelyan G 44

veganism 11, 21, 30, 36, 82, 132, 143, 144, 188
vegetarianism 11, 27, 30, 72, 82, 97, 124, 128, 132, 135, 140, 143, 174, 188
vitalism 44, 128
Vogel S 17

Wall D 52, 217
Watson L 168
Weber M 51

Weston J **48, 102, 204**
White L **7**
Whose World? project **24**
Willington S **74**
Wood A **215**
work sharing **146-7, 154, 155, 171**
Weyer R van der **41**

Young J **17, 22, 38, 55, 208**

Z to A Project (New University Project) **3, 69, 72-3, 74, 77, 89, 95, 115, 133, 137, 138, 149, 164, 189, 195, 206, 215**